Nationa

2025 LITERARY JOURNAL

NWS

National Writers Series

Traverse City

NWS
National Writers Series

Published by National Writers Series
3301 Veterans Drive, Suite 214
Traverse City, MI 49684

ISBN: 978-1-965278-80-2

Printed in the United States of America
Cover Art: Colleen Zanotti
Book Design: Andrea Reider
Book Production: Mission Point Press
www.missionpointpress.com

For additional copies, please visit
nationalwriterseries.org/raisingwriters

Editor: Audrey Fierberg, Education Director for National Writers Series

Note to Reader:
Some of the work in the *National Writers Series 2025 Literary Journal* may not be appropriate for a younger reading audience

National Writer Series

2025 Literary Journal

National Writers Series
of Traverse City

CONTENTS

Writers Create II

Antrim Raising Writers: Language Lab

Journalism

Sketch Writing Using Improv

Manistee County Poetry Club

Goldilocks Framed Me! Fractured Fairy Tales

This Story

Color the World With Feelings: Sensory Poems

Back to the Beginning: Circle Stories

Fiction Inspired by Myth, Legend and History

Spring Break Staycation! Write 50-Word Stories

North Ed Writers Studio

Introduction by Audrey Fierberg, National Writers Series Education Director

What an amazing year it has been for the National Writers Series Raising Writers program. We have seen young people thrive in our Elementary Poetry Workshops, hosted the tenth year of Battle of the Books, and facilitated classes on a dazzling variety of writing disciplines. What follows is the collected works of our Raising Writers students, who expanded their imaginations and honed their craft learning sketch writing, flash fiction, poetry, journalism, fable and fantasy writing, and more. Additionally, student work is featured from the The Writers Studio program at Northwest Ed Career Tech as well as the work of the winners of our annual National Writers Series Scholarship competition, in partnership with the Grand Traverse Regional Community Foundation.

We'd like to thank our donors, granters, and partners. Thank you to the Dragonfly Fund, Rollin M. Gerstacker Foundation, and the Kettering Family Foundation, as well as to our Raising Writers Mentors. Thank you to Full Tilt Comedy for the learning and laughter. Thank you to the Dennos Museum, the Traverse Area District Library, and to the Alluvion for hosting us. Thank you to Cordia for letting us build intergenerational connections and share important stories. Thank you to the Manistee County Community Foundation, the The Oleson Foundation, The Art and Mary Schmuckal Family Foundation and the Mariel Foundation. Thank you to the Grand Traverse Regional Community Foundation for facilitating the National Writers Series scholarships, and to Bill Unger for providing each of the first place winners with a new laptop to support their studies as they head off to college.

In closing, I'd also like to personally express my gratitude to each of the Raising Writers teachers, whose skill and guidance infuse every page of this journal. Thank you to Nicole Hastings McKendrick and David Thomas,

David Hornibrook, Noelle Riley, Kevin Fitton, Sam Collier, and Ashlee Cowless. A special thank-you to 'Cole Birkett for being such a focused pioneer of our programming in Manistee County, and to Miranda Keskes both for her expertise in flash fiction and for helping to edit this journal, and to Kelly Almer for teaching so many incredible classes. Each of your creativity, expertise, and generosity of spirit makes transformational writing experiences possible for our students. Lastly, thank you to the parents of each of our students. By raising writers, we're writing the future.

2025 NWS Scholarship Winners in Partnership with GTRCF

Introduction: NWS Scholarship Winners by Audrey Fierberg

The National Writers Series is honored to feature the work of this year's winners of our Scholarship Competition, hosted in partnership with The Grand Traverse Regional Community Foundation.

Scholarships are awarded each year in four categories: poetry, journalism, nonfiction, and fiction, to high school juniors and seniors. First place winners received a $1000 college scholarship, and second place winners received $500. To date, $70,000 in scholarships has been awarded to young writers in Northern Michigan.

The following works were carefully selected by a panel of judges who sought works reflecting craft and creativity in each of the four categories. The National Writers Series wishes each of these students the best as they pursue their collegiate dreams and enter an exciting new chapter of their lives.

ANTI-ODE TO STARBUCKS DRIVE-THRUS
by Lola Russell, 12th Grade

First Place Scholarship Winner: Poetry

My sister and I sit
Sit
Sit
In the drive-thru on a clear summer day.

The line moves forward.

She leans her head forward to stare
At her phone, scrolling
Through the sounds of the modern day.

The line moves forward.

The shiny silver convertible in front of us stops,
A beep covering up the words the driver must be muttering
At the annoying stragglers blocking the parking lo-
BEEP

The line moves forward.

Small sections of songs repeat.
BEEP
Small sections of songs repeat.
BEEP

The line moves forward.

The rolling up and down of windows all around
Hisses:
Is this really worth it?
For I am not a sluggish scholar in need of caffeine
Or a doctor seeking fuel to work the evening shift.

The line moves forward.

The worker behind the crackly speaker squeaks out
How can I help you?

The line moves forward.

I do not know that
The worker started just the day before.
The worker has not yet perfected their knowledge of the espresso
machine
Or the shiny silver cash register.

The line moves forward.

The worker is,
As the small sections of song repeat,
Giving the shiny silver convertible two less dollars than the change they
are owed.

The line does not move forward.

A dollar bill drops to the ground having
Slipped from the sweating hands of the worker.

The line does not move forward

Until two dollars are handed over.

The line moves forward.

The worker shoves two plastic cups
To my sister and I,
Stuttering as they slide the glass window shut.
Thank you for coming to Starbucks.

PALIMPSEST
by Elijah Flechter, 12th Grade

Second Place Scholarship Winner: Poetry

We wrote our names in the sand,
knowing the tide would come,
but still, we hoped—
maybe the waves would forget
and leave us, just for a moment, to exhale.

We carved words in bathroom stalls,
painted over, but still rigid,
marking time in ordinary places—
quiet rebellions of the unnoticed,
pyramids half-buried in dust—
a great attempt at resisting time's erosion.

We built small monuments
with hands that trembled,
dreaming of immortality in fleeting acts.
A footstep here, a glance there—
only we remember the stories that didn't stick.

The world forgets all but the loudest voices,
Yet our whispers fill the cracks,
sink into the walls,
half-erasures still legible in the right light—
proof that in in every quiet act,
in every unnoticed gesture, we were here.

FOSTERING NEW FEMALE SPACES ON THE NET by Tess Tarchak-Hiss, 11th Grade

First Place Winner: Journalism

The time had come. My mother's worst nightmare: I had lice. I had lice at the ripe old age of 12, posing two questions: First, can middle schoolers even get lice? And second, how did this even happen?

At the time, we'd been stuck in COVID quarantine for a month. I was placed in double isolation, walking around my house with a hairnet, looking like Chris Farley in SNL's "Lunch

Lady" skit, preventing any jumping joys from springing onto my mother while she plucked through my hair like a chimpanzee looking for a sweet treat.

Despite this situation, there was an upside: nobody from school knew I was cursed, and no anonymous alarm was sent out to the parents of my peers that "so and so" had lice. I was saved from the embarrassment and the shunning. However, I was not saved from countless hours in front of piercing white lights, sitting on the floor in the bathroom while my mom rooted out my infestation. To prevent my squiggling, an iPod Touch was thrown into my hands. An iPod Touch with three worthy apps: Subway Surfers, Bitlife, and YouTube.

I've always adored video games: Sims, Animal Crossing, Sonic, Pokemon, Hello Kitty Island Adventure, you name it. Cute animals and a fun house to decorate? I was drawn to gaming like a toddler with millennial parents glued to the iPads at Olive Garden. Through these games, I developed a further sense of creativity. I made stories about my villagers in Minecraft and mapped out my Animal Crossing island on the big poster board intended for my pre-COVID science project. Despite being stuck indoors, my world was large as my imagination ran rampant.

My mother, who was a survivor of Sims addiction back in her day, was hands-off regarding what I played. Working from home, she had priorities, and her daughter's screen time was not one of them. As much as I wanted to explain to her my Mario Odyssey speedrunning strategies, there was a generational and situational disconnect; she was always preoccupied with her job and the world being on fire.

At the time, the fear of being judged by my real-life friends over the lice situation was immense. Despite that, I wanted a community; I wanted a frequent force in my life I could admire, whom I could share a common interest with. I turned to YouTube to find those figures.

Female gamers on online platforms get a horrible reputation. On account of a few bad apples, a stereotype is perpetuated that all women who play video games are money-hungry, overly sexual, clout chasers. I, and many others my age, found comfort in a specific group of women who knocked down these assertions and provided safe spaces.

These spaces were uplifting to awkward tweenage girls, embracing different backgrounds, interests, and various levels of weirdness. Watching YouTubers such as IHasCupquake, LaurenZside, LDShadowlady, and StacyPlays provided millions with warmth equivalent to a hug in a time where the closest physical interaction one could have was waving at the UPS driver dropping off a package at the top of the driveway.

These women fostered motherlike admiration from their fans, proving that women could be their most authentic selves in male-dominated spaces. Mai Lantz, a sophomore at Traverse City West Senior High, grew up watching these women and continues to incorporate their messages of originality and resilience in how she sees the world.

"There was a lot of guardianship that they provided when I was looking for a figure like that," Lantz says.

"They were parental figures to me. I wanted to be as strong and creative and as funny as they were. They showed me possibilities through my screen. These women, I always thought they were just extremely strong because it takes a lot to put yourself out there, especially on the internet, especially as a woman. But they put themselves out there and were relentlessly harassed because of it. "

According to womeningames.org, "Some 59% of gamers who are women and girls have experienced some form of toxicity from male gamers, with 28% saying that they experience this regularly online."

That's not the only dark side to gaming. Online video games, despite immersive storytelling and visual elements, despite the community they build, despite the creativity that lurches out of it, function as one sole thing: a diversion.

"It's a whole different thing when you're depending on a video game solely for your happiness. It puts a dent in how you learn, how you see things, and how you interact with people. Some people start depending so much on these games. Especially when it's the only thing you have, and it's the only thing you have to live through. It can be a positive and a negative; It's a way for people to distract themselves from what they're going through," Lantz says.

Even though video games provide dopamine to doomscrollers and dungeon dwellers alike, finding a balance between Call of Duty lobbies and the outside world is key. For me, life is a lice-permeated highway; therefore, if shutting down your brain and escaping to the world of the top ten best Minecraft mods while an incandescent lightbulb bleaches your eyeballs amidst a pest pilgrimage on your scalp, go for it. Said highway is full of roadblocks, ranging from mite-sized to a pandemic seizing the globe, shriveling it to a crisp. In moments like those, where the world is so unbearable it feels like a simulation, it's important to stay grounded in your present reality, instead of playing Papa's Pizzeria alone in the dark until 4 AM, losing yourself in your phony nine-to-five.

The communities these female gamers assembled, while helping mold middle school girls into independent and eccentric young women, provided a safety net that preserved certain "chronically online" behaviors. After being forcefully exposed into the world after the first initial lockdown, these quirks shifted into a universal language of love in normal life, tying the string between those who were similarly drawn to these role models, role models who exhibited strength and spunk and passed it down to their viewers. Viewers who developed their own trademark moxie through their personal mettle and transitioned into their own idols, sharing traits passed through their communities and embracing reality standing up, parallel to the women we doted on from our bathroom floors.

2
KATHY KOZACHENKO: LOCAL LEGEND AND UNSPOKEN QUEER HERO
by Keira Wesley, 12th Grade

Second Place Winner: Journalism

Many Americans herald Harvey Milk as one of the first public advocates of LGBTQ+ equality and is widely regarded as the country's pioneer openly queer person to be elected to public office in 1977 ("Harvey Milk"). However, what most Americans do not know is that Milk was not the first LGBTQ+ public official; three years prior to Milk's election, a 21-year-old lesbian student at the University of Michigan, Kathy Kozachenko, was elected to the Ann Arbor City Council. A member of the now-nonexistent Human Rights Party, Kozachenko fought for not only LGBTQ+ rights but also affordable housing, racial equity, workers' rights, and various socialist issues (Compton). Though her achievements widely go unrecognized, Kozachenko's courage to affect change at the local level as a queer socialist woman is undeniable.

Originally born in Alexandria, Virginia, Kozachenko grew up in a very nonpolitical household. Despite Kozachenko's profound concerns for others and their lives, current events were not discussed in her family, and her political interests were not shared by her peers. However, when Kozachenko moved to Plymouth, Michigan to attend high school, her passion for political activism blossomed; at one point, Kozachenko–with the help of a few of her teachers–organized an informational meeting about the United Farm Workers' pay, working conditions, and boycott of non-union grapes (Kozachenko).

After she moved to Ann Arbor to pursue English and creative writing at the University of Michigan, or U of M, Kozachenko almost immediately joined the civil rights movement and was quickly recruited by a student group called the Human Rights Party, or the HRP. The HRP asked Kozachenko to run for city council, and, believing in the HRP's social justice goals, she agreed (Compton). But, unbeknownst to her HRP campaign runners, Kozachenko was already in a battle–one with her identity.

Even though Kozachenko entered college with an openness to exploring relationships with women, she remained confused about her sexuality as many other "lesbians" at U of M were actually straight women trying to prove a point about the importance of decentering men. But, after the Stonewall Uprising of 1969 when police raided the Stonewall Inn and patrons fought back (Blakemore), Kozachenko gained confidence in her identity and knew it was time to come out. Unfortunately, like many American teens today, Kozachenko's coming out experience was less than positive; when she told her parents she was a lesbian at age 20, "they shrugged it off as the declaration of a hyper-political kid caught up in the drama of the times" (Friess). But, in a demonstration of her resilience and tenacity, Kozachenko did not let this disappointment from her parents deter her from achieving her goals.

When Kozachenko came out to her campaign manager, Frank Shoichet, she received a different response. Rather than pushing her identity aside, Shoichet celebrated Kozachenko's identity as a lesbian and suggested she run as openly lesbian for the city council (Friess). When Kozachenko agreed, she cemented herself in the history books as the first openly queer person to run for public office.

A burgeoning socialist, Kozachenko endorsed policies such as rent control, farmworker's rights, racial and gender equality, and LGBTQ+ rights ("Meet The Candidate..."). Since she was still a student at U of M, Kozachenko had limited time to campaign, and while that may have stopped countless others, it only fueled Kozachenko's persevering spirit and her determination to win. She campaigned in residence halls and student neighborhoods and ultimately won the city council position by a margin of 52 votes, making even more history by becoming the first openly LGBTQ+ person to hold public office ("It Happened at Michigan...").

In her acceptance speech,Kozachenko stated that "10 years ago, or even three years ago, lesbianism would have meant automatic defeat..." and her campaign "forced some people to... re-examine their prejudices and stereotypes" (Compton).

Today, only 0.17% of all public officials are part of the LGBTQ+ community (Reese); when Kozachenko won her position in 1974, that percentage was 0. Her trailblazing efforts not only represent her incredible courage but also her commitment to improving the country and making it more accepting of queer individuals.

Kozachenko only ended up serving one term as a city council member. Noting that she saw the HRP as more of a vehicle for change rather than a political party with staying power, Kozachenko decided not to run for re-election (Compton). But her career in representing those without a voice, in fighting for queer liberation, was far from over.

After graduating, Kozachenko moved to New York where she was involved in several socialist and LGBTQ+ organizations. Most notably, Kozachenko was an organizer for the 1979 March on Washington (Friess) in which more than 100,000 Americans marched in front of the White House demanding LGBTQ+ rights, representation, and equality ("1979 March on Washington..."). Then, in the 1980s, when Ronald Reagan became president and he, along with his cabinet, ignored the raging AIDS epidemic (Bennington-Castro), Kozachenko continued her activism by volunteering with political and community groups (Friess) and remains a staunch advocate for all kinds of queer causes to this day (Kozachenko).

When asked to join the HRP, Kathy Kozachenko could have rejected it. She could have spent her life hiding and suppressing an identity she was afraid of facing. Instead, Kozachenko chose to be bold. She chose to run a campaign with her queerness at the center of it in a time when being openly queer could mean losing your job, your family, your friends, your life . She chose to put everything on the line with the vision of a better future, deciding that–even though it would be incredibly difficult–choosing courage over fear could change our country for the better. She was right.

DYING FLOWERS
by Katelyn Popp, 11th Grade
First Place Scholarship Winner: Nonfiction

In the bitter winter of my 4th-grade year, my teachers and friends changed left and right, but my home and family were always constants I could hold onto. Tedious five-day weeks and weekends flew by, occasionally broken with visits to extended family, usually my grandma. There, I knew a breath of fresh air from the monotony of elementary school life could be taken. Granted, my time at my grandma's miniscule apartment wasn't riveting by any means, but it was something different and that was enough for me.

One Saturday, I was playing with my American Girl Dolls in my room, slowly brushing the long black hair of the retired Josephine doll. I braided the signature, over-the-shoulder plait she came with, and tucked a fake yellow flower behind her ear. I was calmly admiring my work when my mom called out to the family.

"Kids? Can you come to sit down at the table?" The sound echoed in the open-concept house my parents always disliked. My brother and I raced to the table, curious as to what the matter was.

"What is it, Mom?" My brother inquired; hesitancy filled his voice at what would be in answer to his question.

"Sit down, kids," my mom instructed. Her eyes flitted to my dad's for a brief second, a subtle display of her unease; other than that, she was a statue. "Your Grandma," she didn't have to specify which one, for my other had died several years prior. "She has cancer, stage 4."

"Is that bad?" I questioned. I knew what cancer was, and its sometimes deadly consequences, but I never imagined it would happen to someone I knew, so why wouldn't she be okay?

"It isn't the best, but I'm sure she'll be fine," my mom reassured my brother and me. "She is going to start chemotherapy soon. It is supposed to get rid of the cancer." My young mind couldn't pick up on the slight deflection and lie in Mom's words. I didn't cry; my brother didn't either because my mom said that my grandma would be okay.

Over the next few months, my grandma got sicker and weaker, but I assumed that was normal. After all, my dad had told me that chemotherapy tries to target only cancer cells, but it can kill others also, so it would all be fine once she stopped. In the meantime, my mom and her sister visited often. It was a two-hour drive to the hospice house, but that never stopped her from making it.

By this point, I should have accepted the truth that my grandma was going to die, but I was incapable of thinking that way. My undying optimism completely shunned the potential fate that lay in store for my grandma. Nobody in my family that I knew closely had died, so it was nearly impossible for me to imagine a world in which someone had. Therefore, life moved on as normal for me. I never visited my grandma frequently anyway, but I had not seen her since she was in her little apartment, crocheting blankets and slippers at the speed of light. I had no idea of the changes that had occurred in my absence.

We went camping in the summer. For four days we were going to have an RV and the time of our lives. Campfires became an evening tradition and on the third night, we were sitting around in big green chairs, all aligned in a little circle. Then, my mom got a phone call; it was from the hospice house my grandma resided in.

"Hello, do you have a minute?" The modulated voice asked, just audible enough for me to make out the words.

"Yes, I do." My mom answered. She left the circle of chairs and walked inside. Through the windows, we could see her pace back and forth, the embodiment of stress. Eventually, she set down the phone and motioned for us to join her inside. Her features were taut, and even though no tears fell, they were not needed to show the extent of her sadness.

"I'm sorry kids, but your grandma is not doing well. I think it would be best for us to visit her." My mom told us. The words "for the last time" were not said, but everyone could still hear them. My optimistic self, however, thought there was still no way she would die, not that I had even grasped what that truly meant, but why would she? She had cancer, but she'd been doing chemo, something that gets rid of it, right? So why wasn't it gone? Why would she die?

These thoughts plagued my mind as I sat in the backseat of the 2014 Chevy Tahoe my dad had recently gotten. The slight squeak of the brakes and the wind rushing by as we zoomed down the highway were the only sounds that filled the car. Activities to keep us children entertained—notebooks, puzzles, and an array of Twistable crayons—were hastily shoved in a bag and thrown back in the seats.

When we arrived at the hospice house we were ushered to a large room with nothing but a folding table, two folding chairs, and the hospital bed with my grandma on it. She was sleeping when we arrived, so my brother and I were instructed to keep quiet and play with our toys. A half-finished puzzle already sat on the bumpy gray surface of the table. Decadent desserts in the form of cakes, sundaes, and eclairs were photographed in the 500-piece puzzle. The bright pink frosting that lathered each of these desserts was painful to look at in comparison to the brown walls and somber mood.

There was one window in the corner where flowers and grass could be seen. A hummingbird zoomed by and I thought of how much my grandma loved hummingbirds. With their bright colors and constant energy, it seemed almost impossible not to. But her eyes were closed and she couldn't enjoy the sight she once loved so much. Eventually, a nurse came into the room and tilted my grandma's bed up. The nurse wiped her eyes and helped her open them, a common task so simple I had never even thought about it before, never considered that it could be so challenging for someone.

The old woman who sat on that bed was unrecognizable. She was removed from the familiar apartment, the kitchen with white appliances, and the floral perfume she always wore, and was reduced to a person completely reliant on others. Her eyes seemed to see nothing of the world in front of her. If the hummingbird flew by again, it would go unnoticed by her once more.

My mom told my brother and I to greet her, but it seemed there was nothing left to greet. Nonetheless, we tiptoed over to the side of the bed and held her hands, shaking like paper in the wind, as we told her how much she meant to us. The same hands that used to crochet and knit endlessly, now seemed like somebody else's entirely. No sign of recognition was ever shown in her eyes as we spoke.

Eventually, we retreated to the bright pink puzzle and put it together slowly as my mom greeted my grandma too. But I think at that moment it was really a goodbye. Soon, the puzzle was finished, and I pulled out my 30-page sketchbook with an ugly watercolor butterfly on the front and wondered what to draw. I sat there for minutes, pondering what I could possibly draw at a time like this. The beautiful terrain outside the window could never truly be captured; one must be in it to grasp the experience. But I wasn't in it. I was inside a desolate hospice house watching my grandma die. Still, flowers were drawn and hummingbirds were too, by dusty crayons with childish dexterity.

After a couple hours my dad, brother, and I left, but my mom stayed. Her sister joined and would give her a ride back to the campsite after everything was over. The car ride back seemed even colder and more somber than the house.

I woke up on a Thursday morning and my mom was there, crying. I hated to see her cry and had no idea how to comfort her, so I didn't. I stayed in my little bunk and thought of all the memories I had with my grandma. Baking brownies, going to butterfly houses, museums. My face became hot and my throat felt like it was closing, but no tears came.

Soon after, the funeral was held. As everyone piled out of the car, I didn't. I stayed in the car with my dad. My stomach hurt so badly, for a reason that I couldn't place my finger on, so I just sat in the car for hours. I think I knew that if I went in there, I would start crying, and I despised crying in front of people. So, I sat in the car with the guilt of my dad missing his mother-in-law's funeral stewing away, not helping my stomach ache at all.

The car door opened suddenly and I climbed into the backseat to let my mom take the passenger's.

"It was a beautiful funeral," my mom lamented. "She would have been so happy." It seemed all my parents could talk about was the funeral. She was talking on the phone with her sister about headstones, ashes, and memorials. It was a lot, but I never cried.

A month later, my family and my mom's siblings gathered for a memorial in the cemetery. In the middle of August, the heat was suffocating me; I was wearing black, my mom wouldn't stop hugging me, and it was all too much.

My breathing shortened and quickened, my hands tingled, my vision blurred and I couldn't feel anything except the heat. I felt my knees weaken and my mom tightened her grip on me. I tried to push away, to get away from the heat.

I ended up in the back of the car, the AC blowing on my face, a plastic water bottle in hand, and my dad beside me. He told me, "It's not good to keep your emotions bottled up like that, you have to let other people know what you're feeling."

I just nodded and breathed in and out. In and out. I unscrewed the lid to the water and took a long sip. The metallic tang of the water, warmed from the sun, didn't make me feel any better. My mind was flashing through all of the memories, and it was hard not to become overwhelmed. I tried to think of all the good memories, the baking and crocheting. I tried to remember the smell of the brownies, and her laugh as I tried to taste the batter. I wanted to remember the soft pink wool that I knew would become the afghan I keep in my room to this day. I really did try, but the flashback of her in the hospice house played front and center, over and over.

In that moment I truly grasped the concept of death. The irrevocable and unavoidable fate that someday everyone I know will face, including me. Even with all the signs, death always strikes the revelation that one second a person could be alive and the next they aren't, and there was nothing I could do about it.

Flowers and grass surrounded the car, and finally, I was in them. But unlike in the hospice house, I could see the imperfections. No hummingbirds or butterflies danced around the sky, and the flowers were brown and dead, lying on a bed of yellowed grass. The tulips placed on the headstone had already wilted from the unrelenting sun, and soon they too would die and turn to dust, and there was nothing I could do to stop it.

BEHIND CLOSED DOORS
by Elyana Marschner, 12th Grade
Second Place Winner: Nonfiction

Content Warning: Child Abuse, Suicide

Growing up, I didn't think much about how my family wasn't like other families. I grew up in Kingsley, Michigan in a three-story house that was white with green shutters. From the outside, my family looked just like a new other family.

My parents fought a lot; I could hear it from my room. I'd sit on the first step of the stairs, out of sight, hoping they wouldn't notice me. One time I saw my dad grab my mom and pin her against the wall. He yelled at her: she looked terrified and had a look of not knowing what would happen next. My parents mostly thought about three things: my dad's drinking, how his drinking affected the family, and how he needed to be a better father.

Until I was three, my dad was my favorite parent. I loved him more than anything. We'd go for adventures outdoors or go on family trips together. Around four, he started becoming distant. By the time I was six, he started abusing me.

It all got worse when my stepmom, Jennifer, moved in. She was his high school girlfriend who had recently gotten divorced and was moving back to Michigan.

My dad used to say, "The dogs are part of the family, treat them like family." He stopped saying that when Jennifer moved in. She was allergic to every furry animal.

She constantly complained about them, saying things like, "I can't sleep with them here," or "They need to get out." My dad did whatever he could to make her happy, even if it meant hurting the dogs. My father locked away the dogs in the garage. I only saw them when I was sent to the garage to fetch a beer for him. They were always shaking, and I never saw food or water for them. I still remember the last time I saw them. It was an overcast day, and Jayger, one of the dogs, licked my hand. It was something he'd never done before.

My father says they died of old age, but I believe it was because of neglect.

My dad had a short temper, especially when he was drunk, and he often took it out on me. There were times he'd send me to my room without dinner, making me stay there until the next day. He took the back of my neck so hard it felt like I couldn't breathe, or he'd grab my arms with such force so I have marks from his fingers.

I remember the first time Child Protective Services came to the house. I was in my Hello Kitty pajamas, watching "Chowder" on Cartoon Network. My stepmom was putting my sister to sleep and my father was in his room when there was a knock on the door. I looked out to see a police car and a white car in our driveway. "There's police here," I exclaimed.

My father and stepmom rushed down to the front door, refusing to let them in. The CPS worker, Ashley, was taking notes as I peeked through the window and locked eyes with the officer. After forcing their way through, they searched the house and found things that became usual notes taken in the CPS reports over the years.

The notes always said this: "Cabinets full of alcohol, fridge full of beer in garage, garbage can filled with cans of beer, plastic water bottle covered with electric tape filled with tobacco, and father of the house is slurring words."

The police decided it was best that my mom picked us up and we stayed with her. My father tried to protest and say people hated him and were making up lies about him. As my step-mom took me back to my room where my sister was sleeping, she made a comment about how it was finally good that we weren't sleeping on a blow up mattress anymore and that we finally got on a bed. After we had gotten changed, we waited in the driveway for our mom. I was looking down the driveway, red and blue lights flashing, standing next to my sister, the CPS worker behind us, watching the police officer talk to my mom. He gave her something to breathe into at the end of the driveway while my dad and stepmom stood behind the storm door. My step mom had a slight smirk on her face. They told the authorities my mom was a heavy drinker hoping to get her in trouble as well.

Going to my father's house after that day was terrifying. I didn't want to go, but the court wouldn't let me decide where to live until I was 18. Even though CPS had been called a number of times, the court didn't think there was enough evidence to do anything about it. The situation didn't change until I tried to take my life when I was eleven.

The last time I saw my dad was five years ago. I was twelve when we had a big argument. I said everything I could possibly say to hurt him. I've seen him cry a lot but it was because he thought everyone made him out to be a bad guy to me or because he was just drunk. This time, he cried because I called him a joke of a dad and a horrible father.

"I WOULD RATHER DIE THAN BE IN THIS HELL HOUSE ANYMORE!" I yelled at him, "YOU'RE A HORRIBLE PARENT, YOU DON'T DESERVE KIDS!"

He looked shocked to see those words come out of my mouth. I wanted to stop. I knew my punishment would be severe, but the words kept rolling off my tongue. I was letting all my anger and hatred onto him.

"Just call my mom to come pick me up please," I said as more tears started to form in my eyes.

"NO, YOU'RE STAYING HERE AND YOU WILL NOT LEAVE THIS ROOM UNTIL TOMORROW," he yelled back.

"FINE," I said, gaining some energy, "I'LL WALK!"

"WAIT TILL YOUR MOTHER GETS HOME!" he said angrily walking out of the doorway of my room.

She's not my mom and this is not my home,' I thought to myself. I knew not to say anything else because everything I had already said, I would be severely punished for. I stared out of the window in the room waiting for my stepmom to arrive. I thought I was ready to face her anger and my punishments, but as soon as I saw her drive up the driveway I was crippled with fear. I had never felt this kind of fear as I was paralyzed and started to have a severe panic attack. He told her everything. She came into the room and dragged me out and made me apologize to him.

"We'll deal with your punishments later, go back to your room, and don't come out unless I say you can," she said to me. It had been two hours of sitting alone in silence when Jenifer came into my room again.

"We need to go Your father got in a car accident," she said while rushing in through the door.

We were almost to where he had crashed when we saw the car: the whole front half of the car had been totaled. I wondered what had made him crash and what the other car looked like.

We stopped in front of the middle school where we saw the police car and that's when I saw what he hit.

A parked car.

This is so embarrassing for him, I thought.

I couldn't believe it. Could that day have gotten more chaotic?

It did.

"LOOK WHAT YOU CAUSED," she yelled at me.

You've got to be kidding me, what I caused, she's gotta be kidding, I thought.

My stepmom got out of the car and helped my dad into the car. As she was talking to the police officer, I wanted to jump out of the car and beg the police officer for help. I stopped myself, though. I knew it would create more problems, and he most likely wouldn't do anything.

As soon as Jenifer got back into the car she started yelling at me, "LOOK WHAT YOU CAUSED YOUR FATHER TO DO, YOU PUT SO MUCH STRESS ON HIM, YOU'RE LUCKY HE'S OKAY."

Guess she wasn't joking.

We got back to the house and I was sent right back to the room. The next time my stepmom had come into the room, the sun had gone down and she was putting my sister to bed. "Come down to apologize to your father and we will talk about your punishment," she said.

I didn't want to apologize but I knew I had to. I climbed down the bunk and walked out of the room she followed behind me. I looked around the house.

The house was in lockdown.

There was a curtain rod in the sliding door of the sun room so I couldn't get out that way.

I walked down the stairs and saw heavy objects in front of the front door and garage door. They put chairs, a bag of golf clubs, boxes, and totes so I couldn't get out. The only places that weren't in lockdown were the basement and my room. There was a rock in the room I could throw to get the screen door out. I would have to jump out the window if I wanted to escape.

"Keep going down the stairs, he's on the couch in the game room," she said, still close behind me.

I walked down the stairs into the game room. I saw him sitting there, but I couldn't tell what he was feeling. He was looking at me blankly as Jenifer sat next to him.

"It hurts me and your father that you acted that way. You were rude and disrespectful to him and he has done so much good for you. People tell you bad things about him," she said to me.

I was just standing there awkwardly not knowing what to say. All I could think about was going home and telling my mom everything, remembering things so I could write them down to tell her everything. My dad started crying; he definitely had drank more.

"It just hurts me so much," he said to me. It wasn't the first time I heard him say that while crying, "You cause so many problems and I don't know why."

"Your mother—" I didn't let my stepmom finish.

"You have no reason to talk about my mom the way you do, and neither does your mom.

You and your family, especially your mom, act like my mom ruined this family and that she brainwashes me. SHE'S DONE NOTHING WRONG. I'm so sick of everyone acting like it's her fault, when most of it was you, YOU'Re A HOMEWRECKER. YOU DIDN'T EVEN CARE THAT HE HAD KIDS, and then you cry when we don't say I love you back. Ever think it's because we don't love you?"

Shoot, I shouldn't have said that last part. Now I'm in even more trouble, I thought to myself.

A few minutes later I was walking back up the stairs to my room. Tears were starting to form in my eyes, but I refused to cry.

I lay awake all that night waiting for morning to come. I was paralyzed by fear of what would happen if I fell asleep. It felt like hours before I drifted asleep.

The morning came, and I was still filled with fear. The car ride to Culvers was completely silent. He had cut off the door lock so I couldn't pull it up and get out anymore. As soon as he parked, I grabbed my things and jumped out of the car as fast as possible.

I got in the car and told my mom everything.

THE DOLLHOUSE OF SHATTERED WALLS

by Solé Demeuse, 12th Grade

Honorable Mention: Nonfiction

For the entire month of August, a DIY mini dollhouse that took hours to glue, tape, and piece together sat in the center of my dining room table. Its delicacy once frightened me, as its walls could collapse at any moment if someone accidentally bumped it in the wrong spot, and the precious time I spent meticulously building that home could be washed away in a matter of seconds. But as I looked closer through the inch-wide plastic window, I noticed a little girl. A girl bruised with stress, anger, and confusion; and at this moment, I realized that the girl wasn't living the life she's always dreamed of in the lovely abode I created for her. She wanted to be let out — she wanted to be free.

At 7 years old, I found myself nearly suffocating inside my own house after finding my dad unconscious on the couch with a bottle of pills sitting next to him. The air was thick with the scent of cheap vodka, the butter-yellow couch looked a little more worn, and dark clouds painted the living room grey. At this age, I vaguely knew of my dad's drug addiction because of his constant visits to rehab, but seeing it with my own eyes felt like I was using all of my limbs to try to stop the walls from closing in on me, crushing me to death.

But after several long years, I slowly began to feel like I could breathe again. Right around my dad's 5th anniversary of sobriety, he bought a home after years of not being able to afford one. From there, every bike ride, family dinner, and camping trip was accompanied by a liberating gust of fresh air. The smell of fresh cut grass and the warm breeze in these moments sent me to a safe haven I could never experience inside a small space. Although I physically had brand new walls built around me, I didn't have any enclosures to worry about escaping anymore. I was free.

However, the universe had other plans for me. After the most glorious three weeks of my life in my father's new home, he was placed in the hospital after suffering a severe stroke. Walking into the hospital felt like walking into a tiny chamber barely made for one person; I began to suffocate again. The relentless buzz of the cold white lights drilled into my skull as I sat down next to him, with his pale body hooked up to endless machines. Every day of those four weeks, I just hoped that he'd get right back up and tell us it was all just a joke and that he was actually fine, but he never did. Although his recovery was going somewhat smoothly for a stroke victim, another one unexpectedly hit him and claimed his life. I was demolished by the weight of my father's death, imprisoned in a space I could not escape.

The next day, I pulled myself out of bed to go out and buy some sort of craft, desperate to distract myself from the fact that I had just lost my best friend. Under the fluorescent Hobby Lobby lights, I found myself standing before that mini dollhouse. I felt drawn to it, just like how I felt compelled to build tight walls around my mind to protect me from the cruelty of the outside world. So I did exactly that; I went home and assembled my quarters. When building my compact house, it dawned on me that each room was a reflection of my own mind. One filled with fear, one filled with sorrow, and one filled with memories. Each room, however, had one commonality: the tiny restrictive walls had no doors, no way to escape.

A couple of weeks later, I woke up to the ballad of "The Good I'll Do" by Zach Bryan — my father's favorite song — as my alarm. On any typical morning, I would've immediately turned around and pressed "STOP" on my phone, annoyed that I had to get up, but this time, I didn't. Instead, I laid in my bed for the entire 3 minutes and 31 seconds of the song, digesting every single lyric, replaying every memory of my father I could remember. And once it was over, I finally turned off my phone, got up, walked downstairs, and smashed my mini dollhouse. As I watched all of my tiny cardboard furniture explode into a million pieces, the weight of the walls around me lifted.

Every hour that went into building that dollhouse was gone within seconds. My dining room table was covered in scraps of glue, paper, and wood that formed the dollhouse. At this moment, however, I realized that peace doesn't come from constructing high walls to protect ourselves; it comes from the courage to break them down and unleash ourselves from the restraints of grief and sorrow.

As I step beyond those shattered walls, I no longer feel trapped by grief. My father was never constricted by enclosures that tried to trap him. Now, I feel his presence in every gust of wind down every open road. Now, I follow in my father's footsteps, running free and exploring the world with bravery, never to be trapped behind those tiny windows again.

THE BIG LAKE SURF SCHOOL
by Jack Schripsema, 12th Grade
Honorable Mention: Nonfiction

As I was admiring the beauty of the nearby pier and the picturesque background of the dunes, a large mass of water took up my entire sight and soon after, engulfed me in a frothy tumble of foam. Seconds later I stood up, pushing the ice cold water from my eyes, laughing with my friends about the epic wipeout. We were out doing one of my favorite activities: surfing Lake Michigan.

The first time I went surfing was in a small town in Costa Rica when I was twelve where a local surf instructor helped me catch my first waves. My performance wasn't pretty, but it got me hooked. After that, I was only able to surf a couple more times in Florida, so when I was fourteen and found out that I could surf Lake Michigan, only an hour from my home, I was ecstatic. Although surfing the Great Lakes isn't easy, especially without salt's buoyancy, the people I meet and my love for nature makes it worth the extra effort.

When I make it out to the "big lake," I am always greeted by numerous smiles, how you doings, and nice to meet yous. These greetings and people are what come to mind when I picture the Lake Michigan surf scene. I've built many small but meaningful connections with other surfers and I love it. I meet all kinds of people, whether from out of state like the middle-aged women from Indiana who was unprepared for the cold water, or the older guys who paddle surf, pumping us up for the waves, or even the guys in their mid-20s who travel around in search of surf and stop and tell us how excited they are to see even younger guys surfing. We all have something in common as a small, special, tight-knit community in northern Michigan: we love to surf!

Because the weather in northern Michigan is so unpredictable, and because I could only surf on non-school days, there weren't many days when I could improve my surfing abilities when I first started. To make the most of my time, I aimed to learn as much as I could. I watched countless YouTube tutorials. Then, when I was more comfortable, I would sit on the beach and examine the other surfers to pick up on anything they were doing that could help me out. Eventually, I got in the water and met so many amazing people. From there I utilized my relationships with those people to get any tips on how to improve my abilities. I had not only found my new happy and social place, I had found my new surf school. Soon enough my drive and motivation paid off.

I changed from trying to paddle against the too strong waves to simply jumping past them off the pier. Instead of being intimidated, I felt comfortable with the friendly veteran surfers. I switched from riding the white wash of the wave to angling my board and riding the face of it. I was really surfing.

From there I would invite friends to come out in the frigid waters to surf with me. I taught them the basics and then everything else I learned so that they too could enjoy the water. This is one of my favorite things to do, and I still get excited whenever I get the chance to pass on my knowledge.

What started as a one-day lesson for a twelve-year-old in Costa Rica has turned into a passion. It encompasses the happiness my friends on our surf trips and those in the surf community bring me, the excitement of teaching others, the combination of my determination and utilization of all my relationships and resources, and my love of nature. Surfing the Great Lakes is not only a sport, but also an ever-changing, passionate learning adventure.

DROWNING IN THE DEEP
by Annie Stempin, 12th Grade
First Place Winner: Fiction

Like smoke, Dad was gone. He'd always been fleeting. Since Georgia and her sibling were teenagers, he was never a constant. Sometimes he'd disappear for days at a time and then suddenly turn up, ready to wreak havoc on the house and the lives inside it until he'd leave again. However, he'd vanished for good this time. Only a few reminders he'd ever lived in the house remained. There were empty beer bottles and piles of records in the living room. Old clay magnets still stuck on the fridge after all these years, holding up photographs stained with time. His few items of clothing were left in the closet upstairs, waiting to be boxed up and shoved into a dusty attic. The old surfboards they used to take down to the beach, leaning up against the backdoor, just how they'd left them years ago.

The wooden porch, now rotting, the dark oak color rubbing off in certain spots, creaked just the same as it always had when Georgia sat down on its stoop. The chilly Oregon air blew across her face, reminding her of the times she'd sneak out here in the middle of the night to meet up with the friends Dad always disapproved of. The thought that he disapproved of what she did always baffled her, even more so that he would comment on it.

She wrapped her cardigan around her now smaller frame and sighed, breathing out into the fall breeze. It was cold outside, but not so much that it forced her back inside. Honestly, she'd rather sit out here until her eyelashes froze if it meant she could skip out on reliving her childhood through cracked picture frames and dusty knicknacks.

"Too much for you?" Christine stepped out of the door, looking down at Georgia. When she met her younger sister's eyes, Georgia caught a flash of her father. The dark green, the same shade she met countless times during heated arguments that turned into screaming matches with him, the same shade that drained from his eyes after he drank himself to unconsciousness.

Georgia always ended up at his side, praying to any god out there that he would wake up. Sometimes it was hard to look Christine directly in the eyes, no matter how much she loved her. In fact, when Georgia moved out the day after her 18th birthday; it would be five years before she was forced to face her little sister again. It wasn't Christine's fault that she looked so much like dad, and it also wasn't her fault that Georgia and his relationship only got worse over time..

"I guess so," Georgia quickly turned her attention back to the view in front of her: tall trees with the sandy shore and crashing waves just beyond them. Every time her eyes met the sight beyond her, she was taken back to the Oregon summers of her childhood. Dashing out the screen door in her wetsuit, her little siblings right behind her, with Dad carrying their tiny surfboards. "It's so strange being back here, Chris. I know that we lived our whole childhoods here, but I can't get rid of the feeling that it's not our home."

"Yeah, I know." Christine took a seat beside Georgia. "I feel it too. But then I found the bowls we used to eat cereal out of every morning before the bus came, the sand buckets that we played with so much they cracked, and the deck of cards we learned to play euchre with... and I remember that I was a kid here, we were kids here."

"I never fought with him back then," Georgia sighed, reminiscing on the times she actually got along with her father.

"He was just... Dad," Christine agreed. The sisters sat in silence on the front porch for a moment, the only sound coming from the water crashing against the shoreline, making the waves seem violent. However, the ocean had always been the least violent thing in their lives.

"I never should have left you and Elliot," Georgia muttered, her quiet voice breaking.

"What are you talking about?" Christine wondered.

"I should've scooped you both up in my arms and taken you away from this place. I could've saved you. Don't you hate me for leaving? I'm your big sister... I-I'm supposed to be your protector. And I left you, and I left Elliot."

"I could never hate you, Georgie, not for anything," Christine turned to face Georgia, whose brown eyes gleamed with tears.

"But I was selfish."

"I think you deserved to be selfish for once."

Georgia broke into sobs, folding over on herself as she cried. She wept into her hands for a long time. She didn't know if she was crying over her dad or her siblings or both. Then she felt scarily unfamiliar arms wrap around her body, leaning into her sister's side as Georgia heaved with tears, most of them likely drenching Christine's shirt.

Georgia couldn't believe she was the one crying on her baby sister's shoulder. She'd always been the person her siblings leaned on for comfort. She'd always been the person they ran to when they were sad. No matter how much Christine and Elliot bugged her growing up, Georgia would never turn them away. Instead, she'd invite them into her room, scooch over, and cuddle with them under the covers until they were fast asleep, safely dreaming in the comfort of her arms.

"You didn't need to save us., We got out eventually," Christine started, cradling Georgia close. "All you could do was save yourself, and you did. You lived your life, Georgia. It doesn't matter if you were selfish. Growing up, Elliot and I always had our big sister looking after us, but you didn't. You needed to be that for yourself."

"Still–" Georgia sat up, sniffling as she wiped her wet face, "What if I had waited a little

longer, saved up a little more? We all could've left."

"What if? Georgia, we will never know." Christine took Georgia's hand, squeezing it lightly.

"Elliot could..."

"Don't even say that."

"It's true, you know it is."

"Yeah, it probably is. But you can't change the past, and you certainly can't blame yourself for it."

At times it seemed like it was the three of them against the world, stuck together on their own little island, especially when Dad would go off on his own. They were unsure of the world beyond their bubble, but they were together.

"I hate how broken our family is," Georgia sighed, resting her head on Christine's shoulder.

"What makes you say it's broken?" Christine asked, peering down at Georgia.

"We have no parents and our brother is dead. Plus, this is the first time I've seen you in two years."

"I think our true family was really me, you, and Elle. He's always with us, I know it. So, how can a family be broken if they are stuck together for life?"

"All these years and... maybe we never did leave each other's sides."

"I know I've always been with you."

Georgia had tried for years to bury her childhood, doing everything she could to block it out. But she never could forget the times she spent with her siblings, how far she'd go for them. They were truly the only people she loved unconditionally, without ever having to think about it. Those memories of the Oregon coast, their little cabin they called home for many long years, Georgia could never truly shake them. But, why would she ever want to shake her baby brother and sister? They were irreplaceable, unable to be remade. Georgia would forever be a sister., Nothing, not even the most terrible things, would change that.

RABBIT TRAP by Sam Milks, 12th Grade

Second Place Winner: Fiction

Dead leaves and gnarled sticks crunched under the heavy steps of Jacob's worn-down converse. He was in the forest on a dare. The camera was turned on to prove he was actually doing it. The last thing he wanted was to lose his lunch to Harris again, the jerk. Jacob cursed himself out as he slowly got closer to the crumbling building ahead. Local legend told that those who visited it were never heard from again, seemingly deciding to be a permanent resident. Some sort of feeling allured its guests to never leave. Of course that was only a tale, Jacob knew, but as he scaled the camera up the twisted, molding planks that made up the wall of the house, he couldn't help but listen to the fear welling in his gut. Jacob shook his head, swallowing his anxiety and looking at the building with a new determination. He had a dare to fulfill. It's not like anybody was inside, and his pitiful shaking was spoiling the footage.

Tentatively, Jacob pushed the deteriorated door open, gritting his teeth as the high- pitched squeal of rusted hinges pierced his ears. He fumbled to turn on his flashlight before stepping inside and getting the best shot he could of the terribly damp, empty interior. It was odd.

From the outside, the building looked like an old, worn-down house, but the inside was gutted of even its partitioning walls. The snap of a twig and the calls of a frightened bird had Jacob quickly backing out of the building. The slightest visage of beady, gleaming eyes and a shape all too unnatural choked Jacob. He turned and ran, lungs working overtime to keep him moving. He only stopped when a stump that seemingly appeared caught onto the toe of his shoe and tripped him. He hissed at the burn in his knees and mourned at the dirt and grass stains in his beloved jeans. Had he been allowed to change, he would've. Another snap of a twig and suddenly he didn't care that his new jeans got dirty. He watched a rabbit, pale as snow, run across the clearing and suddenly, he couldn't see much of anything at all.

Pam wailed as she repeated the description of her son to the officer again. "Long, black hair, birthmark on the corner of his eye, fair skin, baggy clothes." Over and over, she repeated, pleading for help, for progress, for anything. She even whispered Christ's name, beseeching for an answer.

Officer Stalts sighed as he calmed the sobbing woman he was stuck on call with. "Yes, ma'am, we know he's missing. We've been looking just like you asked. My fellow officer just informed me that they may have found his camera, and they are bringing it in to be searched."

Pam only wept harder. Stalts hesitated before grumbling, "I suppose you and your husband can come down the station and look through the camera with us. You'd be better able to identify it than we would."

The woman's head snapped up and she stared at her phone in disbelief. "We'll be right there, sir. Thank you. Thank you so much," she bawled, elated and yet mulling over the pit of dread that had hardened in her chest.

It didn't take long for Pam and her husband to arrive at the police station. The officer couldn't blame them, he supposed. Their son was missing, after all, and it had taken him and his crew weeks to find a lead as to where Jacob had gone. The poor old woman had sounded utterly distraught over the phone. Upon seeing her, his observation couldn't have been more correct. Her eye bags sagged, her brown hair frazzled, and she heaved heavily, almost looking as though she had run a marathon. Her husband, however, looked none the wiser. Regardless, Stalts motioned them over to the table his fellow officer currently sat at, going through the camera they had found. The officer's white gloves contrasted against the scuffed black material of the thing. Pam covered her mouth, choking back a sob. "That's it," she whimpered, "That's his camera."

Stalts tilted his head a little. "Right." He turned to the other officer, "Play the most recent video for us, will you?" The officer nodded and pressed play. The entire room was transfixed on the tiny screen of the camera. The lens was to the ground. Dead, grey grass lightly obscured its view of the forest around it. The trees blew peacefully, even if the branches heaved and groaned. A blood curdling scream erupted from the speakers of the device, interrupting the peaceful silence the scene radiated. Pam gasped and looked away. Her husband simply stared blankly as the screaming continued. Each time it started and stopped it caused a new lump of disquietude to settle in the stomachs of the poor people hunched over the tiny camera screen.

Pam bleated, "Please, please make me listen to this no more! This is torture!" Stalts nodded and gripped the other officer's shoulder until he skipped through a significant portion of the video.

It wasn't until the screaming stopped that the sound of rustling leaves presented the possibility of a warm body. Perhaps a survivor. Perhaps Jacob. Pam waffled between cowering away and staring at the screen with hope and shock. Her next peak made her breath hitch. A pair of perfectly shined black dress shoes entered the frame, gleaming in what little light escaped through the gaps of the leaves above. Beside them dropped a rabbit, bearing a mark of brown over its eye, marring the near white coat that flashed in the few escaping lights casted from the moon. Blood seeped from the rabbit's nose and more pooled around its limp body. The shoes stayed perfectly still. The wind howled through the trees. Leaves stirred and whipped around the camera, and yet, the figure held its ground. It was as though he were a wolf presenting the observers with a successful night's kill.

LOVE ALL YOU CAN
by Ani Free, 12th Grade
Honorable Mention: Fiction

The days of man were long lost, but their echoes forever haunted the pages, suspended in time. The libraries of the world did not mourn their loss, relieved from their obligation. The bookstore, however, loved humanity for all it was. The same heart capable of great cruelty could also love to endless depths, forever imprinted in the memory-bound books–waiting to be found. A small girl with pigtails just touching her shoulders walked through the door as the bell above announced her presence. To her amazement, it was as if the walls themselves had come to life with an unfamiliar warmth. She didn't know how she'd found this place when all that remained was left in ruins. But inside the bookstore, the rest of the world eased away, and the horrors of reality were only a distant thought. She had come looking for something, proof that there was more.

As she ran her fingers across each binding, she could feel them humming tunes of different melodies. She stopped at one, and upon opening it, the room was filled with a somber sound. The pages were filled with images of desolate fields., She could hear the cries and pleas as they echoed off the walls. Sounds that haunted her dreams.

She shut the book closed with a loud snap as the tears welled. The little girl sank to the floor feeling hollow, as if the wind would cut right through her.

She hadn't noticed how the lights had dimmed, filling the store with a colder hue. On the shelves above she could hear the books rustling against each other until one fell from the top shelf. It hit the floor with a clear thump, appearing the same as the previous book she first picked.

Hesitantly, she approached, finding it to be opened to the same page as the last book, but this time there wasn't a rush of cries and the music didn't swell in a bottomless pit.

Instead, the room was filled with lights, and the music was airy as it lingered in the air with each note. The pages flipped as she held the book between her palms, creating a moving sequence.

In front of her eyes a story was unfolding., It wasn't just the barren wasteland that she'd call home or the constant yelling and pointed fingers. There was a little girl playing among a group of kids with her mother watching in the distance with a faint smile seemingly illuminated by the sun.

Even from the other side of the page, she could hear the lively laughter of childhood. As the pages continued to flip, she was brought to another scene. An older couple with bread in their arms was welcomed into a small home. Upon entering the dining room, they were met with a makeshift of tables and chairs. Pieces that'd never belonged with each other, and frankly the ugliness was laughable, but when a large tablecloth cloaked all the tables, they all sat in unison.

The room was lit by a few small candles, but the bright eyes and growing cheers would've made you believe the world was under a spotlight. At the center of it all, stood the women from before with the same recognizable smile.

The book was nearing its end as it flipped to one final scene. The mother and daughter sat in darkness, foreheads pressed together. The mother whispered something—soft, fleeting—before fading into the unknown—a message she wouldn't understand until much later. The daughter's breath wavered, lost to the deafening silence.

As the book closed, the girl sat frozen, her mother's words still clinging to her much like the darkness. But even then your love never stopped. And that same love called on her once more. She blew the remaining dust off its cover and folded the corner of the first empty page before tucking it in her coat. She drew a new breath, one that was strong and sharp. Unshakable. Her tears had slowly dried and even to her surprise, a small smile crept across her face.

The girl gathered her things before making her way to the door. As she lingered at the entrance, she looked back, giving the bookstore one final look.

"Thank you. I found what I was looking for," she whispered, before gently shutting the door, leaving everything she'd come to know. She walked through the world with her book under her arm, always keeping it close to her heart. The once-cruel winds no longer hollowed her; they carried her forward with her mother's words steady in her bones.

"Love all you can, and do it well."

And so, she did.

TAPPING ON THE TANK
by Salome Flowers, 12th Grade
Honorable Mention: Fiction

As Laurie lies on the scratchy tan carpet of her bedroom, she hears the light "tink tink" of raindrops on her window. It's a November day, but her mother has insisted everyone crack their respective windows. Her mother loves a freezing home. She loves having fall air through the window and the smell of wet leaves in each room. She wants it to be just cold enough that they have to turn on the gas fireplace in their living room. Laurie can hear everything outside. It's the evening, not necessarily late but dark due to the season. Wind hisses through her window and into her room, rustling the sheer white curtains framing the oak-sided pane of glass.

Her head rests on her arm that has begun to fall asleep. Her lower body is wrapped in a plush knit blanket, little fingers wrapping around the thick yarn. As she gazes up at her fish tank nothing else bothers her, possessing the blissful ignorance of the world that only an eight-year-old girl can have. The goldfish she has affectionately named Rudy mills back and forth, combing the bottom for extra food. He intakes pieces of gravel and spits them back out methodically, over and over again. The light from the tank illuminates her face and her dark bedroom.

She got Rudy when she was four. Her father refused to put him in a bowl and instead opted for a twenty-gallon tank with live plants and an expensive filtration system. He said that if they were going to trap the fish in a monotonous life, they had to at least try and make it interesting. Due to the extra space and extra feedings Laurie routinely gave him, Rudy became glutinous. He was large, about four-and-a-half inches long with a swollen belly. His nutrition had made his skin bright orange and his face expressive. Laurie loved this fish unconditionally. She loved in watching him aimlessly sift through gravel for hours.

Her friends found it strange that she had not asked for a dog or even a hamster for her fourth birthday, but instead begged and pleaded for a fish. However, what her fellow second graders didn't understand was how extraordinary Rudy was. She felt he was the most intelligent goldfish to ever live. She had detailed conversations with him upon getting home from school, explaining to him the trials and tribulations of Mrs. Elmgrens' second-grade class. Though he never spoke back, he would sit behind the glass motionless, seemingly hanging onto her every word.

As Laurie lay there, studying Rudy, she noticed he had sucked a rather large piece of gravel into his mouth. He was making the effort of trying to puff out that piece of gravel but it appeared to be stuck. Just as she stood up to investigate further, she heard a loud clatter coming from downstairs, accompanied by yelling. Startled, she ran down the carpet-covered stairs of her two-bedroom home. The thick shag runner made her stumble so she gripped onto the wooden railing for stability.

Just as she got to the bottom she decided it would be best to not make herself known right away, just in case. She tip-toed into the living room, her sock-covered feet making no sound. She rounded the corner into her kitchen, peeping her head in. First, she saw the shattered glass of her favorite plate, one she had made in a summer camp pottery class. She had meticulously painted an ocean scene on it. Bright green reeds drifted in the water surrounded by colorful fish. She now saw these brightly-colored shards lying around her feet, one of which had a chubby orange blob on it modeled after dear Rudy. As she followed this trail of blues and greens, she saw her father, his back turned to her. He was standing, his right hand holding the sides of his head with a firm grip, massaging in the way he did when he was stressed about work or solving his daily crossword. His shoulders were slumped and defeated.

It seemed to Laurie that if he hadn't been holding on to the island in front of him with one hand he would melt to the floor. Laurie had never seen her father like this. He was an exceptionally stoic man, perpetually composed.

Her mother was on the other side of the island. Laurie's parents were the gospel of "opposites attract." Her mother was a frazzled woman while her father was trim and put together. Her hair billowed out on all sides of her head, brown frizzy coils that seemed to emulate her aura. She had a high shrill voice that was often too loud for the setting. Laurie never minded. Laurie's father never minded. Her three-person family unit was firmly bound. Laurie's best friends were her parents, delighting in any extra time she had the privilege of spending with them. But now, standing in this kitchen, she saw two people who only faintly resembled her mom and dad.

Tears streamed down her mother's face in clear rivers, her cheeks pink. Laurie looked at her. Her normally happy and frizzy mother. Just at the sight of the damp-faced woman, a lump formed at the base of Laurie's throat—a kind of tightening that means if someone were to ask,

"Are you okay?" the only answer would be a wracking sob. Laurie's father stood there, his hand fell from his temple. His shoulder blades pinched together, reaching a silent resolution.

Laurie suddenly experienced the overwhelming feeling that she was not meant to be there. She was not meant to see this, whatever this was. She slinked back into the dark corners of her home, the same way she came in. Socks silently brushed the plush carpet up the stairs. As she rounded the corner to her room, she didn't spare Rudy a glance, deep in thought about what she had just witnessed and the implications of what may rise from it.

The next morning, she found that her mother had left—her things packed, and her car gone. Along with this, she found Rudy, belly up in his tank, a large piece of gravel still lodged in his mouth.

Memoir Moments

Instructor Introduction
by Kelly Almer

Special moments in life that define who we are as humans, leave permanent marks in our hearts and minds. This memoir class helped writers dig deep into their lives to uncover defining times that held positive and impactful lessons with each of them. Each memoir took the writer down "Memory Lane" to discover the person, place, or thing and its significance in their life.

It is our hope from this class that as you read these stories you will understand not only why the event or item was special to each of them, but may it also strike a memory moment in your life that helped shape you into the person you are today.

EVERY SUMMER
by Lincoln Montgomery, 4th grade

Every summer in June, July, August, or part of September either my uncle, my grandma, or my mom would take me to their house at Duck Lake. Most days we would go on their boat and swim and do a lot of stuff including kayaking, fishing, paddleboarding, and a whole lot more.

That's really the reason I look forward to summer. I enjoy being with my cousins and I love water activities. Me and my cousins use their paddle boards and pretend we are a tour ship in their lake. We pretend we are talking to imaginary people coming to secure their ships at the dock. I love boats and it brings this to life for me. We also fish every day and kayak at least once every time we go.

I remember one time when we were getting ready to go kayaking, one of my cousins was in the teal kayak a little ways from the dock and found out there was a wasps' nest in the bow! We yelled at him to jump out of the kayak into the water but he didn't. He didn't want to get wet and he was fairly close to the dock so instead he paddled toward the dock and got out of the boat as quickly as a cheetah trying to avoid the wasps.

If I'm not at my cousin's house it takes ten minutes to get to the nearest lake from my house. The moment I see the bay, I feel yearning to run into the water and swim. The water hits my chest and I feel as cold as an ant buried in the snow. Jumping up and down to get warmer, or standing still until I feel used to the temperature, I walk into what feels like a bottomless well.

Duck Lake is a gorgeous lake because the Northern Lights shine bright on the water. I've never been there during the late nights when my aunt, uncle, and cousins go out to see them. They are very bold in the sky along with really pretty sunsets. And my grandma shows them to me through my aunt's Facebook page.

One time on the 3rd of July my cousins' neighbors were having a party and right before they were about to launch the five thousand dollars' worth of fireworks, me, my aunt, my uncle, and my youngest cousin went on their rowboat and saw the pretty sunset that night and my aunt said that she called that a fire sunset.

The last time I went to my cousins' for the end of summer my aunt, my uncle and all four cousins wanted me to jump off the boat but I was too scared. The reason why I was scared was because I felt like I wasn't going to pop back up to the surface of the dark murky lake and I was going to drown. I also felt like a fish would bite me or I was afraid of getting stuck in the long stringy seaweed.

So that afternoon we went out onto the Pontoon boat.

Finally, I promised myself I would do it.

I would jump off the boat.

While my Uncle was still in the water he said that I would have to sit down off the front side of the boat and then put my feet on his shoulders. I felt really nervous but I slid into the water anyway. When we both popped up to the surface he asked me, "How was that?" He also asked me how I felt. I said I felt really, really proud of myself and that the plunge was fun!

After I practiced jumping off the boat in the water...

I finally did it!

I ran and jumped off the boat into the deep end!

I was really proud of myself! After all my cousins cheered for me while some of them were on the boat and in the water, the cousins that were in the water got out and together the five of us jumped in.

Then later that night when we got back to the dock I was happy but sad. I was sad because I had to go home that night, and I was happy because I jumped off the boat.

We went inside. I brought all of my swim stuff, including my lifejacket and my goggles. That night I was really sad because the next day I had to go to school.

I felt I could do anything in the water now that I could jump in. Before I jumped in, the lake was a place where I could have fun, but I was missing out on the fun of jumping in. Rising to the surface for the first time, I felt really excited because the water was no longer what I could lose to. I felt like a bit of a pro.

HOT DOG SUIT
by Wren Gotts, 5th grade

Hi, I'm Wren Gotts. I was dressed in a hotdog suit in a room full of adults and kids who all wanted a part in the community theater, and I was the only one that looked delicious! Well let's go back to the very beginning.

Ah yes, about three weeks ago we were looking for Halloween decorations at Target. Yes, that's right we were looking for tiny skeletons to ride pink plastic flamingos as we were living in Florida temporarily. Mom probably saw the idea on one of her apps that old people use like Pinterest. Anyways I was hoping to get a good look at the toy aisle, but the future had different plans for me. Now more about my hot dog suit and when I first saw it...

It was beautiful!

It was the chef's kiss of Halloween costumes!

It was soo...oh what were the words the French use again, *tres magnifique*. It was pure perfection, I just had to wear it, had to have it, had to be IT!

That hunky piece of meat with perfectly toasted buns had to be mine. Whoever designed this costume is a genius and I wanted to be wearing their masterpiece.

The only thing standing in my way was Mom and that it was on the pricey side of Halloween costumes. She found a much cheaper costume of a banana made for an XL dog. "What about being a banana?" she said. I'm practically eleven but on the smaller side. Of course Mom had to try to stuff me into a costume made for a dog. I thought my life was ending not that you would want to know or anything, but it was a banana costume made for a dog like a German Shepherd or Golden Retriever, not a human child.

When Mom finally realized the potential in the hot dog suit I was so relieved! It was the wiener! For a second, just a second maybe the first time EVER I felt embarrassed trying it on in the store, but then I thought to myself, no, I'm just kind of a weirdo and feel fine with that and started to feel better. I actually felt invincible, flabbergasted with amazingness. I couldn't stop laughing and smiling. The hot dog suit actually repelled negative energy and inside it a new world was opened. I didn't want to take it off. People around me, complete strangers, smiled and pointed. A kid in the store said, "Look Mom, a funny hotdog!" while I did a little dance in the store. The cashier smiled and laughed when we purchased the suit and I wore it out the door.

A few days later I went to get new headshots for acting. Yes that's right I'm an actor on TV and theater. This particular photographer was fun. She asked me over the phone if I wanted to bring anything that shows my personality. Hmm, I wondered if she had photographed something as amazeballs as my hot dog suit. After telling her my ideas she said, "Ok, You need to bring this hotdog suit."

A week later we showed up with the hot dog suit in tow. The makeup artist and photographer were inspired and even had to go and get mustard packets to make a Hulk Hogan mustache on me to complete the look. Everyone in the studio that day was laughing, smiling and had funny ideas as I strutted my stuff in costume.

Soon the hot dog suit had a new entry as a star. I wrote a monologue dedicated to my hot dog suit. Once I put the masterpiece on and was as confident as ever I rocked my audition but I had to wait, so I waited.

and waited,

and waited,

and waited,

until I received the part of Flick in the show, "A Christmas Story."

I am now known as the hot dog girl and live up to that name and it will go down in history just like Rudolf the Red-nosed Reindeer. Whenever I think about the hot dog suit, it brings me joy. It changes how people look at me. If they see me in the hot dog suit, they think I am a really cool kid. I think I am and it's all because of a lot of meat in between a bun. There is so much more to me than "meats" the eye.

REPAIRING THE SAW
by Wyatt Wagner, 4th grade

One Sunday at church, Mrs. C walked up to me and said, "I have a broken saw, would you mind trying to fix it?"

I replied, "Sure, I'll fix it."

Earlier in the summer, I had fixed a fan for her daughter. It was a really old fan, made of all metal, and the cord was frayed which kept electricity from going into the fan motor. My mom and I took it apart, we studied how it worked, and then we decided it needed a new cord.

Once it was apart, I realized it would be really easy to fix. We replaced the cord, and the fan worked better than before.

The saw was a Black and Decker jigsaw. It was an old, red saw, and the cord was frayed so badly the wires were exposed. At first, I had to take the saw apart to study how it worked. As I took it apart, I told myself I needed to remember how to put it all back together. We took pictures and video so we could reassemble it.

The next day I went to my grandpa's house, and he helped me cut the damaged part off the cord. My grandpa is a really smart guy. Grandpa is always taking care of things. He knows a lot about fixing items, and he likes helping me. He served in the 82nd Airborne and ran his own business for 42 years, realigning large paper mill roller machines.

He also has a shop full of tools that smells like oil.

Grandpa's shop is a special place.

It is full of tools!

I see a metal lathe, a work bench full of tools, hand wipes, and a big air compressor. There are bins full of metal pipes. He has a display shelf full of old-fashioned cars. He gave me three of them. One of them is a Ford. It's a minty-ish blue color. I keep it on a shelf in my room now. I love it.

The tools have been used many times because he has taken apart a whole car and sold the pieces. Next to the shop there is a garage full of lawn mowers, a dirt bike, tractors, a zero turn, and more things. I like being in Grandpa's garage. The smell makes me think about the many times I've been inside of it, working on the saw, and looking at his tools.

I had a toy tractor and my sister had a jeep at Grandpa's shop. We raced and we raced in the yard for hours at a time, driving back and forth. Some rounds I won and some rounds she won. My cousins now live in the old house and the tractor and jeep are still there while my grandparents moved to a new house on a lake.

One summer morning my family and I went to visit Grandpa. I took a black plastic box holding the jigsaw into the garage. I hoped my grandpa would know what to do. We were going to have to order a new cord for the jigsaw but Grandpa suggested we might be able to fix it.

Grandpa looked at the saw and said, "Oh we can fix this." He grabbed wire cutters and cut the broken part of the cord. Then we took wire strippers, and stripped the plastic coating off the metal wire. We then had to take the end of the wire, dip it in flux, and then solder the wire into the saw. I was nervous about the hot metal dripping onto my finger. I felt relieved because Grandpa was helping me and I was spending time with him. This was the first time that Grandpa and I worked on a project together. What I enjoyed the most was using the soldering gun. I had never used one before but Grandpa was a patient teacher. He didn't rush when he was giving directions; he took his time. He taught me the steps it would take to solder the wire. I was surprised at how easy it was. The first step was dipping the wire in flux. Flux is a cloudy brown color and looks like wax. The second step was to touch the solder to the tip of the soldering gun and drip it on to the wire. The soldering gun heats up quickly and creates terrible burns. We were cautious not to drop the solder on our fingers or drop the gun.

We took the saw home and eventually we figured it out. Mom and I put it back together after three attempts. The next Sunday, we gave it to Mrs. C. She was happy that I fixed her saw, and said, "Thank you."

Fixing the saw was exciting for me because I enjoy helping other people. I also like spending time with my grandpa. The knowledge my grandpa shares with me, I can use again. I used the soldering gun to fix a part on my bike with my Grandpa Wagner. I remember the smell of the solder and it wasn't good!

Each time I use the soldering gun I remember the steps and more importantly spending time with Grandpa. He is an amazing man and making things with him is more enjoyable. I love him.

Writers Create II

Instructor Introduction
by Kelly Almer

What makes a story a story?

That answer is simple. Any imaginative event or storyline the writer wishes to record, enjoy, or leave for posterity is a story. Stories have been handed down through the ages, told orally then recorded for future generations.

The stories created in this class were exceptional and wonderfully crafted. Every story was told with enthusiasm and knowledge of storyline and character development. It was a pleasure and honor to work with these talented writers and it is my hope they will one day be #1 NYT best selling authors. Enjoy each tale and the richness captured inside their words.

PROLOGUE: POLAND, WARSAW, 1939
by Reagan Bulloch, 6th Grade

Lina Potrofke walked home with a terrible feeling in her stomach and she knew something was wrong, but what? Normally the word holiday was joyous and welcome, but something felt grim and unsettling this time...

One year earlier.

Lina laughed so hard that she almost cried when her best friend Helen made a funny joke as they were walking home together. They did everything together. They walked together to and from school, they ate lunch together: they were inseparable. When they got to Lina's house, they waved and said goodbye. As soon as Lina entered the house, she walked out to the patio and there found her mother. Mrs. Potrofke was sewing and drinking iced tea. Lina said hi and kissed her on the cheek. Then she picked up her sketch pad and started to draw. Lina was an amazing artist and she drew everything. Friday was Lina's favorite day of the week because Helen's family always came over to eat dinner with them. Mother always made the most delicious home cooked meals on Fridays. Lina loved her mother's Pierogis.

Just then Father walked through the door dressed in his crisp police uniform. Father was a tall man with brown hair, kind brown eyes with a strong chin, broad shoulders and a gentle voice. He always made Lina smile and laugh at his jokes.

He took his coat and hat off and hung them up on the coat rack. Then he hugged Lina and kissed Mrs. Potrofke and sat at the table with Lina to look at her drawings from the day because he was the one who had taught her how to draw in the first place. He asked Lina how her day was and just as she started to answer Lina heard a knock on the door.

It was Helen and her family!

She ran to the door to greet them, opened the door, and welcomed them inside. Lina ran upstairs with Helen while the grownups talked, as the two of them always did this. As they were talking, Helen's mother said that dinner was ready. After everyone was full and tired, Helen and her parents left and not long afterward Lina and her family went to bed.

The next morning Lina woke up feeling happy and well-rested. She got out of bed, brushed her hair and teeth, got dressed, and washed her face. She walked down the stairs to find her mother in the kitchen cooking breakfast. Lina headed straight for her sketch pad and started to draw. She decided to draw her mother today.

Helen came to Lina's house Sunday later that afternoon. Helen was the kind of girl who always looked neat and orderly. Her hair was combed neatly compared to Lina's which was constantly messy no matter how hard she tried to keep it neat.

When she knocked on the door Lina invited her inside, and the first thing that Lina noticed was that she was wearing a yellow star on her jacket, but she paid no attention to this because she was more concerned when she noticed Helen wasn't laughing or smiling as she usually did but instead she looked anxious and on edge. However, Lina knew it would only make her friend uncomfortable if she mentioned this so she said nothing. That night she lay awake thinking about her friend; why was she so anxious? Little did she know that over the course of the next few weeks she would learn why.

It was Monday morning time and time for school. Lina packed her backpack and walked to school with Helen. Lina realized that she was wearing the yellow star on her jacket again. When they arrived at the school they entered the big brick building; it looked so cold, lonely, and uninviting. As the two girls entered their classroom they walked towards their desks when their teacher Mr. Kristas stopped Helen and said that she would be sitting in the front of the classroom from now on. When Lina heard this she was confused and thought, "Why Helen? Has she done something wrong?" Bashful Helen walked to the front of the room and sat down.

The next days were not much different. Lina was still confused at Mr. Krista's meanness towards Helen who was a good student and never did anything wrong, unlike Lina who inevitably seemed to be in trouble for one thing or another, from drawing instead of listening to getting into fights with Marcus (a boy who Lina disliked).

When the bell rang and the teacher told the children that school was over, Lina and Helen packed up their books and exited the school grounds.

As they started walking together towards Lina's house she could not wait any longer. Her curiosity got the better of her. She asked Helen about the yellow star.

Lina had been trying not to say anything for days, but finally she could not wait. Lina had to know.

As they were walking home Lina asked why Helen was wearing the yellow star on her jacket. She also said that she thought that the jacket looked better without it. At first Helen did not say anything. Then she started yelling. She was mad.

Lina knew this much, but why?

Then she got her answer.

Helen was now sobbing. Each tear that rolled down her rosy cheeks was laced with rage and disgust. She asked Lina if she had ever just stopped and looked around, if she had even noticed the German soldiers, and if she had seen how cruel they were to Jewish people, like her.

That is when it hit Lina... the Nazis.

She had heard Mother and Father arguing about them one night through the vents. Lina felt so stupid. How could she not have noticed? She knew their opinions about Nazis, and she knew about how they invaded Poland and took over the government. Helen and her family were Jewish. Suddenly the yellow star made sense. Helen had no choice but to wear it. It was not an accessory; it was a way of knowing who was Jewish and who was not. The ones who wore the stars were treated significantly worse. Some restaurants would not let them dine, certain stores would not sell to them, and Jewish children were humiliated or expelled from school (which explained Mr. Krista's sudden meanness). In the time it took Lina to figure this out Helen had kept walking, leaving Lina standing there looking positively dumbfounded in the middle of the sidewalk.

Lina finally snapped out of it and ran to catch up with Helen who would not even look at her. Lina did not blame Helen for not talking to her. How was she so blind to the awful things happening to her friend's family? She was ashamed of herself. They walked home in silence. When Lina got home she did not grab her sketch pad. Instead she went to her room and cried.

The next day she walked to school alone. But when she saw that Helen was not at school, she knew something was wrong. Helen's mother never let her stay home from school, never. She decided to ask Mr. Krista because he would know. However all he said was that she was on holiday. The words themselves were not bad but the way he said them, with a grinch-like grin and a chuckle, made her feel sick. Lina Potrofke had a terrible feeling in her stomach and she knew something was wrong, but what? Normally the word holiday was joyous and welcome, but something felt grim and unsettling this time. After school she raced to Helen's house, but when she arrived at her house she saw something that made her heart skip a beat. On the front of the house in big black letters were the words JEW. She knocked on their door and nobody answered. Then she tried to open the door; it was unlocked. Helen's family always locked their door. When she pushed it open, she saw things that would haunt her forever.

Helen's family's belongings were torn and broken, paintings were ripped off the walls, chairs were smashed into pieces. She looked everywhere but there was no Helen or her family.

By now Lina was undoubtedly worried. What had happened to her friend? And why was the neat house such a wreck?

All Lina could remember was that the hot tears streaming down her face made her vision blurry and the sound of her rapid heart beat was all she could hear. Lina's knees started to buckle and she felt faint, then everything went black.

When she gained consciousness Lina couldn't remember where she was for a moment. She then realized that she was at Helen's house. It all came flooding back. She got to her feet and walked to her house. When she entered the front door, she found her parents in the kitchen with worried looks on their faces. Her mother had tear stains on her cheeks. When Mrs. Potrofke saw Lina, she hugged and kissed her daughter. Lina's mother told her how scared she had been when she had not come home from school.

Lina knew that she owed her parents an explanation so she told them the whole story about how she and Helen had gotten into a fight, how Helen was not at school, how their door was unlocked, how everything was disheveled, and finally how there was no Helen or her family to be found. After she had told the story Lina asked her parents where Helen's family was, and with this question her parents looked at each other and then at her and their faces said it all.

FIVE LITTLE DUCKLINGS
by Nora Bruinsma, 4th Grade

Five little ducklings and their mom lived on a farm. The farm was in a small town in the country. The ducklings were yellow and fluffy like marshmallow candies with orange beaks. Every day they followed their mom around the lake flapping their wings. The momma was very caring and always watched over her ducklings. The momma and ducklings lived on a tiny island in the middle of a lake on a farm.

One day they decided to go for a swim. One of the ducklings, Dave, was scared of the water so the momma had to push him in with her wings. He was splishing and splashing because he didn't like getting in. He liked being warm and the water was very wet and cold.

The other four ducklings loved the water. They jumped right in and started to fish. They put their heads into the water, their cute little butts in the air. Dave saw his siblings having fun and decided to join them. They each caught one fish for lunch.

After eating the delicious fish, their momma decided they should swim over to the other side of the pond but as they started to swim, it began to rain. They turned around and went back to their nest in the reeds. There was an egg in it! "Look Momma! The egg must have washed up on the shore!" said Dave. Looking around they saw animal tracks leading to the nest. The little ducklings hid in a huddle behind Momma. They all peered around her to see the egg. It was sort of small, smaller than a duck egg and was white with brown speckles. The baby ducks slowly walked up to it, put it under their feathers, and made a little huddle over it.

Mamma was surprised and confused! She knew it wasn't her egg because it was too small. So, she made another nest and put the egg in it. Then she took some reeds and put them over the egg to keep the egg warm.

Tomorrow she would find the owner of the egg. The ducklings then snuggled into their nest and fell asleep. They fell asleep, dreaming under the warmth of their mom's wings, hoping they'd find the egg's mom.

When they woke up, they wiggled out from under her to wake her up. Then they pretended the egg belonged to them. They sat on it like their mom sat on them. She gently grabbed the egg and tucked it under her feathers. They swam over to the other side of the lake to search for the egg's home.

When they got to the other side they visited the swan's nest. "Is this your egg?" said the momma duck.

"No, it is not, I only have three eggs," said the swan. So the momma duck and her ducklings moved on to the farm on the edge of the lake.

They found a beaver's nest that they had never seen before. "Is this your egg?" said the momma duck.

"No silly, I don't even lay eggs," said the beaver.

When waddling onto the shore they stepped on a hole in the ground and out popped a groundhog. "Is this your egg?" said the momma duck.

"No way! I don't lay eggs," said the groundhog.

Then they asked the grandma chicken, "Is this your egg?" The grandma chicken said, "No way! I haven't laid eggs in years!"

They waddled up to the fence determined to find the momma. A big brown head appeared. The mom duck asked, "Is this your egg?"

The cow said, "No way! I don't lay eggs. I am a mammal, silly!"

"Oopsy daisy, sorry to bother you ," said momma duck. They waddled up the hill to the chicken coop. There were lots of chickens. The momma duck asked the smallest chicken, "Is this your egg?"

She said, "No." Then all the chickens started to gossip, "Is this your egg?" they repeated, running around in circles like rice spilling all over a kitchen table.

No one claimed the egg until one fluffy white chicken stepped forward.

"Is this your egg?" asked the ducklings.

"Yes! Yes! It is!" exclaimed the fluffy white chicken. All the ducklings cheered. The momma duck slowly moved her wings to the ground, gently releasing the egg. The fluffy, white chicken picked the egg up with her wings and carefully added it with the others in the nest inside the chicken coop and sat on them. She was so happy to have her egg back she jumped into the air as high as she could go. The ducks waddled back to the pond happily and the four of them jumped in. Their mother and Dave followed behind. He waddled into the water and swam off happily. Their mother followed behind Dave, joining them. They formed a line and swam across the lake to invite the swans to their party.

"Hello Swan," said momma duck. "Would you like to come to our party?"

"I would like that very much. Thank you!" said the swan.

Then the ducklings swam and invited the mallard ducks, who also decided to join them. They even invited the fish swimming in the pond. The rabbits, groundhogs, beavers, and other farm animals joined from the shore. They all celebrated, happily dancing, clapping, and hopping, their quacks and chirps to be heard from afar. The cow was so excited he even tried to swim. They were all so happy the egg was returned to its rightful place.

It was just as the celebration ended that the egg began to shake. Then there was a crack! Out popped a foot, head, and a tiny pair of wings. The ducklings leaned close. They thought it was so interesting! The mother chicken scooped up the chick in her wings and spun around to show off her baby. They all went home with joy in their hearts. They had completed their mission.

ROSE
by Lily Wagner, 6th Grade

I walked along the dirt road, kicking at small rocks carrying my school books. I was fuming. I was so mad that I couldn't even notice the exploding, vibrant fall colors that garmented the trees. Those mean older kids had been teasing me that I couldn't ride horses and I wasn't good enough. They were all boys. They tormented me that I was a girl and girls shouldn't ride horses. Tom Bower was the worst of the lot. "Hey Redhead!" He would say, "Betcha you can't even sit on a horse without falling off!"

I'll show them. I'll show them what I can do!

I ran home the rest of the way, my knee-high skirt catching my legs. When I arrived at home, I thrust open the door and stomped my way to a chair. Mama was cooking something over the old stove: stew and biscuits. We didn't have much money, but Mama could always cook something good.

"Jane, how was your day at school?"

"Not so good" I huffed. "Those mean boys were saying I couldn't ride a horse because I was a girl!"

"Well," Mama said, "you can show them what you can do. Just make sure you're humble about it."

"Yes Mama," I said.

"Good, now run off. You need to feed Rose," she told me.

I always loved taking care of Rose.

I ran out to the pasture to greet her. Rose was an old and kind mare. She was a workhorse, but I liked riding her. "C'mon Rose, let's feed you some dinner." I led her to our small barn, scooped out a bucket of grain, and let her eat. I liked the soft sound of her munching as she nuzzled my arm softly. It helped to soothe me. I leaned against the big horse's side, and breathed in the warm, sweet scent of her and closed my eyes. My Mama and Daddy had gotten Rose as a workhorse when I was young. They said

I was scared of her then, but I learned to love her as I got older. She never got spooked when I fell off. She just stood there as I got back on. Because of this, I could easily ride her. Over time our relationship had blossomed and grown.

Outside of the barn I heard the wind shivering through the leaves of the big oak that stood in the middle of the small pasture. I heard honking geese as they descended on their journey to the south, for the cold weather was approaching. The grass rustled in the evening breeze and I heard my older siblings playing outside. I smoothed down her tangled, black mane and pulled out burdocks that had embedded into it.

In one day, after school, all the kids who had horses would gather up and have a race. It was small, and to be held in the fields behind the school house.

I was so excited!

When Rose was done eating, I took her out to the pasture and started riding her bareback. I loved the feel of the wind rustling my red hair, and the thrill of the ground rushing below her. I felt the strong muscles of the horse bulge and move. Rose may be an old horse, but she was a strong runner.

Later at dinner, Daddy asked, "Jane, how was your day?"

"It was fine until that jerk, Tom Bower, said I couldn't ride, but I'm gonna show him on Friday!"

Daddy smiled and said, "I know you will."

After we were done cleaning up after dinner, we all went outside and I went over to the big maple tree standing in the middle of the yard. Its huge crown of golden leaves waved in the cool breeze, and I walked up to it and started climbing it. Its large limbs were very easy to climb because they were rough with old bark, and years of waving and swaying in the wind. Years of children of the Brown family climbing the tall, wide tree. As I traced my fingers over the bark, a small ladybug crawled on the surface. The shell was glistening in the sunlight as it crawled on over the bark.

I heard a whinny, and looked over to the south side of the house. Rose was rolling in the pasture, covering herself in dirt to keep the bugs away and flies off. She seemed to be enjoying herself, rolling, twisting, turning in the Kentucky dirt. I grinned and hopped off the tree and walked over the fence and sat on it. Rose stopped rolling and sat up. She turned, saw me, and trotted over. I scratched her velvety soft ears and she lowered her head for me to pet. We sat there for a while, enjoying the moment.

I used this special time to walk to the barn and clean Rose's stall. As I entered my favorite place, I smelled the familiar scent of leather, horse, and straw. It was very comforting. I went over to her stall and scooped out the old straw and put in some new bedding. Her water needed to be topped off, so I went out to the well and scooped out a bucket of water. I went back to the barn, the water sloshing and splashing my dirty skirt. I emptied it and went to take Rose to her stall. I led her into it and she took big gulps of water.

Finishing the work, I walked back into the house to end the day.

The next morning I woke up before the sun, as usual. I pulled on my dress and went downstairs as Mama was getting breakfast ready: oatmeal and bacon.

I went outside to feed Rose and the other farm animals. It was still dark, and I loved the scent of an early fall morning. The moon still faintly shone in the sky, but there was a light in the east; I must've woken up later than I normally did. I shivered because it was cold. I entered the small barn and lit a lantern. Rose was waiting for me in her stall. I gave her some oats and topped off her water. As she crunched on her oats, she nuzzled my arm as she always did. I scratched her soft belly. Rose finished eating, so I led her out into the pasture. As the sun was rising, it cast golden light down on the grass, lighting up the morning dew like diamonds that were sprinkled across the ground. The buttery light crested the treetops with sunshine, and the clouds were shades of pink and red. I turned around and walked inside. I quickly ate my oatmeal, then hurried outsided, almost forgetting my lunch pail and reader. I walked to the schoolhouse, taking the short way with Molly through the field.

Molly walked silently, pushing through the tall grass waving in the early fall breeze, stooping down to pick a pretty flower every now and then. We came to the creek that passed through a small section in the field. It shimmered, and I bent down to pick up a glittering stone shining in the water and tucked it into the pocket of my skirt. I decided to give it to Rose—maybe it would brighten up her stall.

We crossed the road and came to the schoolhouse. Children of all ages were playing outside. I went to sit down on the schoolhouse steps. Only a few minutes after, the teacher, Miss Ross, came out and rang the school bell. We all went inside, and I sat down next to my friend Sarah.

There was lots of chatter in the room so I said to Sarah, "I can hardly wait!"

"For what?" she questioned.

"The race!" I said excitedly.

"Oh!" she said "I almost forgot!

"Class, quiet down please," Miss Ross, our teacher, said. All the chatter went away, and I stopped talking. I didn't pay much attention in class. I was too busy daydreaming about the race. When I was FINALLY done with school, I burst out and ran outside with Sara. "I can hardly wait!" I said biting into my sandwich.

"Me too!" she exclaimed. "Even though I won't be in the race, I'll still be rooting for you!"

I smiled and said, "Thanks."

I finished my sandwich and was just about ready to leave when someone tapped me on the shoulder. I turned and saw it was Tom Bower. I glared and said, "What do you want?"

He grinned and said, "You actually think you can be in the race? You're a girl! You should be sitting down doing your sewing!"

"Well, I'll tell you this Tom, who says you're going to win the race? And also go step in some cow dung." I turned and walked away.

"You should have seen the look on his face!" Sara exclaimed. "It was as red as a ripe tomato and steam was practically blowing out of his ears!"

I grinned and said, "Well I better run back. I gotta get Rose ready!"

"I'll see you there," she shouted after me.

I ran home. Molly was talking to her friend so she didn't mind that I was leaving early. I stopped at the creek to get a sip of water and ran for the house. I entered the house greeting Mama then headed outside to the barn. I led Rose into her stall and put on her bridle. No saddle was needed as I was going bareback. She nickered and touched her nose to my arm, seeming to sense my nervousness. I put her bridle on her and rode out the barn, and my hands were sweaty as I gripped the reins. I couldn't help but feel a little nervous. I pushed the butterflies that were in my stomach out and focused on the pretty tall golden grass waving in the wind. The small stream in the distance looked like a silver ribbon lying on the ground. The tall trees were waving in the distance, garmented in fall colors. I didn't want to be late so I hurried Rose into an extended trot.

We arrived with a few kids already lined up. Tom Bower wasn't there. I lined up next to a girl, the only other one there, who had brown hair chopped short, and she was riding a young mare. Tom Bower showed up, riding a stallion. Its coat was a deep chestnut red and was very big, though the horse looked a bit intimidating. It seemed nervous as it pawed the ground, and its ears lay flat on the horse's head. Rose sat calmly, staring out at the grass. The race path was lined with logs and old, rusty barrels which kids sat on in the grass, cheering and shouting. I noticed Sarah. She was waving her arms around and shouting my name. I smiled and waved back. A boy standing on a large tree stump was shouting stuff.

Suddenly he said, "Racers, get ready!" I braced myself and he said, "On your mark! Get set! GO!!" I kicked off starting off slow, pacing myself. All the other racers were far ahead. Then I sped up. Rose's hooves pounded against the ground pulsing forwards, faster and faster. I passed in front of a kid, then the next, and the next. Rose was speeding up! "C'mon Rose! You can do it!" The other girl was in the lead. I started passing others. Tom Bower was startled! He scowled and went faster but I easily bolted past him. He was urging his horse too much, so it quickly slowed down. Now the girl and I were right next to each other!

Then something went wrong.

A log must've rolled out of place onto the path and Rose either tripped on it, or she just stumbled. Either way, Rose fell. It seemed to happen in slow motion. Her left front leg rolled and I heard a sickening crack. I put out my arm to brace myself for the fall and then I heard another crunch; this time it was me. I laid on the ground and closed my eyes. Pain flooded through me, and Rose laid on the ground a few feet from me, still. I heard the thunder of hooves as all the others passed me and felt the ground shake. I got up, looked down at my arm, and shuddered. It was bent and definitely broken.

I looked over at Rose.

What would happen to Rose? My heart sank all the way down to the bottom of my stomach.

Her front leg was bent and broken and she was breathing heavily, laying on her side.

Tears flooded from my eyes and I cried. I cried because I knew.

I didn't notice Sarah sitting there trying to comfort me, or Mama fussing about my arm. Papa came over and had to wrestle me away from Rose to get me to Dr. Morris's office. I remembered people crowding around me. The girl who won the race stood there staring at me as I walked away, not knowing what was to become of Rose.

Was she in pain?

Would she be OK?

An hour later, my arm in a cast, we returned to the farm. I ran up and fumbled with the door trying to get it to open with one hand. I burst in and ran to Rose's stall. As I entered it, I saw she was laying down, breathing heavily, and her eyes were closed. When she opened them to see who was there, they looked like an old shadow had fallen over them, but they lightened up a little bit, and I sat down next to her. She nuzzled my arm, and I petted her ears where she always loved to be petted. I picked up one of her stones and felt it with my finger rubbing its smooth surface. It sort of reminded me of the race, and I was surprised that I still had it.

"I love you Rose, I will miss you but your time has come." I couldn't believe what I was saying at all. Tears welled up in my eyes and I leaned against her side feeling her breathing, relishing the little time we had left together.

Hours dragged by with me by Rose's side. I fell asleep in the soft, sweet hay.

I soon woke up to someone shaking me awake. It was Mama. "Come on Jane, let's head inside," she said. I got up and pulled some straw from my tangled braid. "Mama, may I sleep here tonight?" I asked.

"No, you've got a broken arm, and it's far too cold to sleep out here" she said.

I got up, but just before I left Rose I put her nose to my arm and rested it there. She laid it back down, and then I walked out of the barn. It was dark, but the moon shone brightly in the sky and a curtain of shining white stars hung across the vast open darkness. I shivered. As I was about to fall asleep I saw a bobbing light shine through the window. I got up from my bed and looked outside to see Daddy walking slowly into the barn.

He was carrying his gun. NO!!!! My insides screamed at me.

I knew what he was about to do and I dreaded the moment. I plugged my ears waiting for the gunshot. It came.

Cracking through the calm, it echoed through my mind and I fell on my bed and cried and cried. I would never ride through the pasture. I would not be smelling her sweet smell and there'd be no more of her leaning her nose against my arm. I felt like I was in the deep, dark pits of sadness. I ate breakfast but my stomach felt hollow inside.

I got up from the table and somehow walked outside.

It was a very pretty fall morning but despite my sadness, everything was covered in a sparkling, glittering frost in the early morning sun. I looked over to the far side of the pasture and noticed a mound of dirt that hadn't been there before.

I walked over to it and pulled up a very pretty golden leaf that had fallen from the maple tree.

It was then I remembered the stone that I had pulled out of the creek the day before and placed in Rose's stall. I walked back to the barn to retrieve it and set it on the leaf.

It still glistened even though it wasn't wet. I looked down at the leaf and the pebble and smiled.

I loved Rose very dearly but her time had come.

I will forgive Daddy. I know it wasn't his fault Rose died.

I will always have Rose with me. She will always be in my heart and I know that she knew I loved her so dearly.

YOGI
by Desmond Andrick, 6th Grade

Yogi's chipped iron pickaxe bit through solid rock, one block of stone after another, no ores anywhere in his little mine.

Down he went carving a narrow staircase and placing torches to light the way. Then, after so much mining, a glint of gold met Yogi's eye.

Out of the rock came five pieces of raw gold, awaiting a warm furnace.

Yogi eagerly ran up the spiral staircase to his little house. Yogi had built this house with his own hands; he was proud of it. With a brick foundation and two stories made of oak and birch planks, he had spent many tiring days cutting down trees and digging for clay. Yogi's favorite part was the outdoor, rooftop balcony where he could watch the moon and stars all night. His house also had a secure iron door, keeping any monster at bay.

He slid the gold into the furnace with some sticks from a nearby chest. Then he pulled out a watermelon slice from a different chest and sat down to wait for the gold to morph into solid ingots. The furnace's flames died as Yogi finished the juicy treat.

He pulled out the warm gold and bent over to put them in a chest with a few other semi rare ores. He would bring the gold tomorrow to sell at the weekly fair which was held in the nearby village, a short walk away. Gold was a shiny but soft metal, good for decorating but not for making tools. Yogi already had iron tools and weapons, so he would sell this gold at the fair for emeralds. Villagers would buy almost anything, funny people, and sell interesting things too. As he opened another chest (he had a lot of chests) he saw the stack of a dozen emeralds that he had been saving over a week's time. Better bring them tomorrow, he thought, and get some rest.

Yogi slowly climbed the stone staircase to his bedroom, yawning all the way. After a quick chapter of his favorite book he drifted off to sleep, with dreams of heroes, battles, and legends from long ago. The next day was hot and sunny, but it was cool in the patch of forest that snaked from Yogi's house to the village. In the huge trees Yogi strode peacefully on the worn dirt path. His heavy backpack was full to the brim with things he intended to sell at the village fair, his destination.

He also brought the emeralds that he had been saving. The huge spruce and oak trees loomed from far above, and mossy logs littered the fern-covered floor. A few birds swooped through the trees. Other than that the forest was very quiet and still. Perhaps the animals knew that danger was coming. After a while, he saw the village, out on the endless plains with stone towers and peaked wooden rooftops shining in the afternoon sun.

Villagers, travelers, and merchants crowded in the square, awaiting the opening of the market. At the corners of the packed square stood a still stone statue. But this was nothing like a statue because it moved. This friendly stone giant was one of the village's defenders. Inbound with some ancient magic, it used its huge stone fists to smash monsters to bits. As Yogi walked down the bumpy cobblestone streets, a large dinging bell sounded the opening of the fair. Yogi walked behind the crowd as people rushed in to get first dibs on good ware.

First, before he got distracted with cool things at the market stalls, he went to the traveling merchant. He sold almost everything and bought almost everything too. Yogi plopped all the things he was carrying onto the table and explained he wanted to sell them. Then the trader nodded and produced emeralds for each item, for Yogi had brought a few other things to sell: mostly stone and ores. When the robed trader put the emeralds next to the five gold nuggets Yogi said, "Two emeralds for five pieces of gold? Are you sure that is right?"

The trader shrugged. "Metal is not in high demand since the end of The Great War." Yogi sighed and left with his pay to go shopping. He purchased his normal week's worth of food: bread, apples, beef, pork, pumpkins, rice, chicken, beets, and flour. He also allowed himself a few sweet treats, and, for two emeralds, he got another book from the book store and returned another book to the library. Then, at sundown he hauled his things back to his house through the dark woods. That night he read his new book and fell to sleep with dreams of sword duels, stone giants, and portals.

THE DEVIL'S AQUARIUM
by Ziva Erlenbeck, 6th Grade

Cautiously, my friend and I darted around a corner. When I saw the coast was clear, we silently sprinted down the hallway to a heavy iron vault door which hung slightly open. Wow, I thought, Dad must have been in a hurry. He's never left the vault door open before. We weren't supposed to be in the lab, but we were only going to have a quick look while going by, and I really wanted to show Eleanor.

We slipped into the room and Eleanor gasped in awe at the large, blue lit room cluttered with parts and contraptions. Finally, Eleanor spoke, "What's that big machine over there, Rosalie?" I turned around, being careful not to bump tools and parts with my heavy backpack to see what she meant.

There, in the middle of the room was a large, cylinder machine that could fit four people and was covered in buttons with numbers and letters such as Mid-Jur-147-Mya and other strange combinations. I inched closer to stand next to Eleanor who was closely examining the perplexing machine. As she turned to speak to me I saw her elbow hit a button labeled Earl-Dev-390-MYA. There was a blinding flash of blue light, and we were gone.

Next thing I knew, I found myself face down in the cold, wet dirt. I got up and started wiping the mud off my clothes. "Where are we?!?!" Eleanor yelled in astonishment. I looked around and to my surprise, we were in a forest of tall bushes and plants. "Did your dad's machine teleport us here?" asked Eleanor, her eyes wide.

"I don't know," I replied, continuing to glance around. I took a look at the ground and stopped a small silver gadget that read, Laurentia-North America, early Devonian era, 290 million years ago.

As I gaped at it in surprise, Eleanor came over and picked up the gadget as she asked, "What does that mean?" while examining the screen.

"I think it means my dad's machine sent us back in time 290 million years ago in the Devonian era!" I answered, scarcely able to take it all in.

Eleanor's eyes widened. "Do you really mean that your dad invented a time machine?" "I think so," I said slowly, trying to take it all in.

"What are we to do?" Eleanor asked, echoing my own thoughts.

"Maybe we could look around a bit," I suggested, taking the little gadget and putting it in my pocket.

We started squelching across the muddy, swampy area. "Shouldn't we keep an eye out for dinosaurs?" asked Eleanor worriedly.

"No, the gadget says we're in the Devonian. Dinosaurs didn't appear until the Triassic, 45 million years from now," I said doing the math in my head.

"I'm so glad that you study this thing a lot. If it was just me I'd be completely lost, though, we kind of already are, with this whole time travel mess," Eleanor said. "But what are we to do? We don't know how to get back."

I thought for a moment. "We should keep walking."

For a few minutes we walked in silence, both of us trying to think of a way to get ourselves out of this strange predicament. We started walking through another bush forest.

"How come we haven't seen any trees?" asked Eleanor, who was looking around.

"It's because trees haven't evolved yet," I replied, remembering the tree evolution book I borrowed. As we pushed the last leaf fronds out of the way, we were greeted by the sight of a huge body of water stretching out across the horizon. I breathed out, taking in the sight of the shining turquoise water, hued gold in the light of the now setting sun. "It must be the Western interior seaway," I said to Eleanor, who was also looking out upon the beautiful scene. "Also called the Hell's Aquarium," I said wryly as a huge mosasaur leaped out of the water with a shark thrashing in its jaws, sunlight glinting off the beast's armored exterior.

"It's home to Xiphactinus, Enchodus, Cretoxyrhina, and Deinonychus which were all pretty large and terrifying: to name a few."

I would have been more startled, but the shock of being sent back in time 290 million years had not yet worn off. We prepared to set up a camp with the supplies in my bag but suddenly there was a luminous flash of blue light and we were gone once more.

We found ourselves in a dense forest with thick vegetation and sprawling ferns. "Where are we?" asked Eleanor, looking around.

I pulled out the little silver gadget and told Eleanor, "It says Germany-late Jurassic, 150.8 MYA, so it appears we not only traveled in time but also teleported to Germany." I wasn't really surprised because if it's possible to go back in time, why wouldn't it be possible to teleport?

Eleanor asked, "What are we to do? It's not like we can control where to go, or when we go."

"Then I guess we can explore. It's not every day you can look around ancient Germany, may as well make the most of it," I replied.

We headed off in a random direction brushing ferns out of the way and stepping over decaying logs. After some time we heard a chirping call from under the ferns a few meters away. We headed towards the sound and saw a pack of four brownish-green Compsognathus creeping up to the fern.

Then I saw it, a nearly fledged black chick cowering beneath. I ran forward and the little dinos scattered and fled, leaving me to pick up the tiny chick and examine it.

"What is that?" Eleanor asked. I took a look at the chick and it had teeth in its beak, and a long tail.

"I think it's an archaeopteryx!" I said breathlessly.

The archaeopteryx was my favorite species of prehistoric animal as they had many bird traits, such as feathers, wings, beaks, and a wishbone; and also dinosaur traits such as teeth, a bony tail, claws on their wings, and belly ribs.

"What are we going to do with it?" said Eleanor.

"We should probably look for the parents," I replied as I looked up into the trees. There was a distant chirping sound and the little chick replied with a high trill.

"Look!" Eleanor exclaimed in a loud whisper. A pair of archaeopteryx were gliding through the trees, their silky black tails flowing behind them. They perched in a nearby tree as they regarded us silently. As Eleanor watched the parents in awe, I gently placed the chick next to the fern and slowly backed away. Eleanor followed and we watched a good distance away as the family hopped off together into the vegetation.

As we continued on our way, I couldn't stop thinking about Compsognathus and Archaeopteryx. We were the first people to ever see them alive! Then something occurred to me: if there are dinosaurs like Compsognathus around, aren't there going to be other, larger predators?

I walked up to Eleanor who wasn't taking her gaze off the trees. "Those archaeopteryx were so amazing! We're the first to see them alive!" she exclaimed with enthusiasm.

I cut straight to the point. "We need to be careful! There could be other dinosaurs in the area. Who knows what's lurking around? There could be Pterodactyls, Dimorphodons, or other scary things!"

Eleanor's eyes widened. "I didn't think about that," she said.

We walked more quietly and didn't speak. The incident with the Archaeopteryx had reminded me of the time when I was younger, about seven. I had found a little duckling. It had its webbed foot stuck in a tangled fishing net on shore and was chirping pitifully for help., It's parents were on the other side of the large pond and likely couldn't hear the baby duck. I gently picked the little creature up and untangled the net. I had really wanted to keep it and knew my parents would probably let me, but the duckling already had a family, so I had decided to do the right thing and with the duckling cupped in my hands, walked to the other side of the pond.

At my approach the family of ducks had grown quiet and stopped splashing about. I put the little duck in the water and watched it happily reunite with its parents and siblings.

Now, I continued walking with Eleanor and we eventually came across a small cave on the side of a cliff; it fit us and our bags nicely. After taking out and unrolling our sleeping bags, we leaned some sticks against the entrance of the cave to make the opening smaller. Then, we ate a small can of chicken soup and went to bed, though sleep would be hard to come by.

In the morning we began rolling the sleeping bags up and were about to go out of the cave when a shadow fell over the entrance, and a large theropod stepped out from the nearby trees. It had its nostrils to the ground, sniffing for a scent. I took a look at its three horny crests and deduced it was probably a Ceratosaurus. We sat there motionless, gazing out of the small gap in the sticks we had put over the opening. The Ceratosaurus looked around one more time before tromping off to the forest. As soon as it was gone Eleanor spoke, "I'm so glad we took the time to make the entrance smaller with sticks. If we hadn't we'd be in a lot of trouble."

"Yeah," I agreed, "Though it's still pretty cool that we got to see it. No one else has ever seen a living Ceratosaurus specimen."

"That's true." Eleanor replied, "Though it was terrifying."

We grabbed our bags and started heading out when, yet again, there was a flash of blue light, and we were gone once more.

We landed in a field of tall grasses and wildflowers that shone like precious jewels from the morning dew. I pulled out the little device and read out loud, "Utah-early Cretaceous-122.8 MYA. Guess it appears we're still in dinosaur time."

We began to walk towards the nearby forest and spotted an orange-hued rock formation. "Looks a lot like modern Utah," I said looking out at the scene. We continued walking through the forest in the direction of the rocks. As we went by, I saw movement out of the corner of my eye. I turned around and saw a large raptor, slightly taller than me, only seven feet away.

I froze, standing as still as possible. Eleanor turned around to look at me and froze as well. The raptor cocked its head and examined us curiously before taking a tentative step forward. Quite suddenly, a loud barking call rang out and the raptor ran off, leaving only a feather behind. After a moment I realized that I had stopped breathing, and we made our way to a rock to sit down. "That was crazy!" Eleanor said in a frightened voice, "Why didn't it attack us?"

"It was probably curious, it's never seen a human before." I replied, heart still hammering.

I picked up the raptor feather and put it in my bag. "Due to its size, that raptor was probably a Deinonychus. If we're encountering those, there's probably Utahrapters around as well."

"What's a Utahraptor?" asked Eleanor.

"Utahraptors are the largest raptors, about 6-10 feet tall."

"Then let's just hope we don't meet any," replied Eleanor. nervously.

We continued walking through the open woodland, when suddenly I tripped over a root hidden in the grass. I stood up brushing the dirt from my clothes. "You all right?" asked Eleanor as she came over.

"I'm fine," I replied. Then I turned and saw a mound of dirt and twigs about a foot high and three feet in diameter.

"It's a raptor nest!" I said in a loud whisper as I stared at the smooth, white eggs. "We don't want the parents to catch us here. Maybe if we climb up into the tree, we can observe them."

"Okay" replied Eleanor, a hint of nervousness to her voice.

We made ourselves comfortable up high in the tree. After a minute or two, we saw movement to the left and a tall, sandy-colored raptor stepped out. It had some white splatters dappled about. It looked around majestically before carefully sitting on the nest like a mother hen would. A little while later a second one appeared with a small dinosaur in its jaws, which it dropped for its mate to eat.

Then, in a flash the peace of the scene vanished as a pack of deinonychus leaped from the shadows, about nine in all: they far outnumbered the pair of Utah raptors. The deinonychus attacked and started driving the raptors away, slashing and biting the whole time. We watched from the tree in shock as the fighting raged on. The pair of raptors managed to kill three of the deinonychus, but they were not strong enough to defeat six more. I couldn't help but feel sad, but that was how nature worked; predators had to kill to eat. We sat in silence as the six remaining deinonychus dragged away their kill triumphantly, disappearing back into the shadows.

Once I was sure they were gone we descended from the tree, lowering our packs first. "We should probably take the eggs before some other creature finds them. Without their parents they're all alone," I told Eleanor.

"But how are we going to take care of them? We don't know how to incubate them, and what are we going to do once they hatch?" asked Eleanor dubiously.

"We can only do what we can and hope for the best," I replied after counting the eggs (ten in all). I used my sweater as cushioning for the eggs as I lowered them into the empty pack. I took out the gear and put it in Eleanor's. I still wanted to explore, despite the danger and we set off after finishing our snack of granola bars.

The trek through the woods was rather uneventful, and we quickly came upon a large clearing with a watering hole from which a group of sauropods were drinking from. Most of the large creatures were around twenty-six feet tall, and they were a light, dusty tan color. We watched, hiding at the edge of the forest for some time. Just as we were about to leave, a pack of eight Utah raptors sprang out of the forest and ran to attack a smaller sauropod at the edge of the group. They cut it off from the others and chased it, nipping at its heels and driving it toward the forest where the brush was thickest, and they were soon out of sight. With another dazzling flash of blue light, we were gone once more.

We landed on the interweaving roots of a mangrove tree, and I pulled out the gadget and read, Egypt-Late Cretaceous-95.8 MYA. "Still in dinosaur time, and I don't really remember what carnivores lived now." The only noise Eleanor made was a sigh. We sat there for a bit, so I put my hands gently on top of the eggs so my body heat could keep them warm. After looking around for a couple of minutes I declared, "We should probably get going, but let's stay out of the water."

I saw a few immense fish circling below us. Using the roots to stay above the water we went from tree to tree, spotting many strange creatures such as a small plesiosaur preoccupied with fishing and a huge mawsonia fish big enough to swallow one of us. The water beneath us seemed about seventeen feet deep and there were more large fish. I soon spotted a large piece of land serving as an island and pointed it out to Eleanor. "That'll be a good place to rest."

Eleanor said, "These fish are creepy," and indeed, the fish from earlier were still following us. We quickly jumped off the roots and onto the island, and as soon as we did the fish swam away at top speed in what appeared to be terror. A shadow fell upon us and we turned around and soon saw the reason why.

There, a large theropod stood, adorned with a huge sail and the color of river-bank mud.

A spinosaurus.

To be continued...

A SONG FOR MY SISTER
by Maggie Forsman, 4th Grade

There is no way my ten-year-old little sister, Victoria, is going away to art camp instead of making music with me! I mean come on! That is just a whole lot of drawing and finger painting while we could be making music together!

That morning she looked at the big yellow bus, turned around, and started to say goodbye. When she reached to give me a hug, I whispered to her, "When you get back we are going to finish our album, ok?" She had a red face, starting to cry, nodded and stepped on the bus. She looked a little nervous.

It started to sprinkle when my family and I started to walk back to our house. I started to feel sad that my sister was going to be gone for a whole month. The two of us were so inseparable that we were like two guitar strings in a chord, but when my sister was gone it felt like a guitar that was out of tune.

The next morning I was sitting on the couch with a steaming cup of hot cocoa in my hands. I was thinking about my sister, and I felt so sad. She had only been gone a day, but it felt like one hundred years. I have one particular memory when we were really little. We saw a baby swan swimming in a pond. It was at the bottom of a hill we used to climb. He was by himself in the middle of the pond, trying to look for food. We watched him for a while. He was all white with two black wings. He caught a small fish and once he finished it, he was squawking around with happiness, wings fluttering. We never saw him again but if I did, he would probably be all grown up.

I was going to miss her, but when she returned, we would finish our recording for the album we had been making for four weeks now! We had been writing music together for only two years. I liked music because it can bring cheer to a bad mood, and it can make anyone feel so much better in so many different ways.

One afternoon three days later, I heard a knock at the front door, so I opened it and standing right in front of me was Patrick. I had known him since second grade. He lived just down the street. He was all wet because it had been raining and he forgot his umbrella... again! He looked like he had just jumped into a swimming pool. The water was dripping down his short black hair like a faucet that had been on for eight hours. I asked him, "Did you run here?!" He replied, "Uhh, yeh."

"I have an idea!" Patrick said. "We can write a song for your sister so when she gets back she feels welcome." Patrick liked making music too so I called him to come over.

I said, "Come in. You can dry yourself off and I can tell you what I'm feeling." I went to the bathroom closet to grab a towel from the top shelf. I threw it to Patrick who stumbled, falling on the ground.

He jumped up quickly and grabbed the towel from off the floor and said, "I'm good!" When he finished drying himself off, we went into my bedroom and he sat down on my bed. I put down my book and said, "Ok Patrick, as you know, my sister is at camp..." Patrick interrupted me by playing a few notes on his saxophone. I was thrilled. The notes he played all blended together and sounded to me like wind chimes on a front porch.

He said, "Oh yeah, sorry about that. You are probably sad because you two were inseparable!"

I said, "Well yes, I know we are but that isn't the point I just meant that ... well, that never mind."

We got to work.The fast, upbeat way he played those notes on his sax made me want to dance. We worked hard for hours while we wrote the music for my guitar and his sax. Finally we were at a point where we could record it. It sounded good, but it needed some more "oomph."

We were laying on the floor looking around for ideas. There was a crack of thunder; the rain was pattering on the roof. It reminded me of my Dad's drum set. I quickly sat up. "We can ask my dad if he would play the drums with us!"

I ran to my dad in the living room who was reading the newspaper. "Hi Dad! Patrick and I are writing a song for my sister when she gets home from camp. I need you to play the drums for us. Patrick is playing the sax, and I am playing the guitar. Would that be ok?"

"Sure! Let me finish this article. I'll see you in a minute," Dad said.

"Thank you! I love you!" I said.

A couple minutes later we met Dad in the basement, getting ready with our instruments. Dad's drums were red and silver with chipped paint and scratched cymbals.

Dad shouted, "Let's rock!" We laughed really hard.

Dad listened to what Patrick and I had written already while he got his drums ready. Dad nodded his head, and tapped his sticks on his legs while he listened for a beat.

We tried a few times playing the song with Dad and decided we had to change a few little things. Finally, we were ready to record. We recorded the song on the first try.

It was perfect.

The month was gone. Just like that, Victoria was coming home from camp. Patrick came over so he could be there when she arrived. He was excited for her to hear the song we worked on together. We all waited in the living room for her to walk in the door.

Finally!

My sister arrived home. She set down her things and ran to give me a hug. Her smile was a ray of sunshine! I bragged, "I missed you the most!

Patrick, Dad and I made something for you." She picked up a paper mache swan in one arm, and a large canvas in the other. She told us to gather in the living room so she could show us her artwork.

Victoria said, "I can't wait to hear! First I want to share about my trip. We made a whole bunch of sculptures but most of them stayed there. I could bring one of the sculptures home with me. A few things were put into the camp showcase. I made a rainbow painting on a wood cookie and a couple of origami butterflies. I also made a clay sculpture of a fish! I gave some of my butterflies away. We went on a nature walk, drawing what we saw in notebooks. I made only one friend and her name was Lela. We forgot to give each other our address so we could be penpals."

"Can you teach me how to make an origami butterfly?"

"Of course!"

We turned on the stereo to play her our song. While she was listening to it, she almost cried tears of joy. She thought it was so sweet and reached to give everyone a hug. Victoria picked up her swan, set it on the coffee table and said, "Ta dah!"

Looking closely at the sculpture, I noticed something. The swan Victoria made was white with black wings, just like the one we saw at the park in the pond when we were little. I thought to myself, I couldn't believe she made it! I got up and looked Victoria in the eye and said, "Did you really?!"

Victoria replied, "What did you mean? What did I really do?"

"You made the swan!"

Victoria instantly realized what she made when she heard the word, "swan." She said, "I guess I didn't even realize I made it as that particular kind of swan! Everybody sit down." She ran to her room to grab an easel. She covered the canvas with a blanket and put it on the easel. Everyone was so excited to see what the painting was. She said, "Prepare to be amazed!" She ripped off the blanket to reveal the painting.

Everyone started giggling.

Victoria had painted a picture of the family doing their favorite hobby. Dad was playing the drums. Patrick was playing the saxophone. I was playing the guitar, and Mom played a black and white plastic recorder. Everyone was standing next to each other in the park.

From then on, that picture will hang in the hallway and will never be moved. The swan sculpture sits in the middle of the coffee table from that day as well. We finished the album too! We continue to make music together and that was a song for my sister.

IVY AND TAY TAY
by Irene Hong, 4th Grade

Hi, I am Ivy, and this is my bestie Tay Tay (but her real name is Taylor.) We have been besties since kindergarten. Crazy, right? But we won't be ready for 6th grade. But still, it's summer break and school is in two days! Oh, I forgot to introduce my family. So I have an older sister named Ellie, and she is 15 years old, and I am 11 years old, and my younger brother (aka annoying): his name is Jake, and he is 8 years old. Then there's my mom, but we don't really talk about it because she died two years ago because of cancer, and then there's my dad. He works as a police officer in a town. So it's just me, dad, sis, and bro.

Now it's Friday night and it's time for school shopping, and I am so excited! I am getting all the cool supplies. But my dad says, "No you already have your school supplies, so no!"

"But the people at school always get new supplies every year!" I say with hope.

"No! You are not getting new supplies. You get that young lady?" says my dad.

"Fine." I roll my eyes.

Ivy ran up to her room and slammed the door. She grabbed her notebook and started drawing stuff that's the color red until, "Bang bang!" came from the other side of her door. And then Ivy jumped up like a bunny and said, "Who is there? Show yourself and I am not afraid to use my pencil to hurt you!" The door opened slowly with a creaking sound. She moved slowly towards the door. Her brother jumped out at her from the hallway. He jumped on top of her, making dinosaur sounds, pretending to be a T-Rex. Ivy screamed and she pushed him off, saying, "Why did you do that!"

"Because I wanted to have fun!" said Jack.

Ivy told Jack to get out of her bedroom. Jack went to her art supplies and grabbed the markers, paper. He then started scribbling all over the papers. Ivy ran over to Jack, grabbing the marker.

"Stop doing that!" Ivy said.

"But why!!" Jack said.

She kicked him out of the room. Jack stuck his tongue out at her as he ran out of the room.

Ivy flopped backwards onto her bed. She grabbed her notebook, and continued drawing with an orange pencil. She was trying to make a rainbow of stuff.

Later that night, Dad called her to dinner. Ivy went downstairs into the dining room and they ate pasta with alfredo sauce. Then Ivy finished her dinner, and put the dish in the sink and then she went upstairs to get ready for the night so Ivy went to her bedroom, and then Ivy turned off the lights then Ivy went to her bed and went to sleep. The next morning, Ivy woke at 7:00 a.m in the morning and then Ivy yawned big and got out of the bed and went to the bathroom. Then she grabbed the toothbrush and started to brush her teeth but then her dad said,

"Sweetie breakfast is ready!"

Then Ivy finished brushing her teeth and said, "Ok! I will come down"

Then Ivy came for breakfast and started eating her bacon and eggs then Ivy finished her breakfast and went back upstairs and went to her bedroom and grabbed her phone and flopped on her bed and started texting her BFF and asked if they wanted to go to the amusement park and Taylor said yes so Ivy yelled, "Dad can I go to the amusement park with Taylor pretty please."

Ivy's dad said, "Sure you can go to the amusement park but, can you bring your little brother with you?"

"But why?" Ivy said.

"Because your brother is bored too," Ivy's dad said.

"Fine I will take him but can you ask Jake's friend if he wants to go?" Ivy said.

"Sure we can do that," Ivy's dad said.

Ivy said, "Thanks!"

Ivy ran back to her bedroom and flopped onto the bed and grabbed her phone. She texted her friend back saying she could go to the amusement park but her brother had to go too. Taylor texted back with a picture of her smiling and Ivy turned off her phone. She went to her brother's room and said, "Jake, we are going to the amusement park with your friend and Taylor."

"Yeah ok I would love to go!" Jake said with excitement.

The next day Ivy woke up and got ready to go to the amusement park. Her dad called her downstairs to get into the car so they could pick up Jake's friend and Taylor. They drove first to Taylor's house. Ivy went up to the front door and rang the doorbell. Taylor answered the doorbell right away. She had shoulder-length blonde hair and was always ready.

"I'm so excited to go!" said Taylor.

Ivy said, "I'm excited too!"

They ran to the car and got in. They drove to Jake's friend's house which was nearby. They arrived at the apartment and Jake hopped out. He knocked on the door and Jake's friend's mom opened the door. She said, "Jacob, your friend is here!"

Jake's dad said, "We are happy to take your son with us." They went to the car and hopped in. They drove to the amusement park.

Then they entered the park. They broke into two groups, one with Taylor and Ivy, and the second one with Jake and Jacob and Jake's dad. Taylor and Ivy ran to the big roller-coaster and they had the fast pass so they didn't need to wait in a long line. Jake and Jacob went to the kids' area with Jake's dad and they went to the mini roller-coaster and waited for 3 minutes. Then 3 minutes had passed and they went on the mini roller-coaster and Jake and Jacob screamed "Ahhhhhh!"

Meanwhile Taylor and Ivy were on the roller coaster. "Ahhhhhhhh Ahhhhhhh!" They screamed so loud that they screamed like a police siren. Then they were so dizzy. "That was the craziest experience I ever had in my life," Taylor said with a creaking voice.

"Yeah that was the craziest ride ever." Ivy had a creaking voice too. Then they went to the food area and got some popcorn and ate it and walked around.

Meanwhile, "That was so fun, let's ride a different one!" Jake said with a smile on his face.

"Yeah let's ride the super high ride," Jacob said.

"Ok!" Jake said.

Then they went on the highest roller-coaster and it had a 5 minute wait. Meanwhile Taylor and Ivy decided to wait in line.

"Let's go to the carnival," Taylor said.

"Sure, let's go to the carnival," Ivy said.

"But I am going to call my dad to come ok," Ivy said.

So Ivy called her dad and he said yeah he will come to the carnival. Meanwhile the boys were ready to go. "Guys we need to go to the Carnival to meet your sister's friend and your sister. Then they went to the carnival and Ivy and Taylor waited, then Ivy saw her little brother. She yelled, "Over here Dad!" Ivy said.

Then her little brother and her dad ran to Ivy and Taylor. "Guys, do you want to go to that game?" Ivy's dad said.

"Sure we can go therem" Ivy and Tayor said at the same time like they were twins.

So they ran there and the game was a ring toss game. "Oh. Can I do it first?" Taylor said with excitement.

"Yeah you can go first," Ivy said. The person that was running the game said, "If you put more than 10 rings on a bottle you get 10,000 dollars."

"Ok now I need to make more than 10 rings on the bottle," Taylor said.

"Sure. You do you girl," Ivy said.

But Taylor had 20 rings but she only got 5 on the bottle. Then Ivy gave it a try. "Are you going to do it?" Taylor said.

"Yeah, I am going to do it," Ivy said.

"Ok girl," Taylor said with some sass.

Few minutes later Ivy got 17 on the bottle. "Omg! No way you just got 10,000 dollars. You are so lucky."

"I know what I am going to do. And I am going to use half of the money on me and my family and am going to give the other half to charity for the cancer kids for my mom's memory," Ivy said.

Taylor said, "Oh, that's so sweet of you! I remember your mom making the best chocolate chip cookies whenever I came over." They hugged at the booth and went to the car.

They dropped off Taylor and Jaocb then they all went home. They went to sleep knowing they had a lot of money they would use for each other. The money they'd win would go to the hospital the next day. Ivy's mom would be very happy with what she did.

Antrim Raising Writers: Language Lab

David Hornibrook

Our goal for this class was to mine existing language for "materials" to bring to life our own poems and stories. This was a fun way to get to know each other and enjoy experimenting with words as a group of linguistic mad scientists, wizards, and alchemists. Along the way, we learned some very strange facts: did you know babies have more bones than adults? Did you know there are more trees on earth than there are stars in the Milky Way? We also shared a little history, science and a whole lot of interesting conversation. How did our experiments turn out? Well, I think the work speaks for itself.

UNEXPECTEDLY
by Nora Hornibrook, 7th grade

Unexpectedly

On a day where the sky is clear
& the lake is clear, my mind
is clouded. I am confused.
I hear a meow. Our cat is not
happy so I give her a treat. I cross
my arms & tap my feet. I pick
her up & she whines some more.
What is it you want? What is it
you need? A breathy sigh
comes out of me. I can't understand
what she's trying to say – wet.
My hand feels wet; I look down
to see, in my hand – goodness me!
it's a kitten.

MUSIC
by Levi Hornibrook, 5th grade

Music

Such a sweet thing
it can be anything you want it to
shouting over electric guitars
a dance across the keys
or a musical version of the place you call home:
donkeys outside a warm cottage
cliffs by the sea fields and fiddles
or simply sitting on the front porch
in an afternoon rain

PAINTING VIA METAPHORS
by Jacob Stevens, 7th grade

Painting Via Metaphors

I drag my pencil on the paper, a printer copying, taking notes
My axe hands chisel out the stump of a scotch pine
I am the sacrificer, a bombardment of goblins
My finger, a marathon runner on the page of a book
I am a parent to my pets
Top connoisseur of enjoyable podcasts
Assembler of breakfast ingredients
The chief devourer of apple cider vinegar
I am an elderly person when it comes to giving gifts
I am a god, building my own world out of Legos
To me, podcasts are the new bacon
I am the king of game nights

LONE SURVIVOR
by JuJu Pine, 8th Grade

I wish I knew what happened.

When I woke up, I couldn't remember anything. Not even my name. All I knew was that I was in pain and I was alone. And that there was an annoying machine that kept beeping in the corner of the hospital room. The doctors didn't think I was going to make it. Being in a coma and

having severe burns, heart, and lung injuries did not look good. As soon as the nurse checked my vitals, the police came into my small hospital room and requested to speak with me privately.

"Ms. Jones?" An older cop in his late fifties asked. I hadn't realized he was talking to me until he said, "We wanted to talk about the incident that caused your injuries."

"Oh," I squeaked. Instead of just telling them I hadn't recognized my own name, I told him to come on in.

"So, Cassidy," Old cop said. "What were you doing prior to the accident?" Cassidy. I think over and over, trying to remember it. No luck.

"I'm not sure."

A concerned look crossed the cop's face. "Cassidy? Do you know where you are and why you're here?"

My heart starts beating fast and breathing becomes increasingly harder. "No," I manage to say, barely getting out a whisper. Without another word, the police officer got up.

After the police officer left my room, he talked to the nurse in the hall who nervously glanced at me through the window.

When she entered, she told me the basics of my life:

My name is Cassidy Jones. I am a 17-year-old senior at Eleanor Roosevelt High. I live in Manhattan and was in a subway crash with my parents and two little sisters. No one else on the train survived. I am the lone survivor.

•••

Because I was a minor, I was sent to foster care. I still didn't remember anything, but all of my other injuries healed.

I was placed with a woman named Leanna, whose husband and daughter were on the same train as I was. The car ride to her house was awkward and quiet. She kept glancing at me in the rear view mirror, like she wanted to say something but kept rethinking it. I wished I could have told her something to comfort her. Like that it was all over so quickly, but in truth, I had no idea if that was accurate.

When we arrived, I was given a tour of the house. It wasn't huge, but it was a modest Tudor style just outside the city. She gave me a tour, excluding one room that had flowers hanging all over the door.

Like the car ride, the first day was quiet. I think we were still both in shock. We were running errands when she asked if I wanted to go to the station where it happened. She had gone

everyday, but said she understood if I was uncomfortable going. I decided I wanted to see the

place where my life had changed forever.

•••

It just looked like a normal subway station. It was crowded with people. I don't know why I was surprised. It had been over two months since the crash, so of course they wanted to clean things up as fast as possible. Bright signs aligned the wall.

THE CRASH WAS NO ACCIDENT

I did a double take. The sign really said to stay behind the yellow line, so why did I read it so wrong?

I shivered and looked around. I decided to give Leanna some privacy to mourn. I glanced at the other side of the room where a little girl, no older than 8, stood, soaked in blood. "The crash was no accident, Cassidy." The memories hit me like a brick wall. Flashes of blood, fire, and screams echoed around me.

I remember my little sister Mary wanted to meet the conductor. I was busy texting my friend, but my parents made me take her.

I remember walking through the trains of the cars, the families chattering happily.

I remember wanting to not have to be the one taking care of my sisters all the time.

I remember a dark thought creeping its way into my brain.

I remember acting on it and pushing Mary off the train and her sneaker getting caught on the track, derailing the train.

I remember everything.

I just wanted a few minutes of peace and alone time. Now, all I'd done was condemn myself to a life of always being alone.

I thought of Leanna and all the other families who lost loved ones because of me. I don't know when I sank to the floor. But I was sobbing and Leanna was rushing over. "I'm so

sorry." I sob into her shoulder. "This is all my fault."

Journalism

Noelle Riley

Instructor Introduction

The National Writers Series was pleased to hold its first journalism writing class for area youth in the fall of 2024. Journalism instructor Noelle Riley taught seven students — ranging from 5th to 8th grade — the art of interviewing, how to write a journalism story and the importance of the First Amendment and how it relates to Freedom of the Press.

SHIRLEY MURRAY ENJOYS REMINISCING ABOUT A FULL LIFE
by Gracie Gregory, 6th Grade

Ninety-year-old Cordia member Shirley Murray has lived an amazingly full life with her family, has traveled throughout Europe, and has a strong passion for poetry and reading.

"Somebody once said that living at Cordia was like taking a book off the shelf because everybody lived a long life (and) had so many interesting things that they had done," Murray said.

Murray is a single mother of three daughters, a sister of three, and is a traveler and a poet.

All of Murray's daughters are fully educated with their masters and PHds in library science and technology. Murray believes that her daughters have grown up with the mindsets of feminists, just like their mother.

Murray has long been a dedicated women's rights activist. "I'm a feminist... so it came very naturally to me," said Murray. In addition to being a mother, Murray also loved to read and write poetry.

"I'm not a real poet," said Murray. "But I just like to do that." Despite not being a "real poet," she actually won three Poet's Night Out awards.

The writer that really got Murray interested was Philly Collins, and when she started writing her poems, she always was inspired by things that happened in her life.

In one of her more recent poems, labeled the "Soundtrack of My Life," Murray dug deep into her old memories of music. She incorporated songs into her poems from World War II when she was a kid and was performing old songs like "Over Hills, Over the Dusty Trails" with her sister to her neighbors.

Also included were songs like "You'll Never Walk Alone" from her choir days. Then Murray integrated songs from her daughter's teenage years like "Radar Love." Finally, Murray used the music from when she and her late husband used to sit in his apartment and listen to classical songs.

"That was the soundtrack of my life," Murray said. Her poems were noticed by her granddaughter who is now putting together a book of her poetry.

For her career, Murray was a teacher to grade-school children. Although she was successful in this field, Murray always wanted to do something more.

"When I look at my daughters and grandchildren, there are so many more options for women...I probably would have chosen something different," she said if there were more career choices for women back in her day.

In addition to poetry and her family, she also loves to travel. Murray has been to Europe and back with her late second husband and has a love for Italy.

"My favorite country is Italy," Murray said. "It's where my husband proposed when we were almost ready to retire."

Murray's second husband was her next door neighbor who traveled while he was working for Chrysler. Even when he was not working for Chrysler, he was still a globetrotter. Definitely one of the many things that they have in common. Knowing Murray's love of Italy, he

invited her to come with him to the Chinquatera, meaning "five villages" in Italian. This was where he proposed to Murray.

When Shirley Murray was proposed to by her late second husband, she had him wait for three years before they were married. Murray said that she wanted to wait until her youngest daughter graduated from college. And she wanted her full retirement as a teacher.

She's happy to spend her time now living in Cordia. Murray's late second husband originally moved to Cordia with her, but he sadly died from Parkenson's disease not long after.

Even though her husband passed away, Murray has been having a fabulous time at Cordia. Celebrating her 90th birthday on Oct. 16, Shirley has been staying active and social, sitting with a new person for dinner every night.

"I think that's the philosophy here," she said. Murray often thinks about her time as a kid when she moved from place to place. But one town stuck out to her. Murray loved the town Toledo, Ohio, where she was able to walk all over and take the bus from age eight.

"It was a time that I wish you and my grandchildren could have," Murray said.

In addition to having a good town, Murray sometimes got to go places with her father because of his job. Murray's father worked for the Ford agency, so of course Murray went with him to a few of his meetings in Greenfield Village.

Although it was special to get to go with her dad, it wasn't a huge part of her life. Murray said, "I remember my travels in Europe more. I remembered it more for the small English village, but doing things in Europe is much more stimulating."

Now happily at Cordia, Murray is having an amazing life, with many things to do and surrounded by friends.

JEANIE RHODES' LIFE HAS COME FULL CIRCLE AT CORDIA
by Ronin Wells, 5th Grade

As a college student, Jeanie Rhodes fell in love with music. Little did she know that her workplace as a music therapist would be her future home.

Cordia, which is a retirement community, is housed in a portion of the former Traverse City State Hospital. Rhodes once worked there as a music therapist when it was still the state hospital.

"Music is the international language," Jeanie said.

When in college, Rhodes thought she knew what she wanted to study.

"I thought I was going to be a lawyer, so while I was in college I took as many pre law classes as I did music," she said. "My advisor said to me, 'You have to choose between one or the other. You got to do pre-law or do something musical.' So I went to the school of music, and I took music therapy. And that's what I am: I'm a music therapist."

Because of that decision, she went on to take classes about the psychological benefits of music. Giving people joy was one of the many things that empowered Jeanie. She even wrote a thesis about the benefits of music.

As part of the process for music therapy, Rhodes would take a musical inventory and figure out what made patients at the hospital calm, crazy, or anything in between. Jeanie and the other therapists found out that giving headphones with music playing to psychiatric patients would override voices being heard in their head. Because of this discovery, less patients were locked up and instead given headphones that played music to keep them calm.

"Sometimes we would have people who would compete for attention. We had these two women... who would swallow things. Razor blades, crochet hooks, forks, knives, they were the most memorable," Jeanie said, noting that they were called "The Swallowers."

She was proud of her job in helping people. Although, the hospital would soon close for good.

"In the last couple of years they were trying to get people out of the hospital," she said. "That's how I lost my job here. They closed the hospital."

After years away from the hospital, she came back to the building only to find Cordia, her future home.

"I'd never dreamed that this final chapter of my life would be spent back in the hospital," Jeanie said. "It's very different from what it was, but in some ways it's very similar."

LOVE AND UNFORGETTABLE MOMENTS
by Adrian Reece, 7th Grade

Through adventures on the great lakes, global travels, and enduring life's toughest challenges, Shirley Klegman's family remained her anchor—united by love, resilience, and unforgettable memories.

Born in Detroit and raised in Ann Arbor, she spent her early years working at her father's pharmacy where she fondly remembers manning the soda fountain at just eight years old.

"I had to stand on a Coca-Cola case in order to be able to reach (the register)," Shirley said. It was there, amidst the hustle of the pharmacy, that she met her future husband at 19.

Although she didn't pursue formal education, Shirley's focus was always on building a family and supporting her husband, Jerry's career. The union between them was beautiful.

"While he was in medical school, I did take a few classes in parenting because I knew we were going to have a family and I thought that would sort of be a nice thing to do," she said.

While Shirley's husband continued his studies, she stayed home and cared for their growing family. After the birth of their first child, they moved from an apartment back to her childhood home with her parents.

They had four beautiful children together. Having four kids and living with her parents made it possible for the couple to travel multiple times, visiting sites across Europe and going on multiple safaris in Nairobi, Kenya.

"We did a lot of traveling, and I remember that the first time there was a safari trip to Nairobi, it was right over Christmas time and we said, 'Oh would that be fun to do.' My father said, 'You do it now while you're young and we'll watch the kids...,'" Shirley said.

She and Jerry went back on safaris about three or four times. "It was just wonderful in

Nairobi," said Shirley.

As time went on, Shirley found herself balancing the demands of motherhood with the ups and downs of life. But it was in 1974, when her husband suffered a heart attack at just 47, that Shirley's strength and resilience were truly tested.

Doctors gave her husband a grim prognosis, expecting him to live only a few more years.

"My husband lived until just 3 years ago. He was 89 years old," she said. He went on to live 42 years longer than expected and shared time with her living at Cordia before he passed.

Now, as she looks back on her many travels, Shirley knows that the experiences she's had — from safaris in Africa to sailing on the Great Lakes — are more than just a collection of destinations. They are precious memories, woven into the fabric of her family's story, shared with the people she loves most.

A LIFE OF COOKING, FAMILY AND GOOD MEMORIES
by JJ Brudi, 6th Grade

After a few years working for Ford Motor Company designing classic Mustangs, Harlan (Pete) Peterson became a cooking aficionado and ended up owning a restaurant for 25 years in Northern Michigan.

"I went to college for almost three years and I was hired by Ford, and I moved to Michigan to work for Ford," Peterson said. "But I started getting other interests. I had always liked to cook." As a hobby, he decided to take cooking classes and thought about going into the food business.

"And then I saw something about a school in Paris, France, and I ended up quitting Ford and moving to France," he said. "I took classes over there. It was very cool."

While gaining cooking skills, Peterson was able to see all the interesting and historic sites. "All the historic things like Notre Dame," Peterson said. "You know, taking the boats down the river, going to French bakeries, going to wineries. Just learning. Staying in a hotel. Seeing what kind of diets, what was their breakfast like, and you know things like that."

Peterson was there for just about three or four months before he headed back to the United States and tried to get into the food business.

"So one thing led to another. And I mean big jumps here, but I read about this little restaurant in northern Michigan, which I admired and thought maybe I should try to work there and see if I like this business," he said.

Peterson moved to northern Michigan to work at the small french-style restaurant.

"It was a good formula and eventually the restaurant became kinda famous," Peterson said. "One thing led to another and I started a bigger restaurant."

His restaurant was called Tapawingo.

"The name is a native American name for a place of peace. So it seemed like a good name for a restaurant," he said.

The restaurant was in Ellsworth, Michigan and became hugely popular. "I was written up in a lot of newspapers because it was a good restaurant," Peterson added.

It was so successful that Peterson ended up owning it for 25 years. Eventually Tapawingo closed because Peterson thought it was slipping away.

"I eventually moved to Traverse City to teach one or two classes at NMC in culinary," Peterson said. "I then helped start another restaurant. It was not mine, but a good friend owned it."

Peterson eventually moved to Cordia Senior Living, in Traverse City this past summer.

He now enjoys watching football and basketball and reminiscing about his past love for motorcycles — at one point he had owned four or five motorcycles.

"That was my hobby even though I had a restaurant. After the restaurant closed, I would go through the country roads and it was a good relaxing way to end the day," Peterson said.

Peterson doesn't have a motorcycle any more since he is older and has problems with both knees. He lives in a small apartment at Cordia Senior Living, and he still helps out with dinner and has a place for motorcycles in his heart.

"I just live right around the corner right there and I have a cabinet full of all kinds of motorcycle things and supplies," he said.

Peterson still enjoys learning and reading about motorcycles.

Motorcycles are cool, but family is important to Peterson too. "I have two older sisters and a brother," Peterson said. They stuck pretty close together and were a tight family.

Unfortunately though, Peterson's older brother — who was a highway patrolman in Montana — passed away a few years ago.

Peterson's sisters were both teachers and are very close to him. "We still are a tight family. The sister that is closest to me in years helped me move here, and she will probably come here in the next few months," Peterson said.

They try to see each other more often but growing older has its disadvantages.

"We are getting old so we can't travel to see each other," Peterson said. "We stay in touch and that is very nice for me."

Harlan (Pete) Peterson may be older now, but the legacy he left on Tapawingo and the cooking world will not be forgotten any time soon.

JUDY MAYNARD HAS LIVED A MULTIFACETED LIFE
by Juju Pine, 8th Grade

Judith (Judy) Maynard found out at an early age what her strengths were and what she wanted to do in life, so she went on to become a lawyer, teach, and work at clinics and hospitals helping people.

"Social services is who I am," Judy said.

When she was a young teen, her school gave her a test called the Kuder Preference Test.

"I feel immensely grateful that I had that test when I was 13. I don't know if I sort of remembered it throughout the years, but it defines me," she said. Her scores told her that she was in the 98th percentile in human services, which is significantly higher than her scores in all the other categories.

Years later, Judy found herself deciding what she was going to study in college. She then took another test, which told her that she could be a social worker, a college professor, a lawyer, a dentist, or a physician.

"I grew up in a time when girls couldn't imagine being anything other than a teacher, a retail clerk, [or] a nurse. And I thought for a while about being a doctor," she said.

Following her test results, she went to the University of Colorado to become a nurse.

Her first year at the nursing program in Colorado was filled with social science, arts and sciences degree classes.

"I just absolutely was completely baffled by organic chemistry and fell in love with the social sciences," she said.

So instead of becoming a nurse, she got her undergraduate degree in sociology, and she also got a law degree and a clinical psychology degree.

Judy moved from Colorado to California, where she got a job at First California Rural Legal Assistance. She started as a secretary while going to law school at night for four years.

"I went to law school because I was involved in civil rights stuff," she said. "I got very involved in Mexican-American political stuff in the 60s and 70s."

Her experience in civil rights led her to becoming an employment discrimination lawyer with the federal government.

After practicing law, she went on to make use of her other degrees and started doing social work for Child Protective Services and was a therapist for drug and alcohol rehabilitation programs.

"Most of our clients came from the local psychiatric hospital where most of them had tried to kill themselves. And so the population I was working with were people with chronic mental illness," she said.

Because it was a time when girls had very few socially acceptable job opportunities, not

everyone was thrilled that Judy chose the career path she did. Judy's mother didn't pressure her to do things she wasn't passionate about, which Judy is extremely grateful for. Yet, sometimes she felt her mother did not approve of her occupations. But that didn't stop Judy.

"I think it's really important that you have goals, that you're attentive to them, and that they change," she said. "So there was something in me, thankfully, that guided me through my life in the direction that was congruent with who I am."

Judy doesn't have any kids, but she is married to her husband who currently lives at Cordia with her. Similarly to Judy, he has lived a life full of adventures.

Eventually, they retired. Instead of settling down, like most retired people, they decide to travel around the country and go to Canada in their fifth wheel trailer.

"We traveled to beautiful places," Judy remembers. "This country's amazing." She and her husband had a blind dog, a cat with amputated ears, a cat with an amputated tail, and a third cat who Judy referred to as being "whole."

When they moved back to California, they were constantly on edge because of all the wildfires.

They began searching for a place where they could feel comfortable without isolation. That is when they found Cordia. Judy and her husband have been enjoying life at Cordia for three years, where they have a sense of home, safety, and connection.

JUDY JONES AND HER LOVE FOR LIFE
by Peighton Kelderhouse, 7th Grade

Judy Jones lived on the edge of Detroit in the suburbs where she learned to knit, crochet, and sew as a young girl. She often stayed with her grandmother and there was a yarn shop close by.

"We would walk two blocks down to the yarn shop and then she taught me how to knit and crochet," she said. "I crocheted a few things... and then I switched over to knitting."

When she first started knitting, she made a baby scarf for her first project. She went on to make a lot of sweaters. Sewing was her hobby, as she did not play any sports as a young child.

"When I was younger, we lived in the suburbs (which had) huge open fields and so we did not do a lot of that," she said, but when she was in middle school she learned to play the violin.

She went on to marry her highschool sweetheart — a man named Norm. They ended up having three kids, and she now has four grandkids.

"When I first graduated from high school, I went to Michigan State University," she said. "I was the first one in my family to ever go to college."

After college she worked for Dow Corning in Midland.

She worked in the personnel department and helped schedule job interviews along with other duties.

Before she moved into Cordia in Traverse City, she had already been familiar with the location. "I had a condo next door in the Mercado and my kids lived in Bellaire," she said.

When her children moved to Traverse City, Judy moved into Cordia. Now, her life is full and she gets to see her friends and family more often.

"I have a lot of friends here... I found some of my neighbors are here and from Mercado," she said. "Once you move in here, you make a lot of friends."

ITCHY FEET AND A WORLD OF TRAVEL
by Addison McGrun, 8th Grade

It would be a dream for some people to be able to travel the globe, exploring new things and learning. For Katherine Newkirk, this was a reality.

"I love to travel and say I have itchy feet," Newkirk said. She's traveled to Peru, China, the Philippines, and even the Amazon, to name a few.

While in these places, Newkirk explained that she taught new things to people she met and also learned from them. For example, while she was in the Philippines, Newkirk joined the Peace Corp, and partnered with one of her group members to help mothers in the area.

"We helped teach nutrition, especially nursing mothers and children's nutrition in the Philippines," she said.

After the Peace Corp was finished, Newkirk says that she was sad to leave the individuals she loved, but was also eager to get home and see her family.

"Because I finished my whole tour of duty, I got — I can't remember — several hundred dollars which was enough to spend three months traveling through Borneo, Singapore and Malaysia and Thailand, before going home," Newkirk said.

While she was staying in the Amazon with a native tribe, Newkirk was taught how to keep the ground underneath her tent clear.

"So that no snakes or anything else could get in," she said. Newkirk added that she ended up staying in the Amazon for about a week, but that it's not one of the places she would want to go back to. She explained that her friend, who had recently been there, said the water levels had dropped about 40 feet.

"I would rather remember it as it was," Newkirk said.

Her love for traveling started when she was a kid and enjoys how that really connects back to her life as an adult traveler.

One of the most noteworthy parts about Newkirk's childhood was her family vacations.

Every summer, Newkirk, her family and their neighbors would go somewhere just outside of the Rocky Mountains for her dad's job conference "...maybe Denver or Santa Fe...," Newkirk explained.

They'd spend the next few weeks afterwards traveling up into the mountains, and staying at cottages.

"We'd get a mountain cottage, cook and play cards at night, and the kids would play and go horseback riding." Newkirk said.

Getting to college was the first time she realized that she was going to have to make money and earn a living for herself.

"I thought I might want to be a marine biologist, but I didn't get past organic chemistry," Newkirk explained. "In fact, I took a year off college to try to figure out what to major in."

During her time away, Newkirk said that she did some more traveling "...my friend's parents were professors, and they had a friend who was doing an archeological dig in Peru. He invited us to come down for the summer and help do that, so I saved my money and we bought tickets to go to Peru."

Unfortunately, just before they were about to leave, an earthquake hit the site where the dig was taking place, and it was left in ruins. But Newkirk said that they had already had their tickets, so she and her friend flew down to Peru and started exploring.

Newkirk and her friend spent some of their time in the Incas, and they also saw Machu Picchu, before heading home so that Newkirk could finish college.

All of her experiences put together eventually lead her to getting a master's degree in journalism at 55 years old. Newkirk then went back to China to teach journalism classes and English as a foreign language. She eventually headed back to the United States.

Newkirk explained how she stayed in Kansas until just over a year ago, before moving up here to live at Cordia. She sees each of her grandkids multiple times every week and is very happy to have them closer to her.

"It's embarrassing how lucky this is," Newkirk said.

She is still finding her place at Cordia while being one of the youngest members, but she loves her new home as much as anyone. Newkirk was perfectly content living in Kansas, but she couldn't have asked for a better place to spend her retirement.

Sketch Writing Using Improv

Nicole Hastings McKendrick

Instructor Introduction

Have you ever wondered how some of your favorite sketch comedy shows like Saturday Night Live, Key & Peele and I Think You Should Leave with Tim Robinson were written? Many sketch comedy scenes start their lives as an improvised scene and are then refined through the writing process.

In this six week class in the Dennos Museum Center's Janis Community Room, students used improvisation as a starting point to write sketch comedy. They started every class on their feet improvising scenes as a genesis point for writing great characters and scripting natural dialogue.

WII
by Tess Tarchak-Hiss, 11th Grade

INT. HIGH SCHOOL CAFETERIA-NIGHT: A high school homecoming queen and king enter the dance floor, wearing crowns with their royal positions.

HOCO KING

God, isn't this great? This is straight out of a storybook perfect! Me, the quarterback, and you, the cheerleading captain. Next stop, Prom Court!

HOCO QUEEN

I know babe! What an amazing way to start our junior year. I'm so excited to dance to "Fien" 6 times with the lights on the entire time!

HOCO DJ

What's up North Highschool? It's the best night of the year: Homecoming night! I'm your DJ for the night—the homeless man who throws cans of La Croix at cars on the highway across from the Applebees—and I'm not qualified at all to be here!

HOCO KING

I love this guy!

HOCO DJ

But since COVID, there's been some changes. Since you were on lockdown during Middle school and are socially inept, the administration added something to make this dance worth the 35-dollar ticket: enjoy the Wii! (HOCO DJ starts to play the intro "Fien.")

HOCO QUEEN

What? There's a Wii?

HOCO KING

Babe, they're playing "Fien!" (HOCO KING starts doing the Lil Uzi Vert dance a little too enthusiastically. There's nobody else in the mosh pit.) (MORE) (frustrated) Huh? Where is everybody? (frustrated) (CONT'D) There were like, 5000 Toyota Camrys in the parking lot.

HOCO DJ

(HOCO DJ continues to dance to his music but points in the opposite direction.) I'd check the room over there.

HOCO KING

What? The library, where they set up all the chess tables for the awkward freshmen boys whose science teachers gave them extra credit for showing up for half an hour?

HOCO DJ

Not quite. I'd check your girl too.

(HOCO KING turns around and realizes HOCO QUEEN has disappeared. HOCO QUEEN has appeared in the middle of a new moshpit, with her heels off, Wii remote in hand, facing a tiny TV. HOCO QUEEN does an elaborate Wii-swing and gets a strike. The highschool crowd around her does the Wii bowling spin and woots. Her opponent is a typical scrawny and NERDY GUY, who is clearly nervous about this match.)

HOCO KING

Babe? What are you doing? What are you all doing? This is homecoming, not "Kingpin!"

HOCO QUEEN

(HOCO QUEEN squats on the floor and intently watches her opponent swing his remote.)

At first, I was confused by it. Like, why is this 2006 best-seller here? Then, I was afraid of it. But finally, I embraced it. I found it. It found me. This is my calling.

(NERDY GUY ends up getting a strike. HOCO KING rolls his eyes before synchronizing the Wii spin with the rest of the pit. HOCO QUEEN screams and tugs her hair, before pulling her neat up-do.)

HOCO DJ

Anndddddd that's a strike for the Esports captain with jaundice! It's neck and neck!

HOCO KING

You aren't a sportscaster. You're an underpaid DJ here to get free Fireballs from 16-year-old girls! (HOCO DJ takes a look back and forth defensively before taking a swig and throwing it under his booth.) And babe, this isn't your calling It's just stupid! Football is a calling, Bitcoin is a calling, making out with your pillow of the dad from *Twilight* to "Don't Dream It's Over" is a calling!

HOCO QUEEN

I don't have time to unpack your homoerotica right now. I have a game to win. (HOCO QUEEN backs up, the crowd making room, before she does a cartwheel leading into a flip leading into the splits, before swinging her Wii remote. Everyone watches intently as the bowling ball virtually rolls. She shakes her head) I should have known something was off when you had all those *Brokeback Mountain* TikTok edits saved in your phone. (The ball hits all the pins beside two. The crowd awes. NERDY GUY jumps up ecstatically.)

HOCO DJ

Oof! A rough swing for the Bama-Rush wannabe.

NERDY GUY

YES! What a horrible play. God, I hope your ACL gets absolutely WRECKED.

HOCO QUEEN

(Goes beserk and screams. Pulling out her clutch from under her dress, she continues to scream as she uses her lipstick as an eyeblack under her eyes.) (screaming) THIS MEANS WAR. LET'S GO MACAULAY CULKIN LOOKIN ASS. GET READY TO GET COOKED IN YOUR OWN VAT OF FAT. GET READY TO BE DESTROYED.

HOCO KING

(HOCO KING grabs HOCO QUEEN before she goes off the deep end.) Babe, listen, please. Did I only go out with you because you're 5'2 and I wanted to win royalty? Yes. Do I think you're a psycho-lunatic? Yes. But it's not too late to change that. It's not too late to be a role model. What do you say? Let's go out there, take our shoes off and dance in mysterious wet puddles on the cafeteria floor to Drake and grind right in front of our math teacher.

(HOCO QUEEN gets her Wii remote ready, but swings it backward,hitting HOCO KING in the balls. He crouches in agony. The crowd awes in Wii-sports resort style. The Wii bowling ball flies back into the virtual audience.)

HOCO DJ

And it's a fumble! A fantastic swing in the phallus! Dexter the Scientist is in the lead!

HOCO KING

What did you do that for?

HOCO QUEEN

I'm not going with you. I want to Wii-bowl. I need to Wii-bowl.

NERDY GUY

(NERDY GUY makes his way, strutting with cockiness.) Well, looks like I'm guaranteed an easy win. (NERDY GUY extravagantly swings his remote but forgets to attach the wristband. The remote goes flying and short-circuits the DJ speakers.)

HOCO DJ

Hey, what the hell? ("Fien" starts playing out of the speaker disoriented. NERDY GUY falls to the floor in demise.)

NERDY GUY

Don't do it, don't say it—

HOCO DJ

Destruction of school property! You're disqualified! The Wii-Bowling Homecoming Champion is the Hoco Queen! (Everyone besides the HOCO QUEEN and NERDY GUY Wii Sports spin, then proceed to chant along to the song: "Fien! Fien! Fien!Fien!")

HOCO KING

Okay, you won. You're done. Can we go now?

HOCO QUEEN

No, we're done. And you aren't listening to me. I'm going to be bowling like "The Big Lebowski". You aren't going to hold me back any longer. I don't want to be known as just "that one really hot girl" who is dating the "really hot guy who is totally gay but hiding it." I want to be known as that "really hot girl who is a Wii Bowling Champion and kicks ass. And also makes niche profound video essays about Jackie Kennedy while doing mukbangs.

HOCO KING

(Dramatically) Are you breaking up with me?

HOCO QUEEN

(Points to the Wii Bowling screen, where it reads: YES!)

HOCO KING

(Rips off his crown, scoffing) Whatever. I'm going home to Charlie Swan. We're going to watch the Troye Sivan GAP ad. Charlie Baby does SO MUCH MORE FOR ME THAN YOU EVER COULD.

(HOCO QUEEN and the rest of the observing students jump around Wii-Sports style in synch while "Fien plays in the background".)

FIN

Manistee County Poetry Club

Nicole Birkett

Led by NWS Instructor 'Cole Birkett, the Manistee Middle School Poetry Club was launched in the fall of 2024 to encourage young poets in Manistee County to develop their voices through creative experimentation, metaphor and symbolism. Each class began with an introduction to different poetry styles, followed by a writing exercise, and culminated with a reading and discussion.

PERSPECTIVE IS REALITY
by Thomas Racine, 8th Grade

An ekphrastic poem inspired by the photograph, "Jack Was Alone" by Deb Dila

There are multiple windows in these apartments
Windows with lights on

The one in the middle
Has a man behind it
The rest are empty

and quiet

quieter than the pages of a dusty leather-
bound biography
in an abandoned library

Jack Was Alone

From our point of view
we are in the dark
but Jack is standing in the light

framed in the middle

Watches to our left
not alone
not from our perspective

jack was alone

Goldilocks Framed Me!
Fractured Fairy Tales

Kelly Almer

Instructor Introduction

Most readers have heard and know of the story titled, "Goldilocks and the Three Bears," written by Robert Southey in 1959. The bears found Goldilocks asleep in Baby Bear's bed, after she had broken his chair and ate all his porridge. But, what if she wasn't so innocent? Was the Big Bad Wolf in the other fairy tale really terrible to the three pigs? How about the Giant with Jack and that tall beanstalk or the old witch with Snow White?

In this class talented writers rewrote a favorite or lesser known fairy tale from a different point of view, creating a fractured fairy tale. The talented writers in this class did exactly this, creating new tales full of well-known and lesser known characters, with plot twists readers will want to read again and again.

Enjoy these wonderful fairy tales!

THE PUMPKIN PRINCESS
by Kayla Cosens, 7th Grade

Hi! My name is Drizella, but you can call me Ella, and this is my side of the story. Before I begin, I know what you're thinking: there is only one Ella and it's not me. Well let me tell you something: her real name isn't Ella or Cinderella. Her real name is Cindy Ella. Also, I'm not as bad as everyone thinks. Neither is my mother or my sister Anastasia, who we call Anna. Here is the real story.

I remember the first day I met her. It was the first week of summer and the sun was shining down on Anna's pumpkin patch in the front yard. My mother said that her new husband's daughter was going to come over so that we could meet her and she would get to know the town better because she grew up in a big city. She said her name was Ella and she was in the 8th grade, the same grade as me, but not Anna because she was two grades below us.

It was a beautiful sunny day as I waited in the front yard for Cindy. I looked at my Apple watch. She would be here any minute now. Just when I looked up I saw a black limousine pulling into the dirt driveway. When it stopped, I saw the door open and out stepped Cindy who was holding something in her hand. It was a pink dog leash. She called her dog Bruno, which was funny to me because it reminded me of the movie Encanto. When she walked closer, I saw she was wearing designer clothes and had acrylic nails every girl longs to have.

I was so excited to meet her that I jumped down all eight steps to greet her but when I got to her she asked, "Where's your butler? I need him to carry my stuff inside." After she said that I knew she had never worked a day in her life, but I just simply replied. "Umm, sorry but we don't own a butler." Right when I was about to say I could help carry them in, my mother and my sister ran out to greet her.

"Hi Cindy. How have you been?" my mother asked.

"Good," she replied.

"Ella, why don't you help Cindy with her bags."

"Actually I can bring them in, and I don't like being called Cindy."

"Oh, well what do you want to be called then?" my mom asked, getting a little red in the cheeks.

"You can call me Ella," Cindy answered.

"Well, it's not going to be hard to remember your name," Anna said joking around.

After a few days, my mom's husband moved in. His name was Paul and he was really nice. Paul and Cindy settled in quite nicely and within a week it felt like we were a real family. But suddenly my mom received a call saying Paul had died in a car crash on his way to work. He was a lawyer. We were all devastated, especially my mom. She took three weeks off from her work as she owns a bakery downtown.

But Cindy grieved differently. She did not show any sadness, at least not in public. Everyone kept saying how brave and kind she was, but no matter how much I tried to see kindness, all I could see was loneliness as if she was craving attention. One day some neighbors came over with some food and a sympathy card and she told them that we made her live in the dusty attic with mice. We explained to Cindy and the neighbors that we did not have time to fix the attic up right now, but she refused to share a room with Anna and me. When she moved herself up to the attic, she found Anna's pet hamsters Jake and Gus, which she called mice. After straightening out that lie with the neighbor, a letter came in the mail. It was red with an old fashioned stamp seal that was gold with the letters PPPC engraved on it. My mother ripped it open and nervously read:

To the Tremaine girls, Cindy and Drizella,

You are invited to participate in the Pumpkin Patch Princess Contests. The contest is simple. There will be three contests. One being, making your own pumpkin costume. The second being a pumpkin pie baking challenge. The last being an interview. We hope to see you there. The winner will be given one hundred dollars.

From,

The PPPC (The Pumpkin Patch Princess Contest)

As my mother finished reading the letter out loud, the neighbors said that they should go so I showed them the door. When I turned around I noticed that Cindy had a huge smile across her face which grew bigger by the second. Apparently Anna noticed too. "Hey, Cindy," Anna asked. Cindy didn't hear a thing, but if you knew my sister she would keep asking until she got an answer.

"Cindy."

Still no answer.

You could see the frustration in Anna's face.

Cindy must have been in a different world or something. "ELLA!" Anna screamed. That got her attention; I guess she really won't answer to Cindy.

"Huh, what oh, what?" Cindy asked, confusion written all over her face.

"Why are you smiling like you have an evil plan?"Anna said.

It took her a few seconds to answer Anna's question, but her answer came out like this. "Oh, um well you see back home, in New York City where I grew up, there was a beauty contest and all the girls in town signed up to join. I was the winner of course," Cindy answered, then turned to me and asked, "So, Drizella. Are you in?" After she asked that question, everyone turned towards me. Anna looked at me with her head tilted a little to the right like a new puppy who was just told to sit.

And Cindy?

She had a competitive look in her eye. I never did anything like this before, but my response was, "Sure, why not. I mean how hard can it be?"

Two weeks went by and I found myself pricking my fingers with sewing needles trying to make a pumpkin costume. The contest was in a month and I was nowhere near ready, but somehow Cindy already finished her dress. I didn't think about it too hard because she said she did this before and was a good sewer.

Another week went by and I finally finished my dress. It was a long orange dress with a dark green sparkling bucket hat. For shoes I decided on flats that I painted brown.

What?! You may be asking yourself, if I sewed the dress, why didn't I make shoes?! True, but I can barely sew. In fact my mom did most of the sewing, but before you tell me, "That's cheating" I challenge you to make a pumpkin costume and shoes in three weeks, and not out of cardboard either!

Time flew by quickly, like the good fairies who knew a girl who sleeps a lot in a castle. What's her name? Sleepinging Beauty or something.

Anyways, it was the day before the contest and I was baking the pumpkin pie. I kindly asked everyone not to go into the kitchen because I needed some space to concentrate. However, right as I was carrying the pie to the oven I heard the water tap turn on. I screamed and dropped the pie. When I turned around, I saw Cindy standing holding a cup of water.

"I am so sorry!" Cindy cried.

"Oh it's no big deal. I'll just make another pie," I remarked. I felt suspicious because we do have another kitchen that my mother uses for cooking classes with a perfectly good working sink. After I said that, she turned around and I think I may have seen a smile in the reflection of her glass as she picked it up to take a sip.

The day of the contest came faster than you could snap your fingers and say, "Bibbidi bobbidi boo!" It was six-forty-five in the morning and we were loading up the car to go to the contests. While we were loading, Cindy came out wearing some new clothes while carrying her contest clothes. A little bit later Anna ran through the door and jumped down the stairs yelling,

"Who's ready to win?!" Everyone looked at her like she was crazy!

"What?" Anna asked.

"What?" I mimicked her. "How do you have so much energy?"

"Well," she replied.

"Well what?" my mother asked.

"I may or may not have drank three cups of coffee."

We all stared at her. Then out of the silence, my mom said, "You did what?"

Anna then replied, "Never mind," and picked up the last bag and placed it in the trunk and slammed it shut.

"Who's ready to go to the contest?" Anna asked before jumping in the back seat of the car. We all turned to each other, then shrugged it off because it was too early in the morning.

When we reached our town there was a huge banner that read, "The Pumpkin Patch Princess Contest." Cindy was the first to get out of the car and ran to grab her items as if she was hiding something. When we grabbed all of our belongings, my mother wished us good luck and walked off with Anna towards the bleachers.

"Five minutes till show, five minutes!" a male person said. I went towards the dressing room when Cindy walked past wearing her dress. The dress minded me of one I saw online when I was searching for ideas on how to make my own dress. I didn't have time to question because as you heard the man, I have five minutes.

The town clock struck with a ring. It does this every time the clock turns twelve. "Show time! Get lined up," the same man said. I was ready to win this.

When I walked onto the stage I saw the judges for the first time. One of the judges was an elderly woman. The other was a middle-aged man with a very odd choice of mustache, and the last one I recognized from my class. His name was Prince and I had a crush on him ever since 5th grade.

When we were on stage it felt like an eternity. The sun didn't help either. The judges looked at us in our pumpkin outfits and threw out some "Very Goods." When we got off the stage I looked at my watch and guess what: it had been only ten minutes. It felt like thirty. "You have fifteen minutes until the next contest," the same man said. Where does he keep coming from? I quickly changed into a more comfortable outfit and grabbed my pie. When I started to walk towards the stage, Cindy came out of nowhere and if I did not stop to tie my shoe we would have collided.

"Whoa, that was close." Cindy sighed. I couldn't help feeling that she wanted to run into me and cause me to drop my pie.

"Yeah, a little too close," I responded, staring into her eyes like I was going to see something.

"Well, good luck," she remarked and walked away.

"It's time ladies. Line up for the second contest," the man explained

"Mmm, delicious," the judges said, and as they walked away from my pie, I heard Prince say, "That was by far my favorite pie!"

I could not help but smile and give out a tiny snort. I frantically looked around to see if anyone heard, but when I looked in the direction of the judges I saw that Prince was the only person who heard. I could tell because he had rosy cheeks and turned away from my direction when I looked at him.

After the judges tasted all of the pies, they went in a little huddle like they were a basketball team discussing their next play. When they were done, the guy with the odd mustache yelled, "We will be interviewing you all separately." After he said that, we all walked towards our dressing room.

When I got to mine, Cindy burst through the door and asked in a frantic voice, "Have you seen my cherry lip gloss?!"

"No?" I responded.

"Well...can you please help me look."

"Sure."

After two minutes the loud speaker screeched and I heard Prince say, "Can we please get Kari on the stage?"

"Oh!" Cindy screamed.

"What?" I asked.

"I remember where I left it. It's in the car. Keep looking though. I might be wrong." Before I answered, she scrambled out of the room in a hustle. I just turned around and kept going on the search for the lip gloss, but while I was looking I saw her dress lying on the ground so I picked it. When I picked it up there was a store tag that read,

Pumpkinclothing.com

I turned around in the dressing room to walk out the door to tell the judges what she had done, but that was when I saw that her pie was actually from my mother's business.

"I found it!" Cindy yelled as she walked back into the dressing room.

"Why does the dress have a tag and your pie, and why is it from the same bakery my mom owns?!" I asked her. She must have had this rehearsed because she sounded very convincing.

"The dress tag—I handmade that—and for the pie, I used one of her boxes to carry mine in. Does that answer your question?"

"Yeah."

Right after I said that, another voice came on the speaker. This time, it was the lady. "Can Drizella please come on stage?"

I left the trailer and walked onto the stage. I heard the crowd roar with applause. I could not help smiling. When I reached them, they wasted no time because they blasted me with question one. "What gave you the idea for your dress?"

"Well, my sister, Anna as we call her, has a pumpkin patch and while I was looking at it for an idea, it came to me."

"What is your favorite ingredient that you put in your pie and why?" the man with the odd beard asked.

"My favorite ingredient I use is pepper to give it extra flavor."

"How did you figure that out?" he asked again.

"I was seven or eight years old, and my mother owns her own bakery. And I wanted to try to make my own pie and I accidentally spilled pepper in it."

"What made you want to come here this afternoon?" the lady asked.

"Wow, umm, well I always wanted to try, but I was always too young, and when that letter came my step-sister, Cindy, asked me if I was in. And I said sure, how hard can it be?" I heard the crowd chuckle.

"What is your favorite back-stage snack?"

"Well, probably pizza." This made the crowd roar with laughter.

"Final question. Are you ready?" This time Prince was asking.

"Sure."

"What would be your advice to girls?"

"Um, probably be kind and have courage."

"Thank you Ella. We applaud your honesty. Who doesn't love pizza?" the judges commented.

They then sent me backstage to wait. When I reached my own room, I heard the judges call for Cindy. I listened to what questions they asked her since my room is really close to the stage, and they asked her the same questions. However, she received different feedback from the judges. I heard a judge say, it is interesting you'd make a dress with a store tag attached. I also heard a judge say that your pie looked very similar to last week's special at the bakery shop; it even had their stamp on the bottom crust layer. I felt a little spark of joy as I heard the judges let Cindy know that she could not trick them in this contest and felt hopeful I could win.

After everyone had their chance to be interviewed we were called back on stage. Unfortunately, my shoes came untied again and one slipped off. I could not stop to pick it up because other contestants were walking swiftly behind me. The man with the odd mustache gave a lovely speech, I think. I was so nervous and distracted so I did not pay close attention. Then I heard Anna cheering, "Way to go! That's my big sis!" from the crowd, and Prince was carrying me a crown and my shoe. I did not know which to accept first. The Crown ceremony music was playing and I was staring into Prince's eyes while Cindy was crying behind me.

As you can see, I am not the bad guy. Cindy is learning that people are not believing her fairy tales any more, and Anna enjoys correcting her when she lies. My mom started dating the man with the odd mustache. He has a beard now. Prince asked me to the dance, and I said yes, but I need some new shoes.

The end....or is it?

Ten years later, Prince and I got married and opened our own shoe business called, Prince and Ella's shoe co.

We also have twins, girl and boy, named Charlotte and Jr. and this is my life after the Pumpkin Princess contests.

"MOOOOMMMMYYYY!" Charlotte screamed. I came running because I thought something bad happened.

"What?" I said out of breath. When I looked at them, I saw Jr. wearing Prince's watch.

"Oh nothing," Charlotte responded.

"Then why did you yell for me?"

"Well, you see, Jr. said that you loved him more so I challenged him to see if he was right."

"And," I said, still wheezing from the run upstairs because our house is above our shoe store.

"We tied," Jr. yelled excitedly.

"How did I tie?" I asked.

"Your time for both of us was 15.45 seconds. So that means you love us equally."

I then grabbed both of the little rascals and threw them on the couch and started to tickle them until they started to cry. Just then Prince walked threw the door and said, "Did you know that you left me down there with a woman and a child that sounded like he was in his terrible twos?"

"Well these two rascals were testing me to see who I loved the most."

"Oh really. What's next? Are you going to test me?" Prince asked.

"No, it's pretty clear who you love more," Charlotte answered, pointing her little finger towards herself. Apparently Jr. did not see that.

Me and Prince then excused ourselves, for we needed to go back to work, but before we went back downstairs I called out, "Anna!" Just seconds after I called for my sister, she came walking through the door.

"What?" Anna asked.

"Why did you let them test us?" There was a little pause after I asked.

"They came up and asked who they thought Mom loved more. I said test them. And a minute later they came up to me and told me their plan. I just wanted to see if it worked. Can you blame me?"

I do not know why, but after my sister answered my question, I started balling out laughing.

After closing, we said bye to my sister and ate some supper. It was pizza, my favorite food.

POISONED APPLE CORES
by Gracie Gregory, 6th Grade

The Evil Queen laughed maniacally as she flipped her hair, tossing the long glossy black locks as she—

"Totally unfair," Blanca complained. The prince looked up.

"Why? Because she called you a cosmetic-obsessed sociopath?" Blanca sighed from where she was reading what the kingdom's latest gossip was, which was, in fact, her.

"No, Prince, not that," Blanca said impatiently. "Why does the Evil Queen, allegedly me, have better hair than the actual Blanca Nieve?" She flipped her head in comparison.

Blanca's curly white-blond hair wasn't much like the glossy locks that the gossip magazine article painted it to be. Blanca Nieve, elected queen of the kingdom of Calamvale, was lounging in the dining hall of the lush palace with The Prince. What is his real name? Nothing.

It's just, "The Prince."

Where is he from? No one knows; he just kind of hangs around.

Blanca was reading the article and complaining while The Prince was lurking like a cat with designer boots in the shadows.

"And they made me a stepmother! I am eighteen years old!" shrieked Blanca.

She was reading the story that Snow White had told the locals, and the locals put it into a crazy tall tale.

Blanca was frustrated that the kingdom was turning against their queen just because of some article that a troublesome brat wrote. Snow White used to be Blanca Nieve's best friend, but then Blanca was elected as queen instead of Snow, and so she spread a bunch of lies that Blanca killed Snow White's parents. But it was so wrong.

Blanca was just about to continue whining about the article when a footman stumbled into the dining hall. "My queen!" he gasped. "You have to see this!"

Blanca and The Prince, confused, followed the out of breath footman to the palace balcony, where they saw a small group of protesters gathered at the foot of the gated palace walls. Blanca gasped as she focused on the protester's shouts.

"I'd guess the word got out," said The Prince dryly.

"Y-yes sir," stuttered the nervous footman. He, too, had heard the murmurs that their queen was trying to kill Snow White and was trying to not believe them.

"These protesters have been gathering all over town," he continued. This snapped Blanca out of her daze.

"And you've not alerted the royal guard?" she said testily. This was starting to put her into a bad mood. The footman looked fearfully at her.

"And do what?" he asked tentatively.

"Oh, whatever, just tell the villagers to stop this behavior," she announced. Scowling, she turned on her heel and stalked icily out of the balcony room.

A little while later, in a room deep in the dungeons...

"Magic mirror! Magic mirror! Where the heck are you?" yelled the disgruntled young queen. Blanca thundered into the dimly lit room, lavish royal robes streaming out behind her. She made a beeline toward the large floor-to-ceiling mirror with intricate gold and diamond-encrusted detailing. Blanca stood in front of it and loudly cleared her throat. Slowly, a ghostly apparition of a young man appeared. Stretching and yawning, he glowered at Blanca.

"I thought I asked you not to call me that," he corrected. "Sorry, Liam," Blanca said, not sounding sorry at all. "It's just 'Magic Mirror' is so much more interesting," she said. Liam sighed.

"But it's not my name," he said stubbornly.

"Fine, fine, whatever, that's not the problem here," replied an impatient Blanca. Blanca was already feeling annoyed, but she needed his help. Liam hds known Blanca since she was a kid and Blanca trusted his advice.

"OK, then, someone's grumpy today," teased Liam, but then noticing the serious expression on Blanca's face he relented.

"Sheesh, what is it?"

"The whole kingdom thinks I'm a murderer!" wailed Blanca, spilling out the whole story. By the end, Liam was looking confused. He hesitated.

"Well.... You kind of are."

"What!?"

"A murderer, I mean. You did kill her parents."

"I did not! So what if the basket of apples they had were poisoned? It could have been anyone...And how could I have known the apples were poisoned? I saw them on the front steps and being a good neighbor, I brought them in when they opened the door."

"Yeah, but it wasn't. I've known you for, like, forever. I know that you killed Quartz and Opal White. I know you THINK that you didn't kill the Quartz and Opal, but I guess you're right...It could have been anyone who poisoned the apples. What do you want me to do about it? Snow clearly wants revenge."

"There's nothing to get revenge for. I was proven innocent in court. You know that," said Blanca primly. "She's just bitter that I became Queen instead of her."

"If you say so," Liam paced back and forth as far as the mirror would allow him.

"Tell you what. I think that you should go find the kid. Sort things out. After all, you did kill her parents. Just...be mature for once in your life and try not to murder Snow White."

"Why would I do that?"

"You do have quite the temper."

"So you think I should go find her?" summed up Blanca.

Liam shrugged. "How would I know?"

After that unpleasant encounter with the crabby Magic Mirror, Blanca was stirred into a frenzy. "Bring me my horse and The Prince's too!" she announced to the Throne Room's guards, even though that wasn't technically speaking their job. The guards, though, were too intimidated to argue. They'd heard it from a cook who heard it from the stable boy who had heard it from the footman from earlier that the Queen was quite possibly a crazy murderer. The guards went to get the horse.

Blanca flounced off to wherever that prince was hiding and coaxed him into coming with her on a kingdom-wide manhunt for Snow White. The Prince honestly kind of thought that the queen was kind of off her rocker.

"Remind me again why we are doing this?" he asked.

"Because, Prince, if we don't get Snow White to stop the rumors that I killed her parents and am now trying to kill Snow White, I will probably lose my throne and ALL my power as a queen, we don't want that, now do we?" said Blanca in reply, puffing as she hoisted her saddlebags on the pretty black mare horse that she was riding.

"I just think the whole thing's kind of unnecessary..." trailed off The Prince.

Blanca sighed, "Look, prince, there's something I haven't told you."

"I'm listening."

Blanca sat down heavily in the grass and sighed. She had a sad look in her eye. "It all happened a long time ago....."

3 years ago....

The haunted forest was filled with many creepy sounds of the night, but the two teen girls moving swiftly through the underbrush took no notice. One girl with long black hair and red lips, and the other with curly blond hair and deathly pale skin. The dark-haired girl nudged the blonde one playfully, gesturing to an abandoned mine shaft. A warm glow of lamp light was coming from its depths. Even though the mine was a good half mile away, the girls could hear eerie singing. "Cm'on," the dark-haired girl seemed to say. The blonde was hesitant, but followed her friend anyway. Drawing closer to the mine, the girls heard the rushed footsteps of seven dwarfs and the horrible roar of fire. Looking at each other with shocked faces, the girls raced towards the mine. "Help! Our brother is still there!" the panicked dwarfs shouted. The heat of the fire consuming the mine made tears prick the girls' eyes and made their mouths dry up. "We have to save him!" The dark-haired girl looked wildly at the blonde and started towards the burning mine. The blonde grasped her friend's arm with a terrified look on her face and shook her head. The dark-haired girl tried to pry free and argue, but it was too late. A wall of fire engulfed what was left of the mine and everything went black.

"And so the dwarf in the mine died, and it was all my fault. Snow and I had an argument and never spoke again," said Blanca flatly.

The Prince blinked. He sat down gently on the ground next to her. "I'm sorry."

"It was a long time ago,"

"If you don't mind me asking, why didn't you want to go into the mine to save the dwarf?"

The Prince braced himself for a scathing retort. All Blanca did was say in a small voice,

"My parents died in a fire."

"Oh."

"I couldn't lose any more..." Blanca trailed off, but The Prince could have sworn she said, 'family.'

An hour later, Blanca and The Prince were ready to go. The palace was relieved to see them go; Blanca's odd behavior was really stressing them out and they could use a break. Thirty minutes into the trip, the Prince was already complaining.

Sighing, Blanca stopped her horse. "What is it now?"

"There has to be something under this saddle. It's so uncomfortable!" he said.

"It's a saddle, Prince. That's kind of the point."

Huffing, The Prince said, "Can we at least stop for a second?"

Blanca sharply exhaled. "Fine: just for a second." Blanca was frustrated with the progress that they had been making. She'd heard from a local that Snow White might be somewhere in the Glimmering Forest, hiding with some dwarfs or something, and they were only on the outskirts of Sonnenvale. The Prince and Blanca pulled over by an old oak looming over a mossy old cave. The Prince hopped off his dappled brown steed and started rummaging under the cracked tan leather saddle. Blanca leaned on the old oak tree, thinking about the fateful day that she (accidentally) poisoned the old King and Queen. Oh, did she not mention? Quartz and Opal White were the old rulers of the kingdom! It was by pure, random luck that Blanca was chosen to be the new Queen.

Poisoning had nothing to do with it.

At all.

At least, that's what a sixteen-year-old Blanca thought originally when she inherited the throne. Now she wasn't so sure...

"Aha!" exclaimed The Prince as he pulled a green pea from under his saddle. "A pea! I thought I told that Stable Boy to not eat on my horse!" Blanca, however, was confused. "How could you have felt that tiny thing?"

"Don't know. Suppose it's because I'm royal."

"Well," sighed Blanca. "Now that that's settled, we should g—" A strange, musical sound abruptly cut her off. It was a whimsical sound, almost flute-like, and it was coming from the cave. Blanca and the Prince stopped to listen. "What's a pretty sound like that coming from a drafty cave?" inquired the Prince.

"I don't know," murmured Blanca. This was a rare occasion where Blanca admitted that she did not know something.

"Come on, let's go check it out!" said the Prince, starting towards the cave. Blanca ran up and grabbed hold of his arm.

"Don't! Stranger danger. Who but a creeper would be playing the flute in the middle of nowhere in a cave!" she whispered urgently. Too late. The cave's inhabitants had already heard them murmuring. The flute's music stopped, and someone was approaching, Blanca could hear the footsteps. "Come on, Prince, we have to go!" she whispered, panicked.

A bald head appeared from the cave's entrance, followed by a toothless smile. Blanca made a squeaking sort of sound. An old man with a wooden flute emerged from the mossy cave. "Well, what are two young people like yourselves doing in the middle of a forest?" he said. That was all it took. Blanca and The Prince bolted for their horses. The old man shrugged. "If that's how you're gonna be..." he said, bringing the flute to his lips. An eerie melody floated through the air and...I don't know. Blanca and The Prince were already far away in the distance.

Blanca and the Prince only stopped riding at full speed when they made sure that no one was following them. They had come upon a pretty, sunny grove of apple trees. Weighing down almost every branch were ripe, juicy red apples. Blanca slowed her mare and breathed out slowly. "Well, that was eventful," said the Prince eventually. Neither of them really knew what to say after that.

After riding for about ten minutes, Blanca and the Prince came to the end of the orchard. The biggest, healthiest tree with dark red apples grew from the ground elegantly. Blanca slid off her mount and dropped to the ground with a sigh. She suddenly looked much older than her age and very weary. The shadows of the setting sun against the apple tree played off the angles of her face.

"Prince, I don't know what I'm going to do. I don't even know why I'm doing this. Snow White still hates me, and for a while she was the only person who cared about me. And now I'm trying to do what? Imprison her? Banish her? Even though she's done nothing wrong and has a great reason to hate me for the rest of my life." The outburst was so quiet that The Prince barely heard it. Tears slipped down Blanca's pale cheeks. The Prince shuffled his feet, not really knowing what to say. Blanca drew in a shaky breath. "Wow, I really know how to kill the mood, don't I?" She let out a light laugh, but not at all a happy one. "It's fine, Prince, don't worry about it." The Prince was looking uncomfortable like a cornered animal. He hated it when people cried.

"Here, have this," he said, handing her an apple. Blanca, not looking at the fruit, numbly took it and before she could think about what it was, bit into it, leaving a perfect mark on the smooth red surface. "Than—" she tried to say, but something odd was happening. Her tongue was swelling, and she couldn't get out the words. Blanca fought down a wave of panic and tried to swallow, bBut she couldn't. Her airways had closed off. She couldn't breathe. Blanca gagged, terror overwhelming her.

"Blanca! What's going on?!" She faintly heard the Prince shouting for help, but everything was growing dim. Everything hurts. Then a very, very cold pain on her arm jolted her back to reality. Blanca took a gasping breath in and looked at the villager who had saved her. Black, glossy hair, sculpted features and warm brown eyes, the person Blanca had both looked forward to seeing and dreaded at the same time. "Snow?" asked Blanca quietly. The girl nodded, eyes misty. "Good thing I had some Whistlethorn on me when I heard this prince's shouts. The only cure to a rare Poison Apple." Snow paused. "And you know what I figured out? Poison Apples aren't made. They are a rare genetic mutation to a normal apple. Oh, Blanca, I'm so sorry! I now know you didn't kill my parents," Snow cried. Blanca also sobbed, tackle-hugging Snow White and whispering, "I'm sorry too." The Prince cleared his throat. Blanca looked up and mouthed, thank you.

Three Months Later....

The haunted forest was still filled with many sounds. But on this beautiful summer day the only ones were laughter and chatter. People, royal and villager alike, gathered to see their Queen Blanca Nieve and their Grand Duchess Snow White, head of human relations, celebrate the reopening of the Magical Creatures Foundation, which stood in place of the old collapsed mine that had burned in the fire. Another new addition was the new memorial to the dwarf who died in the mine. "This foundation is for any person, magical or not, to find a home," proudly announced Queen Blanca, "And our wonderful new Grand Duchess will be supervising and helping all she can." Blanca beamed at Snow.

"We will both strive to make Calamvale a better place for all its inhabitants, and try not to leave anyone bitter or family- less. Your queen and I have both felt these things, and we want to make sure no one else does. We have an amazing queen who is going places, and I promise that I will try to help the community as best as I can," said Snow White, and with that, Blanca and Snow cut the blue ribbon and the foundation was officially open. While they were met with cheers, The Prince and Liam (in compact mirror form) were looking proudly at Snow White and Blanca like they were the ones who had made them friends again.

"Do you think they'll ever be the same friends as they used to be?" asked The Prince.

"I don't know. They sure are working through a lot, but I think they will," said Liam.

"It helps that Blanca didn't kill Snow's parents."

"I always knew she didn't poison those apples," said Liam, looking slightly smug.

"What? How?"

Liam flashed a slightly wicked smile. "Because I did."

The End

PLEASE NOTE: NO WITCHES WERE BURNT ALIVE DURING THE MAKING OF THIS STORY
by Addison McGurn, 8th Grade

Once upon a time, in a dark forest, in a cozy little cottage, there lived an old witch. Of course, her name wasn't actually "The Witch." That's just what everybody called her. We'll get to that in a minute.

The Witch (yes, I'm going to call her that, but only because I don't know what her real name is) was collecting herbs and flowers to garnish her baked goods with. You see, The Witch owned the best bakery for miles and miles around, and despite her hag-like appearance, people came from everywhere just to taste one of her specialty blueberry muffins. I can see why they did. Every morning, The Witch creates the batter (making sure to add a little extra sugar and butter), spoons it into three different-sized muffin tins (small, medium, and large), and pops them in the oven to bake. As they rise, the whole area around her cottage starts to smell like heaven, letting her customers know that she's just about open for the day.

And it's not just the muffins themselves that are amazing. The Witch makes her own fruit preserves from what she picks off the trees in her orchard in the fall, and drizzles them on top of her muffins right after they come out of the oven.

Then, she puts them on the windowsill to cool while she cleans up the kitchen. So you see, she's not the green, children-eating monster that she's characterized as (and she definitely doesn't have any warts).

CRASH!!

Oh. Oh my goodness. Something very bad just happened in—ah, yes. That's right. I haven't told you about how this whole thing works yet. Well, I better explain before we get into anything too crazy. You see, The Witch lives in a book in my library, along with every other fairytale character that was ever created. They are kept in this book so that their stories can just keep repeating themselves, over and over again. I suppose they'd get tired of the same incident refreshing itself if they knew it was happening. Now, don't ask me why the book is in my library. It just showed up there one day, and I felt as though it was my responsibility to look after it. Sometimes I like to narrate the stories while they're unraveling because they play out like a movie right on the page. It makes me feel more connected to the characters.

Well anyway, let's get back to the story. I think I'll just let The Witch take it from here if that's okay.

CRASH!!

I dash to the window, only to see my beloved, right out of the oven, blueberry muffins splattered all over the floor. To be frank, I was more confused than angry. Does a perfectly content pan of delicious muffins that were sitting on a windowsill, just suddenly decide to jump off? No. Because that doesn't just happen! So let me tell you, I was a little...ahem... concerned about how my muffins got off the windowsill in the first place. So I did what any normal person would do; I stuck my head out of the window to see what was going on. And what did I see huddled on the ground under my magnolia bushes? Two small children, who looked to be about the ages of five and seven. The older one was a boy with messy red hair. He was wearing what looked to be a canvas sack that had been repurposed into a shirt, and baggy pants with patches of all different sizes and colors on them. The younger one was a girl. She had long, hazelnut colored hair that hung in two loose braids down her back. She also had on a brown long sleeve shirt, and on top of it, a canvas material dress that was ripped at every possible hem. Both of the kids looked dirty and unwashed, and another thing: neither of them had shoes on! My goodness, you just couldn't help but feel bad for them.

"Well, hello down there," I said as sweetly as I could while still sticking my head out of the window. The children looked back at me with innocent, frightened looks on their faces.

"My dears, whatever happened to you two?" Neither of them responded. So after a moment of awkward eye contact, I said, "You stay right there. I'll be right around the front." As you would imagine, I was quite surprised by the idea of some small children sitting in my garden, tipping over my muffins, and who knows what else. But, as you can also imagine, I was concerned for them. So on my way to the front door, dozens of questions were going through my mind. For example, why were they in the woods at this time of day? Where were their parents and were they looking for them? When was the last time they had a bath?

When I got into the front yard, the kids were no longer sitting underneath my window sill, but standing in front of me. Something I noticed right away; both of them had terrible posture. Their shoulders were hunched, and their heads hung just slightly too close to their chests. "Well..." I said, not quite knowing how to talk to children. After all, I have none of my own. "I guess we should—"

Before I could finish, the boy's eyes got wide, and he screeched, "It wasn't us! We didn't do anything! Please don't hurt us, or eat us, or do whatever witches in the forest do to kids!" So, after taking a step back, I was a bit offended by this comment, considering that no one had ever called me a witch before, and frankly, I didn't think of myself as one.

Before I could say anything, the little girl leaped around to face the boy, and said, "Hansel, don't you dare even try to lie! You tipped over this lady's muffin pan, and you know it!"

Let me tell you, I was quite surprised by how powerful this child's voice was, coming from such a small girl. Then she turned to me, and said, "I'm so sorry, Ma'am, we're just very hungry. You see, we ran away, and came across your cottage this morning. My brother," she gestured to the boy behind her, "thought your muffins smelled so good, and he tried to convince me to steal one! Of course, I said no. Because, you see, I'm not one to take or beg for anything. Although my stomach has been grumbling for the past..." She trailed off, and appeared to be counting on her fingers. I took this as my chance to step in.

"Why, it's alright dear. I was just about to pull them out of the pan anyway. Would you care to join me in making another batch?" I said this in the least creepy way possible, although I still think that I must have scared the living daylights out of the poor boy. How do I know this, you ask?

Well, he suddenly turned and sprinted off into the forest, yelling, "I'm going home, Gretel! Have fun getting roasted and eaten by that witch!" Again, offensive.

The girl and I turned to each other, and smiled, "Ah, Gretel, is it?"

"Yes, Ma'am."

"Well," I sighed lightly, "We better get to making those muffins, or they won't be ready in time for my shop to open!" The smile on Gretel's face was as large as a crescent moon, and she giggled slightly before saying,

"You own a bakery?"

"Why yes, I do. And in fact, I think you would be the perfect employee."

"Really?! You mean it?"

"Of course! How would you like to be... taste tester?" Gretel smiled that beautiful moon smile again as we walked, hand in hand, into my cottage.

Over the years, I have gotten to know Gretel as not only my friend, but my family, as she now lives with me. In fact, I affectionately gave her the nickname of Amorino, meaning little love in Italian.

As for Hansel, he has made it his mission to spread all sorts of rumors about me (aka The Witch). Some of them include eating and/or enslaving Gretel, throwing her back out into the woods to fend for herself, and leaving her to get eaten by a pack of wolves. There are lots more variations that are far more gory, but we don't need to talk about that. Right now, I'm just content watching Gretel grow up and having someone to share my recipes with. Although I do sometimes wonder, where did Hansel get the idea for a house made of sweets, because that sounds fabulous!

So over time, as you can imagine, the witch's story has been twisted and turned in every witch way (Ha ha. I'm hilarious, I know). But as for her cozy cabin, and delicious blueberry muffins, well, they remain the same. So no matter what stories you hear about the witch, you know the real one. And one last thing, if you ever find out what her actual name is, do tell me! I'd love to know.

THE STORY OF THE MOST FABULOUS, GREAT, HEROIC, CHARMING, WONDERFUL WOLF OF ALL TIME (ME)
by Ziva Erlenbeck, 6th Grade

I'm going to tell you a story of a time about ten years ago. Who am I, you may ask? I am the silver wolf (the most fabulous, great, heroic, charming, wonderful wolf of all time), and the story to be told is a true one.

One afternoon, I was out for a walk. Halfway through, I encountered a young prince. He told me that he was on a quest to find the elusive golden bird. The prince's father, the king of Gallania, had ordered his three sons to go on a quest to find the golden bird. The oldest son came back empty handed, and the second son was eaten by a hoard of slugs.

Now, the prince, Prince Ivan, wanted to make his father proud (and not get eaten by slugs). I agreed to help him on his journey, but as we set off I had no idea of how hard and complicated this journey would be.

To be continued...

THE BIG... NOT SO BAD WOLF
by Albert Hong, 8th Grade

A long time ago...

The Big Bad Wolf wasn't always bad. He was once a little wolf pup who played outside with his friends and read books. He loved to read and whenever he had the chance, he read and read and read. When he had grown to a wolf teen he started to stay inside and read all day and night. One day, he came across a book that had the title "Be Bad."It was a long book about how being the bad guy is good; it was so interesting for the wolf. He spent hours every day reading and trying to finish the book.

When he finally finished the book, he was so convinced that being bad was good that he went out his room to try to cause havoc. This is when the Wolf found the three little pigs building their homes. He immediately went over to each of the pigs' homes and started terrorizing them until he came across the third pig's house.

He just couldn't blow his house down! After this he was so embarrassed and decided to take a break.

He worked tirelessly for hours upon hours, trying his best to increase his lung capacity. He started a training regiment, swimming the crawl stroke for 300 meters and diving from 21 meters into a lake, 10 days a week up in the nearby forest.

Feeling good with his work, he felt he was finally ready.

30 years later...

One day, the wolf realized he was getting old and lonely. He saw the three little pigs building houses at the nearby village and he remembered how everyone was afraid of him. He decided he didn't want to be the "Big Bad Wolf" anymore. He wanted to show the pigs he could be kind.

When the pigs saw him, they were scared at first. But the wolf smiled and said, "I'm not here to cause trouble. I just want to be friends." He offered them muffins he baked that morning and promised to prove he could change. The pigs were very unsure and scared, so they kicked the Old Wolf out of their village.

The Old Wolf, walking away from the pigs' village, felt terrible. He had really tried this time. Like, REALLY tried. He wasn't there to blow anything down or scare anybody. He even woke up early to bake muffins and not just any muffins; it was his favorite chocolate chip muffins.

But the pigs didn't care. As soon as they saw him, they ran away. When he tried to talk, they didn't even listen. They just kicked him out like he was still the same old Big Bad Wolf from all those years ago.

Maybe I'll always be the bad guy," he sighed.

The next few days were sad. The Wolf stayed in his little house deep in the forest, reading books. He thought about what he could do to show everyone he had changed, but nothing seemed good enough.

What if the pigs never gave him a second chance, he thought.

Then one evening, just as the sun was going down, the Wolf smelled something weird. It wasn't the smell of muffins or fresh bread or anything like that. But it smelled like SMOKE! IT WAS SMOKE!

At first, he thought maybe some pigs were having a campfire party. But when he looked up, his stomach dropped. Black smoke was rising into the sky. And it was coming from the pigs' village!

"Oh no," the Wolf said to himself.

Without even thinking, he started running as fast as his old legs could carry him. His heart was pounding. He didn't stop to catch his breath. He didn't stop to rest. He just ran.

By the time he reached the top of the hill overlooking the village, his jaw dropped.

The pigs' houses were on fire.

Big, crazy flames were everywhere. The pigs were running around like crazy, carrying tiny buckets of water and trying to save their stuff, but it wasn't working. The fire was getting bigger and bigger.

For a second, the Wolf didn't move. He just watched.

This was it. This was his chance to finally prove he wasn't bad anymore. No more muffins. No more fake smiles. He was going to save them for real.

The Wolf walked to the edge of the hill. He looked at the fire and took the deepest breath he'd ever taken. All those years of practicing blowing down houses? Yeah, well, now it was time to blow out the fire.

He opened his mouth wide, ready to blow with everything he had. But then...

Right before he let out the air, he heard something behind him. A voice.

It was quiet. Kind of scratchy.

"You're not the only one who read "Be Bad,"" the voice said.

The Wolf's eyes went huge. He slowly turned around. And standing there was...

To be continued...

KYLAH OF THE WAVES
by Adrian Reece, 7th Grade

The moon hung low over the edge of the world, casting its pale light across the calm sea. On the rocky shore, where the water licked the land with each rhythmic wave, a solitary figure stood. She was no stranger to the ocean, for it was her home and her heart, yet tonight, something was different. Kylah, a selkie, had not been to shore for many moons, and the pull of the land had become a quiet ache in her soul.

Her fur-lined seal skin lay hidden beneath the jagged rocks, untouched by the cool sea breeze that whispered secrets from the deep. Her long, dark hair cascaded like a waterfall down her back, and her eyes, the color of the endless ocean, reflected both the quiet power of the tides and a sorrowful longing for something that she could never fully grasp.

The land, with its harsh winds and unyielding earth, was not meant for Kylah. She was born of the sea, her spirit entwined with the currents, and though she had danced on the shore many times in her human form, her heart had always longed for the vast embrace of the deep.

Yet tonight, Kylah felt something else—a tug in her chest that was neither the call of the sea nor the yearning for her seal skin. It was the call of a song, a melody she had never heard but knew instantly as if it were part of her very being.

Curiosity, like a current, swept over her, pulling her toward the source of the haunting tune. She followed the winding path along the cliffs, her bare feet silent on the cool stone. As she crested a hill, the sound of the song grew clearer. There, sitting by the edge of the cliffs, was a man—a fisher, his weathered face illuminated by the dim glow of a lantern, his hands moving deftly over the strings of a lyre.

Kylah had heard tales of humans and their music, of songs that could bind the soul or mend a broken heart, but she had never encountered a man who could weave such magic from mere strings.

He was singing, though his voice was soft, like the first breath of dawn. The melody pulled at her, and with every note, Kylah felt something deep inside of her stir, something she hadn't felt in centuries—something that called her to stay, to listen, to understand.

The man did not see her at first, so caught up was he in the song he was creating. His melody swelled with the power of the sea, the rhythm of the waves, and the wind's ancient dance. Kylah, her heart beating faster, stepped forward, her feet brushing the cool grass. The man stopped abruptly, his fingers stilling on the lyre, and turned toward her.

His eyes widened as he gazed upon her, for Kylah, with her long, dark hair and haunting beauty, was not like the other women of the land. She seemed like a vision, like something woven from the very threads of the sea itself.

"You—" he began, his voice trembling. "You are... of the sea."

Kylah smiled softly, a distant sadness in her eyes. "I am Kylah," she said, her voice like the wind across the ocean, both clear and elusive.

The man set down his lyre carefully, as though afraid it might break the spell between them. "I've heard of creatures like you, the selkies... but I never believed the stories."

"And yet here I am," she replied gently.

He took a step toward her, his heart racing. "I didn't mean to summon you," he said, his voice uncertain. "I only wanted to sing for the sea, to honor it."

"The sea does not need honoring," Kylah replied softly, her gaze distant. "It is both life and death, the cradle of all things. It needs no songs or praise."

"But I do," he said, his eyes filled with something she could not place. "I have been lost—my heart adrift in a sea of sorrow. I thought... maybe music could guide me, show me the way back."

Kylah studied him closely. There was a deep pain in his eyes, a weight that the ocean could not wash away. She took a step closer, drawn to him in a way that both confused and fascinated her. "What do you seek, human?"

"I seek peace," he said, his voice raw. "My heart has been broken for so long. I thought I had left the sea behind, but it seems I was wrong. I've been looking for something... someone."

For a long moment, Kylah said nothing. She could hear the yearning in his words, the ache that mirrored her own. But her heart was the sea, vast and wild, and she could never belong to the land. Could she risk drawing him deeper into her world, knowing that her time there would always be fleeting?

"I cannot stay," she said at last, her voice barely more than a whisper. "The sea calls to me. It is my home."

"I understand," the man said, though his voice betrayed his sorrow. "But you... you are the answer I have been seeking. Perhaps, even if only for a moment, you can show me what I've been missing."

Kylah hesitated. She knew the pain of longing, the desire to belong, but she also knew the truth of who she was. Her love was for the sea, for the endless waves that carried her across the world. No human could ever truly fill that space.

But as she looked into his eyes, she felt something stir deep within her, something that made her heart ache with a tenderness she couldn't quite name.

"Perhaps," she whispered, "the sea has not only taken from you, but also given."

The man stepped closer, his breath shaky as he reached out. Kylah allowed it, feeling his warmth against the chill of her skin, and for a brief moment, she let herself be human, let herself believe that there might be a place for her on land, just as there was beneath the waves.

But the moonlight shifted, and with it, the call of the sea grew louder in her soul. Kylah stepped back, her eyes filled with an understanding that only she could know.

"I must go," she said, her voice soft but firm. "But you, too, must find your way back. The sea will always be here, waiting, for those who listen."

With one last glance at the man, Kylah turned and ran toward the water. Her feet barely touched the earth as she shed her human form and dove into the waves, her seal skin wrapping tightly around her once more.

For a long time, the man stood by the cliffs, watching the water where she had disappeared. His heart was heavy, but there was something else—something that stirred within him like a pulse he couldn't ignore. He had felt the pull of the sea as well, not just in her, but in himself. It was as if, in that moment, their souls had briefly brushed against one another, leaving an imprint.

Days passed, and the man could not shake the feeling that Kylah's song had awakened something deep within him. He could hear the sea's call now, louder than ever before, and it echoed with a yearning that was not only for the ocean but for her, for Kylah. He could not stay on land, tied to the cold earth and broken memories. He had to find her.

He gathered his things—his boat, his lyre, and a heart full of hope—and sailed out into the open sea. Days turned into weeks as he navigated the waters, guided by the soft rhythm of the ocean and the melody of the selkie's song that still hummed in his chest.

At last, one evening, as the sun began to set and the stars appeared, he saw her—Kylah, standing on the rocks, her hair flowing in the wind. This time, she did not run from him.

He approached her, his voice trembling. "Kylah... I found you."

She turned, her eyes soft with recognition. "You shouldn't have come," she said, but there was no reproach in her tone. Only a deep, abiding understanding. "The sea is vast, and the land is far from here."

But the man shook his head, stepping closer. "I can't live without both. The sea, the land... and you. I am not complete without you, Kylah."

Her heart trembled, for she knew the truth of his words. The sea called to her, but for the first time, she realized that she could listen to both the sea and the man who loved her.

"Then stay," she whispered. "Come to the sea, and stay with me."

The man smiled, and in that moment, he shed the burden of his past. Together, they returned to the water, Kylah shedding her seal skin to take on her human form once more. He embraced her, not as a creature of myth, but as the woman he loved, the one who had brought him back to himself.

The man stayed with Kylah by the shore, where the sea was always close, always in reach. Though the pull of the deep ocean was ever present in her soul, Kylah learned to embrace her new life, and in turn, the man began to feel the stirrings of something ancient and powerful in his own heart. He wasn't merely a fisherman anymore; he had become a part of the ocean's song, woven into the tides alongside her.

As the seasons passed, Eamon and Kylah created a life of both land and sea. In the mornings, she would help him pull in his nets, her feet grounded in the earth, her heart still fluttering with the taste of salt on the wind. In the evenings, they would sit together by the fire, Kylah gazing out at the horizon, her thoughts always drifting to the vastness of the ocean. Eamon would play his lyre by the shore, the sweet sound of his music blending with the rhythm of the waves, echoing across the water. Together, they found a way to live between two worlds, where the land met the sea and love bridged the divide.

One cold evening, as winter's breath began to settle on the cliffs and the moon cast its pale light on the still waters, Eamon spoke to Kylah of his dreams.

"Kylah," he said softly, his voice carrying the weight of a thousand unspoken words, "the sea has taught me that there is more to this life than I ever knew. I've seen how it nurtures and nourishes, how it holds secrets and promises. I want to learn more... with you, beside you. I want to share in the tides of your world, to live as one with you—both the man and the selkie, the land and the sea."

Kylah smiled, a quiet joy filling her heart. For the first time, she felt the weight of her love for Eamon settle in her chest. She had always been a creature of both worlds, torn between the land and the sea, but now, with him beside her, she no longer felt divided.

"I have always been torn, Eamon," she said, her voice soft but filled with certainty. "But I know that love, our love, can stretch across the ocean's edge and bring two worlds together. As long as we remain true to each other, the sea will never take me away. Not fully."

Eamon kissed her then, a kiss that tasted of salt and moonlight, of the deep currents that flowed between them. And in that moment, they both knew that the sea had not taken her from him—it had brought them together, two souls entwined in the song of the waves.

Years passed, and their love only deepened, a love that bridged the gap between the sea and the land, between the selkie and the fisherman. They were no longer bound by the separation of their worlds. They had created their own, where the sea would always be home, but where they could both live and love, side by side, forever.

The days passed slowly for Eamon and Kylah, a gentle rhythm woven together by the hands of both the sea and the land. Their lives intertwined as seamlessly as the dance of the waves with the shore, a delicate balance of love, sacrifice, and shared understanding.

In the mornings, Kylah would rise with the sun, her bare feet sinking into the soft, damp sand. She would watch as the light broke over the horizon, casting golden hues across the water, a familiar comfort she had known all her life. Eamon would be beside her, his weathered face softened by the warmth of the morning, his hand resting gently on her shoulder. Together, they would pull in the fishing nets that lay tangled on the shore, their fingers working in perfect harmony.

Kylah, though born of the sea, had learned the art of fishing. She was a swift and graceful presence, moving with ease between the land and the water. Her presence was a balm to Eamon, her touch light but sure as she helped him lift the heavy nets and sort the catch. Though she no longer dived beneath the waves as often as she once did, the rhythm of the ocean never left her. She could hear the whispers of the tides, could feel the pulse of the water beneath her skin even when she was miles from the shore.

But it was in the evenings, when the sun sank into the sea, that the real magic of their life together unfolded.

After the day's work was done, they would retreat to the small cottage Eamon had built with his own hands. It was nestled on the edge of the cliffs, with a view that stretched across the endless expanse of the ocean. The sound of the waves crashing against the rocks below was their constant companion, the lullaby that would guide them to sleep each night.

As the fire crackled in the hearth, Kylah would sit by the window, her gaze faraway, lost in the shifting light of the ocean. Eamon would often bring his lyre out of its corner, the familiar instrument a connection to the days before they had met. He would play softly, a song that carried the melodies of the sea, the longing of the tides, and the joy of their shared moments. His music, once a solitary pursuit, now spoke of them both—of the love they had discovered and the life they had built together.

Sometimes, Kylah would join him, her voice soft and clear as she sang along with him. Her song was like the wind over the water, free and fluid, yet anchored by the love she felt for him. The melodies they created together would drift out into the night air, carried by the wind over the cliffs, as though the ocean itself were listening. The sound would join the chorus of the sea, weaving through the waves, becoming part of its eternal song.

Their nights were filled with quiet conversations, moments of shared laughter, and the comfort of simply being in each other's presence. Though Kylah's heart was still bound to the sea, she had come to understand that love, too, was an endless tide. It did not pull her away from the shore; it only deepened her connection to both worlds. Eamon, in turn, had come to love the sea, not just for the bounty it brought them but for the way it had shaped Kylah, who she was, and who she had become.

And yet, there were still moments when Kylah's longing for the deep was too strong to ignore. Some nights, when the moon was full and the tides were high, she would slip into the water alone, her bare feet meeting the cool, salt-kissed waves as she returned to her true self. She would shed her human skin and slip into the familiar embrace of her seal form, diving beneath the surface, where the ocean was dark and mysterious, but always home. She could still feel the pulse of the currents and the language of the waves as they spoke to her, pulling her deeper into the embrace of the sea.

But no matter how far she ventured, no matter how deeply she swam, the land never truly let her go. The thought of Eamon waiting on the shore, his steady presence a beacon in the vastness of the ocean, always called her back.

And every time, she returned to him.

Eamon knew when she needed to go, and though the absence of her was always felt, he understood. He had come to love the sea not only because it had given him Kylah but because it had become a part of their bond. When she returned from her swim, her face would be filled with peace, and her heart would be at ease once again. He never questioned her need to return to the waves; he simply waited for her with open arms.

In the years that followed, their bond deepened, and the love between them grew stronger, built on a foundation of respect for each other's worlds. There were no more tears, no more doubts. They had found their rhythm—a life that embraced both land and sea.

Kylah, who had once thought of herself as a creature of the waves, realized that she was not bound to one world or the other. She was of both, and in this duality, she had found a home. Eamon, too, had found a new sense of belonging, no longer lost in the world of his past. Together, they had created something new, something that bridged the distance between the land and the sea.

On certain quiet mornings, when the light was soft and the air cool, Kylah and Eamon would walk along the shore hand in hand, their feet leaving imprints in the wet sand. The horizon stretched before them, endless and full of promise. As they walked, they would talk of dreams—dreams of adventures yet to come, of exploring the farthest reaches of the sea and the wildest forests of the land. They spoke of children, of how their legacy would carry both the wild spirit of the ocean and the strength of the earth. The thought of having a family, of raising children who would grow up knowing the love of both the land and the sea, filled their hearts with joy.

And so, the years flowed by as naturally as the tides. Eamon's hair began to gray, and Kylah's face softened with the passing of time, but their love remained as strong and as constant as the sea itself. Though Kylah had been born a selkie, a creature who belonged neither fully to the land nor the ocean, she had found a place for herself—right where she was, between the two worlds.

One afternoon, as Kylah sat by the water, her feet dipping into the cool waves, Eamon sat beside her, his hand resting on her knee. She gazed out at the horizon, the sun a soft ball of fire in the sky, painting the world in shades of gold and crimson.

"I used to think the sea was something I could never understand," Eamon said softly, his voice filled with wonder. "But now, I feel like I know it better than I ever knew the land."

Kylah smiled, her eyes warm with affection. "The sea has a way of teaching you things you never thought you needed to know."

Eamon turned to her, his eyes filled with love. "And you... you have taught me to listen. To listen to the waves. To listen to the heart."

Her smile deepened, and she reached over to gently cup his face in her hands. "And you, Eamon, have taught me that love is not something you search for in one world or the other. It's something that lives in both."

They sat in silence, the waves lapping at the shore, the wind carrying the scent of salt and wildflowers. It was a peace they had both earned, a peace that only the sea could give.

As the sun dipped below the horizon, the stars began to appear, twinkling in the vast expanse of the night sky. Kylah and Eamon remained by the water, hand in hand, ready to face whatever came next—together.

For they had learned the most important lesson of all: love, like the sea, has no boundaries. And no matter where the tides took them, they would always find their way back to each other.

HANSEL AND GRETEL
by Marin Henry, 7th Grade

"Hansel?" A voice calls urgently, "Where did you go?"

"Gretel? I'm over here!" I call over my shoulder. Twigs break, and Gretel appears by my shoulder.

"Whatcha doin'?"

"Getting dinner ready."

"That doesn't look like dinner," she utters. She's right. We've only been stranded for a day, and I've already messed up. The mushy slosh that's supposed to be soup gurgles over the fire. Bits of chopped mushrooms bubble to the top. My head slumps. I can't do better than this. I only have a limited amount of food left. My only hope is that she doesn't know that.

"Hansel?" she asks quietly. "Are Mommy and Daddy coming back?" I freeze. How am I supposed to answer that? While she waits for an answer, I take a moment to appreciate the silence that has fallen over us. Birds are calling from somewhere in the distance. A bud of hope blooms in my chest. If there are birds nearby, there's got to be people, right?

"Hansel?" Her voice breaks my heart, but I don't blame her. She's scared and lonely. I knew I could never amount to my father, but I thought I had at least had a little of his courage.

Gretel gives up on an answer from me and sits a few feet away from me. I can hear her quiet sobs. I tell myself to ignore it and try to figure out where we are, but I give one glance at the 'dinner' I've prepared and walk over to her. I rub her back just like Dad does when she's upset. I wipe the tears from her cheeks.

"Hey, it's going to be fine." I hope I don't sound as doubtful as I feel.

"Are you sure?" She looks up at me. Her big blue eyes are glazed with tears, and her lips are quivering.

"I promise." I hold my pinky out. She gives me a weak smile and interlocks her pinky with mine. We stay like that for a while, watching the critters move in and out of the trees, watching birds perch on branch after branch. Her breathing slows until she's not crying anymore. For a second,

I believe everything will be ok. We would find our parents, and everything would be fine. After a while, I drift off to sleep.

Eventually, I wake up.

The sun hasn't risen yet. If I had a phone, I would guess it's 2 a.m. Gretal is snoring softly beside me. I gently unlock my pinky from hers. She stirs slightly but quickly goes back to sleep. I breathe in deeply. New day. New start.

My eyes drift around my surroundings. Even the forest seems to be asleep. The air's still and clear. There is no rustling from the trees or bird calls from the distance: just me and my thoughts. Despite the thick tree coverage, I can still see the stars. They look like the night lights I have at home. Suddenly, homesickness hits me like a train. I miss my mom and my dad. I miss my bed. I miss not needing to prepare crappy meals by myself. I miss not having to worry about Gretel. I miss my Dad's hugs and my Mom's smile. A single tear rolls down my cheek.

"Hansel?"

"Holy—Gretel, you scared me!" My voice cracks.

"Were you crying?"

I can't let her know how scared I am. I don't want to scare her, but I know something I shouldn't. I know the reason we're out here, alone. Gretal thinks our parents abandoned us, but they didn't. I ran away and took Gretel with me. I just can't ever say why. "No Gretel." I sigh. "Let's go back to bed."

"But I'm not tired!" she whines.

"Fine, let's make breakfast then."

"In a minute," she whispers. She grabs my hand and drags me to the ground. We lay down on the soft, dewy grass and watch the sun peek over the horizon.

"Ok, I'm hungry." She springs to life and walks towards the fire. I stand up and lazily walk towards what little food is in my backpack. I find one cracked egg and about a cup of flour. I did not pack well enough for this. I thought we would have found somewhere by now. I decide to make a woodman's idea of waffles.

That was a mistake.

After the egg yolk dried on my shirt and I removed the flour from my hair, I make an executive decision.

"Ok, Gretel. We're going to have to search the forest for non-poisonous berries."

"What do not poisonous berries look like?" she asks.

"Uh? I don't know." I rub the back of my neck sheepishly. My brown curls fall over my eyes.

"Ok then, let's go!" She skips off into the woods. I sigh and pick up my backpack. We will probably have to find a new place to sleep tonight. I snuff out the fire and pack up our remaining things. I really hope we find some berries or—

"Candy!"

"What?" I call.

"Hansel, there's candy!" Gretel practically screams. I run over to her and find a packet of Sour Patch Kids.

"Huh. That's weird," I remark.

"Look, there's more!" She runs off following a trail of Swedish Fish.

"Shoot. Gretel! Come back here!" I run off, following her. I don't know how far she ran off, but I'm starting to get a little worried. I've been running for what seemed like forever and still haven't found her. "Gretal!" I yell.

"Shhhhh." I hear a small voice say from behind a bush.

"Gre- What- are- you- doing?" I say between breaths.

"Look, there's a house made of candy!" she whispers.

"There's no—"

And there it was.

A legit house made of candy.

The architecture is impressive, to say the least. Four walls of gingerbread make up the sides. Frosting decorated the windows, with little candies making intricate patterns. Gumdrops line the roof. They each are shimmery drops of pure heaven. The sugar on them glistens in the faint sunlight. The door is decorated with all sorts of things: gumdrops, Dots, and even Chuckles. Sugar Babies are in a straight line up to a squishy, pink marshmallow doorknob. My jaw is practically on the ground.

"I want to go in!" Gretal starts running.

"Wait Gretal! No!" But before she can hear me, the door is opening.

I don't know who I was expecting to live here, but it isn't her. I thought she would be older. Or at least an adult? She looks about my age. Her dirty blonde hair falls halfway down her back. Her eyes are a bright green, and they shimmer in the light.

"Can I help you?" she asks Gretel.

"Can I have a bite of your house?" Gretel blurts. I decide this is my time to step in. I run in from the trees and step in front of Gretel.

"I'm sorry. We'll be going now." I gently pull Gretel away.

"But Hansel, it's a house made of candy!" she pleads. I barely make it down the steps before the mystery girl speaks up.

"It's fine. You can come in."

"Oh, um. OK." I hesitantly walk through the door. She waits until both of us are through, then clicks the door shut. I swallow.

"My name's Emma." She holds her hand out.

"Oh, this is Gretel, and I'm Hansel." I shake her hand. A buzz of electricity zaps through my body when we touch. My face burns red, and I quickly let go. She laughs and holds out her hand to Gretel, which, to her surprise, has a gumdrop in it. Gretal squeals with delight.

"So... I like your house." I awkwardly stammer.

"Oh! Thanks, but it's not mine." For some reason, this gives me an odd feeling.

"Oh. Then who's is it?" I ask. Then, seemingly out of nowhere, an old lady appears.

"I'm the owner of this house," she says coldly. Emma's smile drops when she arrives. Her big green eyes fall to the ground, almost like she's ashamed.

"I see you've met Emma." She glances at her like she's some stray dog she found on the street. For some reason, it makes my blood boil.

"We have," I bite out. The lady's eyes seem to widen at the mention that there is more than one of me. I grab Gretel's hand. The lady only laughs.

"Well, come on, come in." She starts walking towards the back of the house. When I don't follow, she gives me a hard stare. Like I did something wrong. I slowly start walking after her. Emma stays in the back of the line, watching us. The lady leads us to the very back of her house. The farther we go, the more anxious I'm starting to get. There is one final door at the end of the hallway. The lady doesn't stop, so we continue. Something flashes in the corner of my eye, and I spin around. Emma stops walking just short of the door. Her eyes have a pleading look in them. Almost like she doesn't want us to walk in that door. Before I can take my eyes off Emma, a hand grabs me sharply.

"Ready?" The lady asks.

"For what?" I draw out the words.

Before she answers me, the door opens, and light blinds me. The lady grabs me and shoves me into... into... into a what? I still can't see, but I feel... metal?

"Is this a cage?" I scream. The lights go off, and I can barely see. After my eyes adjust to the lack of light, I can see we are in a cage. I can just barely see Emma, but I can tell she's looking at me. Her eyes are full of sorrow and regret. I want to scream, but more importantly, I want to get out of here. I want to get Gretel out of here. I look over at her alone in the cage across from me. Tears are streaming down her face.

"Why would you do this?" My voice is full of hate and disgust. Emma's head drops lower.

"Do you see where I live?" The lady remarks. "A witch has to eat, somehow."

"You're- you're going to eat us?" I stammer. Gretel cries out.

"Yes, but you are a skinny-lookin' thing. Emma! Get him some cake to fatten him up." Her smile widens. She's insane. I feel sick.

"Emma will be up soon," she whispers. The door slams shut. Then the lights go dark.

The silence makes me want to scream or cry or something.

"Hansel?"

"Yes, Gretel?"

"I'll miss you."

"I-I'll miss you too." A single tear descends on my face.

The door cracks, and light pools into a line across the floor. I can hear footsteps. I wipe my eyes. I'm done being sorry for myself. It's time to let that witch know how angry I can be.

Instead of the witch, Emma walks through the door. But I don't relax my angry grip on the bars of my cage. Not for a second will I let them think I let my guard down.

When the door opens all the way, the room is bathed with light. I can see Gretel in her cage. She's shoved up against the corner, her head buried in her knees, silently crying. Seeing her only makes the rage inside me intensify.

Emma comes up to my side of the room. Tears are stained on her face. Her voice comes out as a horse whisper. "I'm sorry."

I scoff. "Sorry? You're sorry? You led us into your house to die, Emma!" The bars are digging into my fingers, leaving angry red marks. She takes a step back and wipes the tears from her eyes. She turns around and sees Gretel. Her eyes well again. Her voice is so small I can barely hear it.

"I'm sorry."

"You know what. I. Give. Up." I slump my head against the wall and close my eyes. "Do whatever you want to me, but don't hurt—" Before I can finish my sentence, the bars on my hand relax, and the door swings open. I lift my head slowly and open my eyes. As much as Emma looks like she'd been crying, her hands are steady as she helps me out of the cage. I stand there. Not quite knowing what to do with myself. I watch as she helps Gretel out of her cage. The key was hanging around her neck. Gretel runs to me immediately. Her embrace is so tight, I almost can't breathe.

"Just get out of here," Emma whispers.

I stand. And against my better judgment, I walk up to her. But before I can speak, she hands me a rope.

"Use this to climb out the window." She sniffs. "I'll be fine here." She turns and walks away. Gretel grabs my hand and whispers so softly,

"Can we keep her?"

I sigh. As mad as I am, I can't just leave Emma here. Somehow, I know that when the witch finds us gone, she won't hesitate to use Emma instead of us for her meal."Emma, wait!" I call. She stops but doesn't turn around. "Come with us."

As soon as I speak, the entire house goes silent. Somehow, the silence is deafening. I need someone to speak. Anyone to say something to get us out of here. Just as I am giving up on her answering, she says something. "Ok."

Something inside me relaxes.

"Well then..." I walk over to the window and drape the rope over it. Gretel walks over and squeezes my hand.

"Promise I'll see you at the bottom?" She holds her pinky out.

"Promise." I intertwine my pinky with hers. I help her climb out the window and grab the rope. I give her a faint smile, then let go of her hands.

I turn to Emma.

"It's your turn," I whisper.

"I know." She turns to me, tears streaming down her face.

"What's wrong?" I ask.

"I don't know." She laughs through tears. "I've been here all my life."

I stop. "Is she your—"

"Oh, god, no." She laughs again. This time full of life. "I guess she found me or kidnapped me or something, but I don't know." Her face falls.

"I helped her kill so many people," she whispers. I'm silent. Footsteps start from downstairs.

"Emma, we have to go. Now." I whisper urgently. She nods, and I grab her hand. The same electricity sparks between us again, but there's no time to enjoy it. I hurdle out the window and miss the rope completely. I land with a thud on my back. I groan in pain. I can barely see Emma slipping down the rope right as the witch's shadow comes into view. I hear yelling and hop onto my feet. A wave of pain surges through my back, but I ignore it.

"Run!" Somebody yells. I break out into the fastest sprint of my life. I look backward. Gretal is 10 feet behind me. Emma is right beside her, going slower, trying to help her.

I don't know how long I've been running, but at some point, I stop. I look behind me and don't see the girls. Even though it's hard to do, I know I need to trust Emma enough to know she won't let anything happen. For some reason, now of all times, my mind wanders to my parents. Even though I almost died, I would rather do it again than go back home. Not after what happened, what they did. But my mind thinks about going home anyway. My parents didn't know that I knew what they were going to do. They would pretend to be worried for us. Lull us into a sense of comfort. Then, boom, they would—

"Hansel!" Gretel's voice comes from behind me. I whip my head around to see them running at me full speed. I don't know how Gretal still has energy, but she does. I laugh and run towards her. We hug so hard that I accidentally knock her over. She giggles and stands. Emma flops on the ground, completely out of breath. She laughs and stands. We all stand there in silence.

"Hansel, can we go home now?" Gretel asks.

"Oh, um..." Emma interrupts, sensing I am uncomfortable.

"Gretel? Can you find me a flower?" she asks.

"Ok!" Gretel skips off into the woods. Once she's gone, Emma speaks again.

"Why can't you go home?" She crosses her arms.

"It's a long story." I rub the back of my neck.

"I found one!" Gretel yells and puts a pretty purple flower into Emma's hand. She smiles but raises her eyebrows at me.

"If we go home….." I start. I eye Gretel, then walk over and whisper in Emma's ear. "Our parents are going to kill us."

Color the World With Feelings: Sensory Poems

Kelly Almer

Instructor Introduction

Did you know there are more than 150 shades of white? Cream, eggshell, ivory, super white...the list goes on. Crayola brand crayons have 19 shades of blue! Orange has over 35 variations!

Students in this fun and engaging class developed a poem about a uniquely named color and all the subtle shades of it, using the five senses to develop unique poems describing colors such as, "Beach Sparkle," "Stillness," and "Positively Pink."

Read these poems to gain a new understanding of these colors and how the poets felt about them.

POSITIVELY PINK
by Hannah Erlenbeck, 3rd Grade

Positively Pink

Positively Pink feels like a fluffy blanket that has just been washed.

Pink feels like soft, squishy pink regular-sized marshmallows, in a cup of hot chocolate.

A fireplace on an evening night in the wintertime is perfectly pink. Positively Pink feels like a tile piece that you just installed. It feels like a soft feather from a flamingo.

Positively Pink tastes like a piece of store bought bubble gum after grocery shopping. Strawberry cake with cream icing is pink.

Holding a popsicle while sitting on my porch in my backyard is positively pink. It tastes like a push pop when you take the first lick.

Strawberry ice cream is positively pink when you first buy it.

Positively Pink looks like rose quartz. Positively Pink looks like the sunset in the front yard or on the beach. It's like Cherrywood fresh from the Cherry tree. Positively Pink looks like a freshly cut watermelon.

Positively Pink smells like Cherry tree blossoms or flowers in the garden. It smells like my mom when she wears perfume. Positively Pink smells like a rose that has just been watered. Hand cream when you just put on is pink. Drawing dragons and flowers and skiing makes me feel Positively Pink.

Positively Pink sounds like a party in a room when a big celebration is going on. Positively Pink sounds like laughter in a friendly conversation.

Cheering for your favorite team is pink too.

Pink makes me happy.

STILLNESS
by Irene Hong, 4th Grade

Stillness feels like cold ice cubes in a glass cup sitting on the table.
Stillness feels like being frozen in the East Siberian Sea near Russia on a frozen quiet morning.
Stillness feels like a Bluejay watching over her babies in the nest.
I feel cold.

Stillness looks like a Spring sky in Paris on a Saturday morning.
Stillness looks like my silky blue pillowcase on my bed. It looks like the big night sky over the mountains.
I feel comfortable.

Stillness sounds like a still pond in the rainforest. A river flowing to the ocean is like stillness. It sounds like a violin playing a quiet song.
I feel calm.

Stillness tastes just like fresh blueberries picked in a forest. Stillness tastes just like a large portion of blue cotton candy at the fair.
Sour Patch candy when you get it for Halloween is stillness to me. A raspberry slushie tastes like stillness as I sip it on a warm, sunny beach.
I taste sweet.

Stillness smells like light blue tulips from the fresh grassy field. Stillness smells like fresh laundry out of the dryer. Flower scented perfume smells like stillness. It is the breeze of the wind on a Spring morning. I smell the clear blue water and I smile.

Stillness makes me feel Bold.

POSITIVELY PINK
by Joanna Bruinsma, 2nd Grade

Cotton candy tastes Positively Pink. It also tastes like a strawberry ice cream cone at the lake. Fresh watermelon from my garden is pink.

Positively Pink feels like the sparkles on my notebook. A kitten's hard tongue as it plays with yarn is positively pink. It is as soft as the small pink pillow on my sister's bed.

Positively Pink smells like the little flowers in my garden. Pink smells like the Peach Bellini candle my mom lights in the school room. The bubbles in the bathtub right after my mom put bath soap in it are pink.

Positively Pink looks like shiny paint in a bowl on the table in the kitchen and the sun rising over the road in the morning. It looks like a candy heart on the table and it looks like a Valentine's day heart that I give my friend.

Positively Pink sounds like roses dropping their petals along the side of the road. It sounds like the pop of a bubble made of gum. It sounds like the rumble of our pink toy vacuum.

BEACH SPARKLE
by Nora Bruinsma, 3rd Grade

Beach Sparkle feels comfy, light, and soft like my favorite blue chair. And sparkling sand between my fingers and feet. Beach Sparkle feels rough like my blue book bag. Painting with blue paint makes me feel happy.

It tastes like blueberry muffins fresh out of the oven. Or like cold creamy

Blue Moon ice cream on hot summer days. And tacos filled with sour cream and cheddar cheese taste like Beach Sparkle.

And Beach Sparkle smells like salty sea air blowing in the wind. It smells like a blue raspberry snow cone, or blue Tootsie roll pops. Blue fruit roll ups smell just like Beach Sparkle.

Beach Sparkle sounds like raindrops dripping on my window and the ice shaking around in my blue water bottle. A crinkling blue pretzel wrapper sounds just like Beach Sparkle. The blue metal stools at my family's bar where we eat sometimes sound like a little blue drummer boy when we hit them.

Waves on the beach at high tide are Beach Sparkle. This makes me want to jump into them when we are swimming. It also looks like the sun sparkling off the water into the sky at sunset. Beach Sparkle looks like the fuzzy part of my little brother's winter boots, sitting on the boot tray by the front door.

Beach Sparkle is love, joy, and kindness.

Back to the Beginning: Circle Stories

Kelly Almer

Instructor Introduction

Children's stories captivate audiences young and old everywhere with their whimsy and in many cases, predictability. Circular stories have the ability to draw the reader in while guessing what might happen next. This class taught young writers the formula for creating a short circular story. Every student came with ideas and enthusiasm. It was a joy to work with them every week for five weeks. Their finished pieces exceeded expectations. Their stories are creative and so much fun to read. Professional circle story writers would be thrilled to learn of these original stories.

ICE SKATING!!!
by Lily Snyder, 4th Grade

I can't wait for ice skating, It's my most favorite thing in the world!

"All right Mom! I'm ready to go! I got my bag ......Wait, I forgot my fuzzy mittens with the gems on them! I can't go without them. I will be right back. Ok, I got my mittens. That means I'm ready to go," I say as I buckle up in the car.

"Do you have your guards, honey?"

"Darn, I forgot my bright teal guards! I'll go and get them. Hey, that reminds me, I need my ice skates and my towel! I guess that means I have to go run back to the house and get those too. Speaking of fabric, I need my sweater and scrunchie. I need the scrunchie that I got in Disney World!!! It's my most favoritest scrunchie in the whole wide world!"

I sprint back into the house and up to my bedroom with the bright yellow door.

I run into my closet and grab my sweater. It's dark brown with orange-ish, light brown pockets.

Looking around, I see my scrunchie on my nightstand. It's a pink scrunchie with pictures of Taylor Swift all over it. The scrunchie is my lucky scrunchie because it helps me do my tricks on the ice better. Grabbing the scrunchie, I run downstairs while I put on my sweater then place the scrunchie in my hair, making a high ponytail.

I remember I didn't have enough time to eat dinner and I'm hungry. So I go to the pantry and grab some cheesy Doritos and eat them right out of the bag. I'm all set to skate. Wait!

Those Doritos made me really thirsty! I need my water bottle. I need my light pink Stanley water bottle! I go to the cabinet to grab it and fill it with pink lemonade.

I need a napkin! My mouth has cheese all over it! Looking around I find a napkin in a drawer and I wipe my mouth with it.

I look at the time but notice I don't have my watch on! I look around the house to find it downstairs on the TV stand. Grabbing it, I put it on then notice...Wait!

I remember I need my locket! I need the locket that I got for my birthday from my great grandparents!! Frantically I look for the locket. Where is it? I find it on my dresser where I put it last night. Putting it on, I notice that I'm exhausted from all of this so I need more lemonade to fuel me up for my fantastic skating!

I head back to the kitchen to grab more lemonade.

I run to the car and Mom is already there, waiting with the engine running. I get into the car and we drive to the rink. When we arrive there the parking lot is packed. We find a spot. I grab my bag, to notice...

"I don't have my ice skates, skate guards, and towel! I got distracted and I didn't grab them." I throw my bag on the car floor.

Mom says, "It's alright, we will go get them." We arrive back at the house ten minutes later. I run back, go to the ski closet, and find my ice skates, guards, and towel on the floor. I grab them and head back to the car.

Finally, we make it to the rink. I see everyone taking their ice skates off. Then I say to my Mom, " We missed the class!!!"

I remember I have ice skating on Wednesday! Yay! Before I know it, it is Wednesday again! Ice skating is my most favorite thing in the world! I need to grab my bag! Wait!

FISHING
by Lincoln Montgomery, 4th Grade

When I go fishing I need a long sleeve shirt, and it's in my room. I put it on. That reminds me I need a hoodie since it's cold and my ears need protection from the cold. I grab it and put it on. It's mint green.

When I get my hoodie, I realize I need my shoes and I need to hurry and get on the boat and sit down. I put on my shoes and run to the dock and sit on the boat. I look around and I realize I need the net!

It's on the dock! I step on the dock and grab the net. I hurry back on the boat and sit down. I sit down and can finally breathe. We close the door to the pontoon and we pull out from the dock and look for a spot to fish.

Once we find the spot to fish, I look around for my fishing pole. I find it and it doesn't have a reel! I grab the reel from the tackle box and put it on my fishing p...! Wait!

Where is it?! I look everywhere and I can't find it anywhere! I figure it fell in the water. I tell my uncle who we're fishing with. We have to drive ALL THE WAY BACK!

Finally we make it and we grab the extra pole from the garage. But the garage isn't connected to the house. So we have to sprint to the garage because it is almost dark.

We run all the way back to the boat and get on the boat, sit down and chill, until we get back to the fishing spot. Finally we make it and we can at last fish.

But this rod doesn't have a reel either!!! So I reach for the tackle box and actually make sure I hold on to it. I grab a reel and it doesn't have bait. I reach for bait but it isn't there. I look all over the boat for it. I finally find it. It's by the steering wheel.

I put the bait on my fishing pole but then my cousin shouts, "I've got a big one I need hel.," We all go to help but by then it's too late. To be continued ...

Fine, I'll tell you! He falls in the water!

My uncle jumps in the water after him. A couple minutes go by but finally they come up with a giant fish while swimming back to the boat. They put the fish on the boat.

They need the ladder! They get on the boat.

They absolutely need a towel! We get a towel for them.

Then we drove all the way back to the dock. Then we grab the fi...!

Where is the fish! We didn't bring the fish off the bow, so it fell off! Well whatever. We go inside all sad because we didn't strap the fish to the boat. I take my shoes off. I'm tired so I go to my bed to go to sleep.

The next morning we decide to go fishing. AGAIN! We put our shoes on and go to the dock with the b...!

WHERE IS THE BOAT! We didn't strap the boat to the dock! I see something over by the place where we look for turtles. It's the boat!

"Get the kayaks!" my uncle yells. We get the kayaks but I get splashed with water.

That also reminds me that I still have my long sleeve shirt on from yesterday's fishing trip. I go inside to take off my shirt to refresh. I need a new shirt to go fishing again.

ICE SKATING
by Irene Hong, 4th Grade

My mom said, "Come down stairs for ice skating practice." Then I went down and went to the car and jumped in and then I remembered I needed my ice skating bag! My bag was in the garage so I grabbed my ice skating bag.

I went to the car then I remembered I needed my gloves. They were in my bedroom.

And I grabbed my pink gloves and I went running down the stairs and went to the car and then forgot a hair tie to put my hair up! So...

I ran to the bathroom and opened up the drawer and grabbed my black hair tie and ran to the car.

I'm excited to go ice skating. I have been skating for a year and am working on a scratch spin. It is hard to do.

I ran to the car, standing by the door when I remembered I forgot my jacket! It is a black scuba jacket I got from LuluLemon. It makes me a better skater. When I fall down on the ice it is easy to clean off. So...

I went back inside to the coat hanger in the hallway and grabbed my jacket. I ran back to the car and then I noticed that I needed a snack if I got hungry! So...

I went to the pantry and grabbed some Nutella sticks, my favorite snack, and then I went to the car again. We were ready to leave when I remembered that I needed my water bottle! So...

I went inside and went to the kitchen and grabbed my grey Stanly and I filled it up with water. Then I went to the car and buckled up. Mom drives me to the skating rink. We make it on time for my lesson.

After the lesson, I had a great time. My scratch spin was good! I asked my mom, "What's tomorrow?!"

"Tomorrow is ice skating again!" she said. I'm excited! I need my skating bag!

I place my bag in the garage near the car. What do I need? My gloves! Wait! Where are they?!

EMERALD
by Autumn Heck, 5th Grade

There once was a girl named Emerald. She loved art. Her classmate Lily hated art and would tease Emerald. Emerald was lonely but then she met Ava. Ava was kind and also loved art and they became best friends.

But they were about to go to middle school. It was scary for Emerald. She didn't know how to be in a different school. So she went to Ava but Ava said it wasn't ok to be scared of a building. So they stopped talking then. They only had 4 months till middle school and Ava was nervous too, so she went to talk to Emerald.

Emerald was disappointed that Ava now felt the same way but when she didn't, she stopped talking to Emerald. Emerald forgave her in hopes she would be kinder. Ava was kinder and they both discovered they HATED homework but it was fine.

Emerald played the violin and Ava sang in choir. So they formed a band. It was awesome! The band was called, "The 2 Besties." It took ten years but the two girls were famous.

They went on world tours and had merch. But they had to say their goodbyes after Ava got married to Josh and Emerald was on her own again.

But then she met Jade who she married and loved deeply. Emerald and Jade adopted a child named Peyton.

One day Emerald wanted to make a song dedicated to Jade and Peyton and so she went to her studio and thought of ideas. Once she got the perfect idea, she started recording.

The first line was was this, "Ooooo, how you make me shine," and she continued, "SO BRIGHT, SO BRIGHT." And more song lyrics, "Oh Jade and Peyton, oooh, I love you so much."And as Jade and Peyton listened Jade remembered first meeting Emerald the love she felt oh. Peyton remembered being adopted and the feeling of having a real home; it was great.

As the years went by they got older and Peyton turned 15. Emerald was 40 and so was Jade.

And a miracle happened.

When Ava returned, Emerald, Ava, and Jade had a LONG chat.

Ava was sooooo surprised to find out Emerald had a child named Peyton.

And so the circle of life continues.

BRACELET MAKING
by Aubrey Babcock, 5th Grade

Today's a sunny day, a perfect day for making beautiful bracelets outside! I've got my string and...

Oh no! I don't have my yarn!

I run into the house and try to remember where I left it. Looking around the room, I see Luna playing with my yarn!

"Bad kitty!" I say snatching the yarn away.

I run back outside thinking I have everything. But I'm wrong.

I need my beads! Dashing back inside looking for beads, I realize I need my flower and heart-shaped beads! I grab them all while spying my sparkly beads. I snatch those up too.

Opening the door I turn to go outside and spot my charms. I can't resist. I grab the charms. Arms full, I run back outside. There! I have everything now!

Grabbing my string... I forgot the scissors!

Running back in again I open up the junk drawer. Reaching in, Mom yells, "Who wants a peanut butter and pickle sandwich?"

After all of that running and searching, I got pretty hungry! While eating Mom asks, "Did you make any bracelets yet?"

Whoops! I was so busy gathering my things I forgot to even make the bracelets!

I will make bracelets this time! Now, where did I put my string?

Beach Day! by Chantry Halt, 4th Grade

I can't wait to go to the beach! I run to my duffel bag that should have all my beach things in it but...it's empty!

So I run to grab a change of clothes, a light blue t-shirt and matching shorts. That reminds me: I need my towel! Can't be soaking wet when I'm changing.

I grab my favorite super soft purple and blue towel. Oh yeah! I need my goggles or else my eyes will be burning when I'm swimming.

I grab my favorite all-clear pair from my bedroom cabinet. I almost forgot a hairbrush!

My hair gets so tangled after swimming, it's awful if I don't brush it right after. I grab the tie-dye brush I got for Christmas. Speaking of hair, that reminds me I need a hair tie to pull my hair back. I grab the teal one from my vanity.

Oh! I need my crocs! I can't walk on the hot sand barefoot! I get the cream-colored ones covered in plant and flower charms.

Sunscreen! I need sunscreen! I grab the sports extra protective sunscreen from the bathroom cabinet because it is really sunny today. That reminds me...

I need lip balm! My lips get super chapped easily, so I usually have a lip balm on hand. I grab the vanilla bean one.

Oh yeah! I need snacks, so I'm not hungry. I grab a chocolate chip granola bar and fruit snacks. Being in the kitchen reminds me I need my water bottle!

I grab my navy blue water bottle that is covered in stickers and fill it with ice, then put some lemonade in it.

I need my watch! I grab my light purple one to track my steps.

I almost forget to bring mints! I grab wintergreen mints to suck on while reading my...Book!

I forgot my book!

I grab the brand new fantasy novel I got yesterday and walk towards the car.

"Great, you're finally ready!" my mom says. "But where's your swimsuit?"

I run back towards the house and grab a swimsuit.

But where's my duffel bag?

IF YOU GIVE A GIRL A BASKETBALL
by Anna Cosens, 5th Grade

I was cleaning my room when I found my pink basketball that I got at a basketball camp. That reminded me that I wanted to play. Then I realized...

I needed to get a hair tie, so I ran to the bathroom to grab my lucky bright purple hair tie. After I grabbed my lucky hair tie, I remembered I needed my basketball shoes. After I got my favorite bright purple shoes from the hallway, I walked outside.

I realized I needed to draw a three-point line! After I found some chalk, I drew a three-point line. I finished drawing the three-point line, my hands were all chalky, so I walked over to the hose.

When I turned the water on it reminded me... I needed my big light pink water bottle!

I rinsed off my hands quickly and ran through the front door, through the living room, and into the kitchen. I grabbed my water bottle and filled it with lemonade.

This reminded me that I should refill my yellow Labrador's water bowl. After I filled my dog's water bowl, I forgot what I was doing and started to play with my dog.

When my dog brought me a toy ball that reminded me of my basketball!

I thought to myself, wait where's my basketball?????

THE DRAWING CONTEST
by Willa Selle, 4th Grade

Mariah was packing for her drawing contest. She needed her fine-tipped pens, but she couldn't find them anywhere, so she looked for her crayons. A 64-pack and brand new! Where were they?!

She went looking until...They were right where she left them! In her desk. Great! OK! Got crayons—Wait!

Thinking of her crayons, she realized she needed something to drink! Running, she got to the kitchen and started the water for some hot cocoa. Got crayons, hot cocoa started—But wait!

There is no way she can go without her easel! She walked into the dining room where her easel was, and placed it into the car. Wait!

She needed to grab the hot cocoa and put it into her lavender water bottle. OK! Got crayons, hot cocoa, easel—But wait! She needs her paint set! It was on the shelf. OK! Got crayons, hot cocoa, easel, and a paint set—But wait!

If you have a paint set you need brushes! So Mariah ran downstairs and found her brushes. OK! Got crayons, hot cocoa, easel, paint set, and brushes.

"Ok Mom, I'm ready to go!" said Mariah. So Mariah and her mom got in the car.

Ten minutes after they left, Mariah realized that she had forgotten her fine-tipped pens! So they drove all the way back home and Mariah ran inside and suddenly remembered

where the pens were: on the back porch! Mariah quickly ran back to the car with the fine-tipped pens. She did not want to be late to the contest!

After the contest, Mariah was walking out the door and she said, wait! She saw a poster that said, "Next drawing contest June 5th."

"Mom, can I please go?" said Mariah.

"Sure!" said Mom, "but you will need—"

A TYPICAL PREP FOR TRACK
by Kennedy Kraus, 5th Grade

Today is the day! It is the all-city track meet! Kennedy is the team's best mile runner and the team won't last a second without her. But Kennedy has a reputation for being late.

"Get ready Kennedy or you will be late to your all city track meet and we don't want that," says Kennedy's mom.

"Don't worry Mom, we won't be late," replies Kennedy. "I just need to find my purple running shoes and white socks."

As soon as Kennedy says that, she remembers that she needs to find her blue tank top and black shorts, so she puts on her socks and shoes without really paying attention.

"I swear I put all that stuff in my drawer!" says Kennedy. She digs through her drawers but can't find the clothes she needs! "There they are!" says Kennedy, after finding them at the very bottom of her dresser. Kennedy gets changed and then remembers that she needs her lucky purple sweatshirt! Kennedy finds a weird trail of purple fabric leading to her puppy Gus's bed.

"AHHHH!!" screams Kennedy. Gus has chewed up her sweatshirt!

After a battle between Kennedy and Gus, Kennedy finally gets her sweatshirt back. The only thing is that it is ripped! So she tapes it back together.

Taping it reminds her that she needs to fill her water bottle with Propel. So she goes to the fridge to find her favorite flavor only to find that there isn't any left.

"Cole, where did you put my strawberry kiwi Propel?" asks Kennedy, who is on the verge of anger.

"I didn't touch it! I hid it in the back of the fridge! Just use your eyes!"

Kennedy looks and finds that she jumped to conclusions because the Propel is in the back of the fridge. Kennedy then fills her water bottle up and remembers that she needs a healthy snack for the end of the race. But before she can grab her snack, her mom calls.

"Kennedy, it's almost time to go! Are you ready?"

"Yeah almost! Yeah how about let's go with that?!" Kennedy calls back. Then she goes and grabs an energy bar and a Gogo squeeze. Then she remembers that she needs her Apple watch.

She goes to her room to grab it but notices that the watch face is wrong and that it doesn't have the case she wants. She fixes everything but it is just draining away her time like getting three kids out the door in time for school.

"Kiddo, you already missed your long jump event and your hundred meter hurdles! Hurry up!" calls her dad who is also the head coach.

"I am hurry-upping!" Kennedy calls back. "Or well, going as fast as I can. Don't rush me!!"

Then out of nowhere... *My hair tie!* thinks Kennedy! They will disqualify me if my hair isn't in a ponytail. So she rushes to the jar where they keep the ponytail holders...but it is empty!

Then her sister Everly walks by and her hair is in a ponytail. Kennedy runs to her and yanks the ponytail holder out of her hair.

"OW!" yells Everly. "What was THAT for?"

"Sorry!" replies Kennedy, "I needed it!"

Yanking out the hair tie reminds Kennedy that she needs to take off her jewelry or she can't run. So she goes to the mirror and starts to take out her diamond earrings. The only problem is that one earring won't come out. Eventually Kennedy calls her mom and together they take out the earring and the rest of her jewelry.

All of that pain and pulling reminds Kennedy that she needs Cotton Candy Hubba Bubba Bubble Gum. It helped her win her last track meet. She runs to her desk and sees that she has almost every type of gum EXCEPT the Cotton Candy Hubba Bubba Bubble Gum. "COME

ON!!!!" yells Kennedy, "Who took my Cotton Candy Hubba Bubba Bubble Gum!!!"

"You mean the piece that you have been saving for weeks for this very occasion?" calls Cole.

"Yes!!" calls Kennedy.

"Never heard of it," says Cole.

Then he storms off to the basement to play VR. That gives Kennedy suspicions and she goes to her brother's room and takes the piece of gum that is under his pillow. Five minutes later she is chewing her Cotton Candy Hubba Bubba Bubble Gum. Chewing her gum, she suddenly remembers what she does before every race to get her energy and confidence. So she goes to the mirror and says "You are enough, you are fast, you are good at what you do." After finishing her mantras, she stretches. Leaving her room she finds her Dad and says, "Get the car and I'll get the rest of the family."

"Ok," he replies and adds, "By the way, you missed your 800m relay!"

"Darn," Kennedy mutters, "but I can still make the mile run!"

With that, she rallies her family into the car.

Once everyone is in the car, it runs out of gas!

So her dad refills it and they are on their way. Riding in the car reminds Kennedy that she needs to listen to pump-up music. "Can you turn on 'Whatever It Takes' by Imagine Dragons?" asks Kennedy.

"Sure thing!" replies her mom. Before they know it, they are at the track!

"I'm ready to run!" says Kennedy.

"No you aren't," says her dad.

She looks at him, and he is pointing to her feet. She is wearing flip flops and pink socks!

"So I have to go all the way home and change shoes and socks?????" says Kennedy.

Suddenly an announcement is made over the loudspeaker.

"The race is cancelled due to the rain. All events will be redone on Friday!"

"So not only did I put on the wrong shoes and socks, but I will have to do everything again?" asks Kennedy.

"Yup," says her mom. "That is just the typical prep for track."

IF YOU GIVE A HIPPO HUMMUS
by Nora Bruinsma, 3rd Grade

If you give hippo hummus, he'll want some pretzels to go with it and the pretzels will remind him of his favorite stick. He will want you to go find his favorite stick.

When you find it he will want to play fetch with it. While you're playing fetch, you will accidentally throw it in your neighbor's yard with an angry cat! Not wanting to get scratched by the cat, you will have to find him a new one.

But he will need a coat, socks, and boots to keep him warm. Digging into the laundry hamper, you will find your things and say it's time to go.

To find a new stick you will have to go on a hike with the hippo. So you search in the creek and under your favorite tree.

Nothing, so you keep looking.

When you finally find it in the woods, he will want to play with it.

While playing, he will get all muddy. He will want to take a bath. So you head back home, over the hill and through the creek.

When you get home he will want his rubber duck. While sitting in the tub with his duck, he will get hungry so he will want some hummus. And the chances are, if you give him the hummus, he will want some pretzels to go with it.

Fiction Inspired by Myth, Legend and History

Instructor Introduction by Ashlee Cowles

In the workshop *Fiction Inspired By Myth, Legend, and History* with award-winning author Ashlee Cowles, middle and high school students looked to the past to speak to the present. Drawing on ancient stories or historical people/events for the seed of their story idea, students also learned why mythic structures like The Hero's Journey can aid in writing a tale with timeless appeal. In addition to focusing on a new topic or skill, each session involved a workshop period where students learned the art of giving and receiving constructive feedback on their work. Our time together culminated in an in-person session at The Dennos Museum on NMC's campus, where students explored the galleries and put into practice a classic exercise found in Julia Cameron's *The Artist's Way*—taking yourself on an "artist date" to search for that next story spark!

DEATH BE WROUGHT IN STONE
by Ethan Konopacki, 12th Grade

A cold wind swept over the courtyard, filled the cloisters, and lifted papers throughout the premises. The sun had yet to reach its zenith, but already the monks and nuns tended to the interminable chores of the Abbey of Gladsmoth; indeed, the horses were to be groomed and the gardens tilled, though not before the morn's fast was readied and yesternight's sup cleared from the refectory. One might find it a queer notion, therefore, that there would be within the belfry of the Shale Tower a lone brother at rest. That he should waste the day away whilst his brethren and sistren fulfilled their duties of maintenance and supplication. But the day went on, and neither hue nor cry was raised for the missing brother, the one known only as Cerlic of Pontsberg. Not for many hours...

"Awake with you!" shrieked Abbess Ensei, loosing a firm smack upon Cerlic's left cheek. "I'll not be having any such indolence in this House of Our Lord Flous." The brother issued an incoherent response, still groggy from sleep. Rays prodded his tender eyes as he attempted to wake. A second blow, harder than the last, came to his aid. Brother Cerlic blinked hesitantly, then quickly pulled down his woolen habit and surcoat to conceal his bony abdomen, returning to the Abbess. Her face was rotund and wrinkled with papery skin. Angry, too, though that was not so unusual in Cerlic's experience.

"Good morrow, Mother," he said, smiling that patent rueful smile of his. "If that it be."

"That it be not, Brother Cerlic. And I do believe you have been twice warned against calling me so."

"Yes, yes. 'May a hundred breaths bear me insult, but that I shan't abide' if memory serves true." Grunting, Cerlic hoisted himself from the groaning chair he had slept in, trudged three uneven steps forward, and peered over the granite balustrade into the courtyard. Only a few stragglers persisted at work, for the rest had most likely quit to supper. He peeked back toward the Abbess, who stood shorter than his five-and-six by a whole head, and her gaze arrested his own.

The face of the Abbess was fringed and freckled by greatness, and none could attest otherwise, not at a knife's point or beneath the liar's masquerade. From a young age, the Abbess had acquitted herself prodigiously in the logics of mathematics and debate. These talents saw her marching through one kingdom and the next for study and lecture. But alas, wealth was not bountiful in her family's lands, where the wintery frontier wove its steely grasp. And for want of fatuous delusions of romance, the young Ensei chose the cloth over espousal.

For a moment, that young, self-assured woman wriggled into the Abbess's face and supplanted the vexation and ire therein with a knowing softness. But almost as soon as it came, it was gone. "Brother Matthew shall need you soon in his office chamber. His eyes are grown too old to operate the abacus."

"Understood, Abbess."

There was an odd tension in the air, and for many long moments, neither spoke. But, when finally one did, it was the Abbess. "You are young, Cerlic," said she, voice seeping mourn. "Do not languish away in this tower on a hope that could be."

The Matron of Gladsmoth Abbey departed wordlessly, cape billowing behind her, and a silence claimed the belfry, Cerlic, and the three-pronged far-eye that overlooked the incessant stars.

Night's earliest darkness was encroaching upon the sky when the convent retired to their bedchambers for prayer; they, however, would not slumber until sunset, at the earliest. The Sepultides were early rousers and late sleepers, as all beknew from coast to coast of the Seagirt Kingdom of Leindor. On this basis, the Abbey was a sterile place after supper, and still as moss besides. That is to say, motionless to the outside observer. Cerlic leapt upwards, established a solid foothold upon the limestone step, and leapt up once again, skipping the next two. As he ascended the serpentine staircase, crumbs cascaded from the heel of rye in his mouth. There was little food left in the refectory when he had stopped by, so he made do with a bowl of strained chicken broth and a half-loaf of bread. He finished the last of it with a gulp as he came to the rough-hewn spruce door which was overlain by iron panels bolted into the wood.

The brother rapped the door twice and when no answer arose, thrice more. "Alder Matthew!" he yelled, "I have come." A confused mess of consonants and vowels spilled from behind the door. Cerlic momentarily thought the old man had croaked his last breath, but a soft click followed that compelled him to believe he had been bid to enter. At a gentle nudge, the door eased along its arc to reveal the chamber in a state of chaotic disarray.

Brother Matthew—Bursar, really, for the old man had never officiated his vows before an Emissary of the Continental Church of Flous—was seated in his armchair, rocking to a pleasant tune. His office was walled in by a cylindrical pattern of lain brick stacked fifty high. From outside it appeared as a turret upon the east corner of the prayer hall. Though from inside it resembled a mighty library. The shelves abounded with liturgical prayer books, thick volumes of history, and even one illustrated copy of the Mithlin, but the space mostly held ledgers, bills of lading, land deeds, and receipts of expenditure.

"Come now, brother—" the bursar broke into a sputtering cough, "—help me up." His armchair was of chequered linen, mauve and chestnut, and the floor was carpeted in a fibrous nettle whose drab brownish color was complemented by the russet bricks and the cerulean drapery hung around the window at the far wall.

Groaning deeply, the old man raised a tremulous hand. When Cerlic grasped it and gently lifted the bursar from the chair, a sickening smell washed over him. The chair's upholstery was stained yellow and dripping. He looked away disgustedly and led his charge to the nook under the mullioned window, gingerly avoiding the loose papers strewn across the carpet. He pulled up two stools, seated the bursar and lit the oil lamp in the nook. The fire shimmered against the ridged, pockmarked cheeks of Bursar Matthew, flickering in his white, filmy eyes.

Taking his own seat, Cerlic unlatched an ornate black box and set it beside the lamp. It had nine smooth sticks for columns, each containing ten shiny pearls. The backboard was fitted with a red velvet lining. He raked the flat of his hand down the columns to reorient the beads.

"Alder." He nudged the snoring bursar. "I am ready with the abacus."

"Oh, oh, uh. Dear Cerlic, you set me on edge," said Brother Matthew, pawing crusted lids.

"Pardon, then. We must settle the tab the Saracins, elder and younger, raised in the town pub."

"Back when I was a boy, long before you were born—heh, and your parents, at that—the peasantry had a little more generosity to speak of." Brother Matthew waved feebly in dismay.

"The Church is dead. Oh. The Lord holds no sway in the realm of men. Lamentable! Truly lamentable!..." Mutter on and on, the Alder did. The clacking of beads against wood and the rattle of loose pearls was drowned out by his lamentations. Decadence and sin seared the soul, he said. The Lord had punished them with plague and diseases venereal, he wept. Lepers ran amuck, spreading misery by the touch. Marauders ran afoul, and the law watched idly with drooping jowls. Lament the present, for the past is sanctified and the future predestined, Cerlic thought bitterly. The Lord will come...and if not, we will.

As things turned out, many of the brothers had outstanding debts in town. Prior Gabriel had been charged five silver half-coyns by an inn near the small inlet Gladsmoth called a port. Cerlic well knew no meal or lodging could garner such a fee, and so he was compelled to wonder if it was, in fact, a house of game. He wished fervently not. Sacrist Issac's was an easier case; four bronze tokens for a wheel of cheese was a going fare. There was a large shipment of herbs from Korbmon in the west. Chamomile, sage, onion, lavender, mugwort: the infirmarian, Belenus, needed all of it. Brother Matthew had the right of it; men and women alike were dying in swathes from Bishop's Bane, pneumonia, dysentery, and diseases far more deadly than the aforementioned. The value of herbs had swelled up as opportunistic merchants monopolized the trade. The shipment meant a few brothers would sleep on empty stomachs for a moon cycle, if luck was with them.

Once again Brother Matthew found himself asnore. The night was of a middling age, as idioms go, much like Cerlic. A full lustrum has passed since the day I arrived bare-back and bleeding, he reflected. The stars shone bright and brilliant. The Mithlin said each contained a fragment of Flous's will and a devout soul to wield it for good. It was common for Sepultides to claim they had seen a lamented one in the stars. And perhaps they had, but Cerlic wasn't privy to the stars.

The bursar slept deeply that night, Cerlic having doused the oil lamp and draped an ermine covering over him. Inching the door closed, he returned to his cell for slumber. Cerlic too slept deeply that night, dreaming of numbers and beads and soft wrinkled paper.

He awoke to a violent tumult. The ground shook beneath him with the force of a Mithlinic avalanche, dust drifted onto his bed from the creaking planks of wood above, and the vibrations jarred his teeth and seemed to rattle his very bones. Without, he heard terrified yelps and wroth pledges. Prior Gabriel attempted to allay the fear and distress in the hall, but the chaos would not be quelled. Cerlic hastily donned his habit and surcoat and covered his hair, black as despair, with his hood.

When Cerlic opened the door to his cell, he saw everyone clearing out of the dormitory en masse. He pulled aside a familiar face from the pack. Brother Saracin the Younger was in full panic. "Brother Cerlic, please, please, release me, oh please."

"What has happened?" Cerlic enquired in a voice as brittle as cast iron.

"Please, brother, plea—" Cerlic shook him firmly and bit his fingers into Brother Saracin's woolen habit. "Ahh...come Cerlic, hurry, to the debate parlor. Abbess Ensei will explain there."

They set off together after the throng of frantic monks and nuns. The shaking had abated to a low rumble, which threatened to unbalance Cerlic if he stepped without care. Through the wide, open entrance to the parlor bottlenecked by the frenzied crowd, they could hear the abbess deliberating aloud with the senior council. After the queue before them slowly shuffled in, Cerlic and Brother Saracin entered and found available seats among the marble benches.

The deliberating had already lost its civility, and it was clear the abbess was as nervous as the rest. From what Cerlic gathered, a host of a hundred score was advancing. The forerunner had heralded their approach from over the high walls of the Abbey. He had said that the Abbey of Gladsmoth was to be dissolved, by orders of the venerable king of Leindor. Cerlic could scarcely believe the word.

"This cannot stand!" bellowed the young steward, John. "On the king's order they say? Preposterous! We have served Leindor well for over eleven hundred years. By what right, I ask.

By what right!"

"Calm yourself, John," Abbess Ensei reproached.

"How shall we calm ourselves?" howled Saracin the Elder. "The abbey cannot bear more than two moon turns of besiegement. How will we defend ourselves, Abbess?"

"We will entreat the king. He must listen," said the abbess.

"This host, damn them, will shoot down our pigeons and deny safe passage to Pellas to see the king," argued Belenus. "I have heard of such things happening in Carpesh and Nrague."

The abbess raised a hand for silence, and the room stilled. She rested her chin on steepled knuckles. "It seems," she began, "as if we are left one option, one route to salvation: we must send forth a rider before the host's van arrives." Abbess Ensei surveyed the room. She was met with downcast eyes and pale faces.

Cerlic made no effort to avoid her eyes, nor to seek them. She was staring at him, he knew. It was decided. "Cerlic," she started hesitantly, "I trust you know your way."

"I do, Abbess," Cerlic responded dryly.

"You are...best suited." Shame crept into her stony gaze, but she did not drop it.

"I agree, abbess. I will go."

As Cerlic left the debate parlor to prepare, a wave of grotesque praise followed in his wake. Cowards, he thought. Fools. Bloody hypocrites one and all. And I most of all...

The heavy, metal lattice began to rise in fits and starts, squealing where rust had grown dense. Spurring the roan gelding, Cerlic rode through the sally port and came out near the posterior wall of the Abbey. The sun hung low to the east and cast long shadows from over the bailey, all but hiding his departure. Hearsay held that the Abbey was once a minor holding of the Duke of Dontril, whose dutchy had ceased to be for millennia. But, whatever the case, it was certainly a sound fortress capable of defending itself by few against many.

There was no trail from the western wall. Or rather, none that were not layered with decades of overgrowth and inhabited by animals sure to cause the roan fright. Cerlic spurred the gelding to a brisk canter north by northwest, through a barren barley field, trampling over furrowed and harrowed soil. It would take him out of town and along the lowland marsh, from which a small, cobbled thoroughfare led to three hundred unbroken miles of paved brick called Hene's Road.

Cerlic squeezed his thighs against the roan's sides, halting the beast, and looked back towards the high-walled Abbey that had foisted its hopes upon him. He would miss it, he had to admit. By horse, a journey east to the capital Kovbeck could last many months from Hiqueby County. A galley was faster, but the only boats in the bay were skiffs and dories. Cerlic checked the knots of the saddlebag. He was prepared: the provisions of coin and victual were plentiful, and the groom's spare roughspun raiment infused his limbs with a warmth. He was ready.

For a time Cerlic rode unmolested. The pariahs that dwelled past the outskirts of Gladsmoth were content to toil away in solitude. Some cast their suspicion his way, a few halloed him, but most dared not show interest, lest he be drawn in like a bear to the shallows in spawning season. In normal times, their lack of courtesy might have affronted him; however, these were no ordinary times, and he was simply glad to proceed unimpeded. When he reached the marsh, the water proved to be low enough to ford. The gelding demurred at first, prodding the sodden earth and whining like a mewling pup. At Cerlic's continuous urging, the roan eventually acquiesced. The water came level with the horse's fetlocks, but even still it rushed to the solid mounds that layered most of the marsh.

A furlong of nervous plodding saw Cerlic to the bank opposite. The ground sank slightly beneath the roan's hooves for another two furlongs, until they spotted Hene's Road. Relief flooded Cerlic's heart when he saw no travelers traversing the thoroughfare. He had expected just as much, but hope could be a dangerous thing to harbor. Passing small huts and animal dens, through the wild he galloped, on towards the main path. As Cerlic and the roan approached, he noted that the road's bank sloped steeply upward and that the gelding would struggle mightily in the ascent. Even through the thick leather saddle, he felt the horse's muscles working with incredible force.

On the brick the roan seemed more surefooted. Many of the horses at Glabsmoth Abbey came to them from soldiers and mercenaries seeking forgiveness, and Cerlic did not like to think his an exception. Unfortunately, hard stone whittles at the hooves, exception or no. Whilst he rode the sunlight passed by the south, and his and his mount's shadows soon preceded him in a stretching form, slightly askew along the road.

The passing miles grew long and weary, Cerlic saddle sore and the roan sagging. A meal of oats and a long drink from a reservoir near the bank did nothing to quell the roan's slowing pace. I must make camp, thought Cerlic, glumly. Best not to risk lameness of leg or body. For a second time, Cerlic visited a reservoir a little off the bank, this time miles from the last. A minor outcropping girdled the pool of pellucid water, forming a partly sheltered camp. There was plenty of smooth earth to sleep on between the jagged rocks and the pool, and a thick willow tree to tether the roan to. Beyond the camp, thorny bushes and ferns marked the land, interspersed throughout by dense groves and a few minute clearings. Cerlic tore himself a chunk of hardened bread, which he ate with thin slices of cheese and stale jerky, staring out into the blurry silhouettes of nature. 'Twas too early yet for stars, but Cerlic needed to rest well and long if he was to brave the morrow's journey, so he slipped effortlessly into a fitful sleep, fens and mourning doves and storming hooves floating pleasantly within his mind.

Mornings were never pleasant for Cerlic, never as never goes, from even his earliest memories. In his youth, spells of insomnia had captured and imprisoned every strand of eagerness and frivolity that a child ought to have within him: only in the dream world—when he did chance upon it—did Cerlic truly feel a green boy. The tutors berated him for a lazy fool, curling their lips, whetting their eyes with contempt, and his mother and father were of a like mind, in all truth. At the monastery, it was no different. They scorned his freedom, envied his birth, loathed his god, chastising and pontificating and fumigating his impurity like ravens worrying at bloated carrion. But the Abbess was kind, in her own manner. She reminded Cerlic of his brother. Of his pudgy cheeks, his innocent smile, the peaceful soul his frail body contained. The mornings also reminded Cerlic of his brother, and he hated that he hated them; though, some were unequivocally worse than others.

A pointy, steel boot clashed against his lower rib cage, collapsing the bony structure down onto his lungs, violently expelling the air. Another landed, striking his spine, and two pairs of hands thrust his face into the soft soil and bound his limbs with rusted gyves. The hands dragged him about the camp and shoved him against the willow tree. Snorting and coughing to free the soil from his nostrils, he hardly heard the roan braying nervously at his captors and their company. Once Cerlic managed to steady himself, he took a good look at them. The two that had grabbed him were short and stocky, decorated with unpleasantries of all kinds. Behind them, there were some fifteen more, by Cerlic's count. Brigands, unmistakably.

The leader, shaven-headed and obeliscal, ambled over to Cerlic. On his back was an elegant arming sword, sheened and sharpened like and unlike the man's pate. Regarding Cerlic, the brigand seemed suspicious, if not troubled. Angrily his men were arguing with one another in a dialect Cerlic did not understand. He did pick up, however, that the bald man's name was "Hyarold" from his men's differential utterances.

"Hwo er tee?" rumbled Hyarold, drawing his sword, flourishing the tapering end under the brother's chin. Cerlic saw a rapacious, hungry desire in the brigands, their hope palpable.

"I am Eleanid, first son of and heir apparent to the Barony of Pontsberg," said the brother, guessing the nature of his question, "and I suggest you treat me thusly, sir." Hyarold's men stared blankly, but when Hyarold himself roared heartily, so did they.

"Pontsberg, eh. Hwere es't?"

"South, bordering Carpesh and Ghole."

Hyarold brought the pommel of the sword down on Cerlic, who yelped frightfully, flinching. The knob came to a halt just before his temple. The men broke out into contemptuous laughter, and a twinge of amusement touched Hyarold's rugged face. "Cittle mak fyor guod ransom, eh!"

"You must release me! You will not escape the law!" Undaunted, the brigands carried him screaming to Hyarold's horse, where he was strapped down behind the saddle. Hyarold had had Cerlic's gelding butchered for spare meat and its bones tossed into the pond. Cerlic was not outraged; far from indignant, he fretted for his own life, not some poor beast's who had only just come into his possession.

As they set out, Cerlic gathered that Hyarold's band consisted of two sub-commanders, Tark and Gor—the fiends that woke him brutally from his sleep—who ranked just below Hyarold, each with charge over eight others, and three seedy scouts he hadn't seen at the camp. The scouts branched off from the main party on light-footed mares, Tark took half his men behind the rightmost, and Gor his behind the leftmost, leaving Hyarold and Cerlic inside an octagonal formation to follow the middle scout. Though the forest grew denser the farther they traveled from Hene's road, the brigands wove around the fallen pines and through the perilous thickets they encountered like seasoned woodsmen. The riding was hard on Cerlic, as when the horse's hindquarters reared up, he was jostled about unforgivingly. After only a short while, he lost all sense of direction; east was west and north was south and the world spun all wrong. From time to time, Cerlic would lapse into a dazed state, his mind spinning like the earth's revolution gone awry.

Tark and Gor returned intermittently to report to Hyarold, never together, and to judge from Hyarold's scathing tone, their findings were unsatisfactory. The greens and browns of the forest seemingly blended into one as the party trekked through; as such, the few landmarks Cerlic did glimpse stuck with him. There was the raised wooden bridge, which spanned the gap of a shallow ravine, the smoky cave that smelled of burnt cedar and venison, a squalid cabin thick with vines and underbrush, and the glade reeking of death, home to a sea of decomposing wretches half clad in boiled leather and chainmail. It struck Cerlic as odd that Hyarold had not searched the cave nor looted the battlefield, but perhaps it was for the better they didn't go off abducting real noblemen or claiming the goods of the dead. They may keep a god after all, thought Cerlic, still tumbling around on the back of Hyarold's horse.

Coalescing for a midday meal, the party rejoined on top of an especially imposing hill and set about business. A large cookfire was erected in the midst of the encampment, wide enough around for all to gather—all but Cerlic, who had been shut away inside a rickety cross- sectioned cage of elm or oak. His fetters, fortunately, were removed and would not chafe at his wrists for the nonce, so long as he made no attempts to escape. Rowdily, Hyarold and his men feasted and clanged their horns of mead, and Cerlic could almost feel the fire roar up with every chortle and sigh. Hyarold babbled nonsense until their meat was gone and their mead all dried up. As much as he tried, Cerlic failed to understand the barbaric tongue they spoke, slathered with a meady deluge as it was. Clearly the brigands were in no hurry, that Cerlic recognized.

They feel safe...unguarded and conspicuous in an uncharted forest... Indeed; the feast persisted on dregs and scraps and dice, the smoke funneling upwards in a lazy torrent and the embers crackling softly before being scattered and stamped into the dirt.

* * *

Bits of iron and transient sparks took to flight as Karlile ground the quartz whetstone up and down his blade, avoiding the ricasso with care. It was a hand-and-a-half sword, if one had the hands of a giant, sharpened for rending chunks of flesh and bone like tearing an autumn leaf down the midrib. Raising the sword, Karlile inspected its every aspect once and once again. He must be prepared for the Earl's command, for it was certain to come.

The porter's boy, Alan, had spotted a hilltop encampment a little ways off the Cabpa river. Thieves or murders, most likely. Possibly both. "These are not our lands, and their numbers are unknown," Karlile warned the Earl, when they heard the report, yet the young lord stood by his family's virtues. With forty strong, armed men, the forest posed no threat to the Earl, but any risk of engagement was bloody idiotic at best. Cavalry made up the larger part of the Earl's troops: only a handful could hold a charge from the ground.

"Karl!" called Alan, crashing into Karlile's leather tent. "The young mast—the Earl has already donned his armor and instructed the men. He awaits you, sir." Alan quickly helped Karlile dress for battle, girdling his belt, strapping on his sword, sliding the round helm onto his head. When he saw the Earl ordering his men into file, Karlile felt an unexpected pride; the Earl was not his own, but he had raised the lad like a son.

"Come, Sir Karl," the Earl said amicably. "Hark; Rosh here has, gods praise him, snuck a look at the camp. There are twenty-three by his count and not a single sober. This spells victory for us, sir. We have two to their one, and even if the odds were flipped, it would make no matter." Karlile frowned but did not speak, as the Earl would only listen through barred ears.

The Earl left with the cavalry, heading downwind of the encampment, his golden locks sprouting from under his helm. Before the Earl departed, he ordered Karlile to take the infantry men, sneak up to the base of the mound, and wait there until after the cavalry's first charge. In his younger days, Karlile might have demurred to such a plan, but the young Earl needed to succeed or fail by his own decisions. A couple of the men might die in the coming skirmish, more like the enfeebled than not. Karlile himself was not promised to see the day's end, and he knew it. Years of frenzied slashing had worn down his shoulders, and his strength had faded long since. Besides, his late wife was ten years in her grave, and his boys and girls beside her. It was said that every godly man should reach his sixties, yet Karlile doubted he would reach fifty...

The approach was simple, harmless, for the forest ran to the base of the mound. Crouching down behind some large shrubs, Karlile hushed his men. As unlikely the band atop the hill was to hear them, caution behooved him. To his right, in a sudden rush the Earl's troops rode up the slanting ground, a standard of five converging swords billowing behind. Battle cries split the skies as the cavalry charged, wielding sword and axe. Karlile could not see the collision, but he heard terrified screams and then a triumphant hoorah as the horses passed by the crest and galloped their descent. "Distract them, but do not engage," he had told his men, yet they were sure to disregard his orders.

Karlile pushed through the shrubs first, scratching the polished armor around his waist. The others, boys young and younger, went after him and broke into a sprint, the grass below their feet short and dry, granting them certain footing. Karlile puffed and gasped and wished the damned thieves would come down to them before the immensity of the slope ruined his knees. At least the sun is with us, he thought ruefully. Any man wishing to face his rush would be half- blind and drunk, an ideal combination.

At the top, he found the camp still recovering their wits. On the ground lay a man clutching at his bleeding shoulder, writhing around in the pooling blood, and nearby the center of the camp, a bald oaf with an exquisite sword of ornamental make who was barking orders fixed his eyes on Karlile and then the footmen behind.

"...forward..." the Earl cried from the distance, audible before even the storm of horses and the roar of man. The thieves shifted their attention to the assault and decided unanimously and without words to disperse. One of the slower groups was caught by the charge and dealt with swiftly by a few swooping blades. The bulk of the fleeing men found themselves penned in by Karlile's force: they too were cut down. Karlile had the pleasure of shortening two by a head himself until he collapsed under the weight of his iron. By the time he rose, the field was a mess, bloody and stinking of relaxed bowels.

His companions routed, the oaf threw his fine steel to the soil and waved the white. Karlile noticed the blade hadn't tasted blood in the battle, and that the oaf hadn't shed any either.

The Earl had the brute bend a knee before him, alongside a squirming black-haired whelp.

"Speak your name, rabbleborne," snarled the Earl.

"Oi er Igris...laird," the brute said. "Ye mus escuse me, fyor oi war farced te roide wit thim. Eh, ye ken—"

"You lie!" interjected the whelp. "Your men called you Hyarold, and they were your men, for certes."

Hyarold—the bald man—snapped at the whelp who flinched back and scrambled to the side while the Earl's men pinned Hyarold down. He struggled in their grasp until one dashed a heavy fist across his chin. "Bind this fool to the wondrous Mother Earth, Karlile. He presumes too much."

Obeying, the Knights' Commander ripped free a short blade from his subordinate's belt and, kneeling low, stabbed the steel down through Hyarold's hand. The blood trickled out ponderously from where the hilt guard met flesh in branching rills, and Hyarold forbore a scream, jaws clenched to one another like a man and his pride. Karlile respected the man's fortitude, but that didn't change what he had to do.

Slowly, meticulously, with great care to avoid falling, Karlile raised his knee up above Hyarold's hand, his leg wobbling involuntarily under the stain of the sky. Release. A powerful and ancient ecstasy bubbled up within him as his leg dropped, and an eternity passed. Blood squelched out. Hyarold screamed like a dying lamb.

Hyarold, the earth, and the blade itself...

...were one.

* * *

Never before had he seen a man die, this Cerłic of Pontsberg, never as never goes. Not all the piss and stained upholstery in the known world could measure up to a speck of a fraction of the disgust he now felt. Seeing a man slain in battle was one thing...and sacrificial butchery another. They had skinned Hyarold's corpse like huntsmen do a deer, removed the organs, and stripped it of the flesh. All that they burned in the cookfire, leaving it to become nothing. The bones were broken into little shards with a hammer, and the shards were then ground to dust by mortar and pestle. For what purpose, Cerłic did not know.

He was held for a time in a tent, whose make and material escaped his notice for a lack of genuine care; it was all grey and drear, not only the tent. After divesting the dead of their minor personal effects and interring them deep within the soil, the Earl returned to his camp to speak with Cerłic.

"I will take it that you are a friend, or at least no enemy," the Earl said, alone with Cerłic inside the tent, dressed still in his armor. "But I must introduce myself, of course. I am Earl Renfri Lirrilion of that ilk, and you have done my house a great service. That man Hyarold has a vast bounty on his head—though I have settled for an ear. I might have buried him like the rest if not for you, friend." Renfri's face lit up with a boyish grin. "I should like to know your name and to where you are headed, if you do not mind."

"Thank you, Your Grace. I am—"

"Call me Renfri, please."

"Certainly. I am Cerlic of Pontsberg, adherent to and lover of the Sepultory faith, resident of the Abbey of Gladsmoth. As to my destination, Kovbeck it be." Renfri clasped the sides of his helm with both hands and slid it off slowly, revealing a vibrant, guileless smile. Curls, like streams of pristine melted gold, tumbled over his face, concealing his eyes, until he threw back his head and fixed his attention on Cerlic.

"My guess wasn't far off then, but the men would as soon trust a sniveling waif than a man captured alive. I trust you, Cerlic of Pontsberg. And I owe you, too, so fear not; I shall take you to Kovbeck."

Spring Break Stay-cation! Write 50-Word Stories

Introduction by Miranda Keskes

Microfiction is a growing genre in literature today. Due to its short form, it's a powerful tool for students to practice all stages of the writing process. In this three-day intensive, students learned what microfiction is, studied models, and practiced writing several of their own microfictions in response to visual and written prompts. As they wrote, they practiced writing techniques such as how to use descriptive language to show emotions, develop setting, clarify genre, and propel a plot forward. Students also practiced essential revision skills and, as a culminating activity, learned how to provide helpful feedback to one another. We hope you enjoy these tiny stories!

THE BY-BLOW
by Ethan Konopacki, 12th Grade

Spurred forth, the horses charged, looked upon by the roaring crowd. The Knight of Nrague raised his lance, facing his contender in this deadly dance...

...Glance...

He was trounced by the Dark Sun's lance, and, staring up at the stygian birds of the sky, realized he had lost an eye.

THE LAKE
by Albert Hong, 8th Grade

On a bright morning, young Oliver joined his dad at the lake. They prepared their rickety boat with fishing gear when a sudden storm cast dark shadows. A mysterious voice shared tales of a legendary fish. Oliver's heart raced as his dad nervously chuckled, casting his line into the water.

CATNAP
by Fionnagan Vandenheuvel, 7th Grade

The cat longs to sleep. She nudges the book off her favorite pillow. It makes a thump when it falls. The tick, tick, ticking of the clock is driving her crazy. She smacks it to the ground. Then the dog walks in and the cat yells at the top of her tiny lungs.

North Ed Writers Studio

Instructor introduction by Teresa Scollon

The Writers Studio program at Northwest Ed Career Tech offers a creative home and college credit for high school juniors and seniors. This is an intensive two-year creative, professional, and journalistic writing program built for students who love to write. We cover many creative and professional genres—poetry, nonfiction, playwriting, fiction, journalism, professional writing—and audio production in a collaborative, workshop-based environment. We build skills and then apply them to real-world situations. Students develop a writing portfolio, submit work to competitions, and seek publishing opportunities. Seniors may be eligible to work in an internship. Visits by published authors and other working professionals help students build a sense of the wider professional world.

Many students come into the Writers Studio with a real love of fantasy fiction, but not much exposure to other genres. One of our goals is to open up a wider sense of the varied world of writing. The pieces you see here were written during the fall semester, in brand-new genres: poetry, creative nonfiction, and playwriting. We really enjoyed the discovery of and experimenting in new forms; we hope you enjoy reading this work.

For more information, visit:
https://www.northwested.org/career-tech/programs/writers-studio/

I BEAR THE ROTTEN FRUIT
by Addison Seivertson, 11th Grade

I sit beneath the shade of the tree
That bears mostly rotten fruit.

And though I have consumed
The trees last pure and healthy fruit,
I fear that it's only fair
To seek out the knowledge of the rotten nectar as well.

As I am at fault here.
I stole all of it,
I sucked it dry,
And now I get mad at it
When its branches are too fragile to protect me from the sun.

It did not cause this,
I did.
I did not notice how withered the tree had become,
I was selfish, and I was greedy.

And though unfortunately
I believe there is no actual tree,
There is only me.
I sit alone.

My anger, and my selfishness I fear
Is only towards me.
I have inadvertently tore myself down,
While trying to understand myself.

I bear the rotten fruit
that is affected by this hatred.

AT AN ESTATE SALE
by Sadie Hodges, 11th Grade

You will you find me in a box
Not thoroughly sorted
Labeled "$0.25 each"
And feel drawn to my leather binding

You will purchase me
From a stranger
Who is as clueless as you
About my contents

You will have a pen in hand
The first time you
Open me
And you will drop it, quickly

You will stare for hours
At my worn pages
Deciphering stories
Through tear stains

You will run your index finger
Along my torn paper
Where secrets too big to face
Had been ripped out

Yet, you will not
Be brought to tears yourself
Until you find
The light at my end

THE BLACK HOLE
by Alex Morgan, 12th Grade

I've been watching you.
From 1,600 lightyears away, I've been watching.
In my carousel of solitude, I've been watching.

It took me a while to see you, but I've been watching.

I've been watching you try to understand.
I've been watching you try to create,
Your arts and unflattering Persona Poetry...

I've been watching you sing, write songs.
You sing to me, ask me to take your rain away.
As catchy as it is, I shall decline.

I've been watching you and your sun.
Your spinning motions make me dizzy.
I've been watching, so lonely...

I prepared jokes for you, should you visit.
But they all sucked...
Not that It matters... It Antimatters.

Yeah, I've been watching you.

You humans and your issues.
I envy you from my colorless cage.
I want to pull you closer and embrace you tight.

But whatever I pull in disappears.
It weighs on me and rocks my core.
So, as if I'm in a pandemic, I keep my distance.

In conclusion, from 1,600 lightyears away,
I've been watching you.
And you don't visit...

FIESTA DEL TORO
by Kacie Blanchette, 12th Grade

The audience roared at my forced entrance
as a torero egged me on
with his red flag
and his gold-trimmed sequin suit.

He sliced and poked
at my bloody body without regret.
I was exploited as the crowd bellowed
"¡más sangre!"

I was fully surrounded
with no way out.
The stench of my own blood was overwhelming
as his estoque cut to the bone.

But with all my trying
to avoid the matador,
he only wanted a pool of shiny red blood
below me and loud applause.

Olive Joy's Life by Hunter Arnold, 12th Grade

I open my eyes before anyone wakes up.
I sniff the air to see if anything has changed,
Nope, all is the same.
In the moments of stillness
I wait meekly.
I let a deep sigh out,

As a reminder
That I am here,
Ready to start the day.

As you wake and pad towards the door,
I am ready.
My tail wags, and my heart is racing.
The reflection from the door always creates a light,
And I always chase it,
And I never catch it.
I guess I wasn't ready.
My fuzzy ears turn towards the chirping birds,
Before my mind catches up
My legs pull me forward.
I was not ready.

I dart towards a yellow ball I lost months ago,
Still smells the same.
My ears twitch again.
A sound I'm familiar with—
It's my owner.
I run home with my ball.
For some reason, the ball isn't allowed inside.

I've never understood why.

My owner scratches my ears,
And I flop on her feet.
She goes back to bed,
So I decide to take a quick power nap.

I hear movement and I jump to my feet.
My tongue is dry
And stuck on the outside of my mouth.
I suck it back in.
I stretch my back and yawn real big.
I run to my owner's room
Those new small cats
Are always
On her bed.
I jump up on them.
They hiss, and my owner doesn't do a thing about it.

I curl up next to my owner,
My nose rests against her side.
All the warmth spreads through me,
And I nudge her gently,
And like always, her hand meets my head.
Her finger brush through my fur,
And the world feels perfect.

BETWEEN LOVE AND MEAD, A PLAY
by Eileen Knight, 12th Grade

Chloe: Twenty-two years old. Kind-hearted, naive, and visibly intoxicated. She is wearing a puffy dress, resembling a loofah.
Lila: Twenty-two years old. Honest and kind of cold at times. Protective of Chloe. Oblivious to Peter's crush, while also having a crush on him. She is dressed as a black cat.
Peter: Twenty-two years old. Has a massive crush on LILA. Extremely awkward and has an obsession with mead. He wears a name tag that reads 'Mark.'

Scene: Lila's apartment.
Time: Present. Halloween night.

AT RISE: LILA and CHLOE are sitting on the couch center stage. CHLOE is sobbing in LILA's arms, who is desperately trying to comfort her. On the coffee table lay a few bottles.

LILA (Pulling CHLOE away from her chest, she cradles CHLOE's head in her hands.) Hey, hey. Look at me. You don't need him. He's just a boy. The streets are crawling with a million boys just like him. (beat) Like, for example, Gigi Davis' party tonight. (CHLOE shakes her head 'no.') Oh, come on. Are you seriously going to let him ruin Halloween for you? This is the best holiday of the year, and Gigi has the best, most exclusive party. I practically had to kiss her feet for these invites.

CHLOE (She sobs.) No, no party. Matthew loves parties. He's gonna be there and I... (She glances at her phone and sees her reflection.) Look horrible!

LILA What are you talking about? (She gestures to CHLOE's runny makeup and messy hair) You look... fantastic. So stunning, actually. (CHLOE shakes her head.) Yuh-huh. I promise.

CHLOE I look stupid. (mocking herself) 'Hey, you know what would be super hilarious, babe? If we went as a loofah and bar of soap for Halloween.' Haha! Ha! So funny! (She breaks down sobbing and gestures to her costume.) Now I'm just a loofah... with no soap. (She goes limp on the couch, like a ragdoll. She places her hand on her forehead, checking her temperature.) (whining) When is your boyfriend gonna be here? I'm thirsty. I think I'm getting sick or something.

LILA (flustered) Peter is not my boyfriend. (CHLOE laughs)

CHLOE (She picks up a nearby bottle, then sets it down again when she realizes it's empty.) There's... no more. (she wails) I just wanted an apology, you know? (beat) He's literally just confused right now. I know him, better than anyone. He's confused. (beat) Maybe he's out buying flowers right now and everything will be okay. He loves me.

LILA (She pats CHLOE's back, looking very uncomfortable) Oh, Chloe... I—You shouldn't get your hopes up. (CHLOE continues to sob. A knock is heard from offstage. LILA jumps up from the couch.) I'll be right back. (She fixes her hair and rushes to the door. PETER enters, carrying a box of bottles.) (exasperated) I'm so glad you're here.

PETER (brightly) Yeah, thanks so much for inviting me. I brought strawberry mead. Well, I brewed it. For you. In my basement.

LILA (Distracted by CHLOE'S wailing.) That's lovely, Pete. Thanks for thinking of me. (catching sight of his name tag) Who is Mark?

PETER My Halloween costume. (LILA looks confused.) It's ironic because my name is actually Peter.

LILA (LILA opens her mouth, then closes it.) You know what? I love it. Very original. (PETER beams. A timer sounds offstage.) Shoot, I gotta pull the cookies for the party. Hey, do me a favor and... cheer up our friend Chloe, will ya? Matthew broke up with her earlier and she's, uh... (LILA and PETER glance at CHLOE and grimace) Not exactly a tough kid.

PETER I see... and you want me to cheer her up?

LILA Yeah, you'll do great. Make her feel like a special gal, you know?

PETER Not really.

CHLOE (calling from the couch) Maybe I should text him.

LILA (turning to CHLOE) Chloe, I swear, I will confiscate your phone. Put it on the table. Now. (CHLOE reluctantly places her phone on the coffee table and sulks.)

PETER Please do not make me go over there. I brought cherry mead, too.

LILA Perfect! That's her favorite, you know. (PETER looks unsure) Let me level with you here, Pete. I have no clue what to do. I need to get her put together enough to get out the door and to that party, or else Gigi will blacklist me for the rest of the year.

PETER Lila, I appreciate your faith in me, but I just can't–

LILA (grabbing PETER's shoulders) Do you know how exclusive these invites are? Do you know how much work went into securing Chloe and I's spot there tonight? How many biology notes I completed? The obscene amount of manicures I performed?

PETER (gulps) Probably a lot, judging by the amount of pressure your hands are putting on my shoulders. (nervously laughs) Wow, you are stronger than you look. (LILA lowers her hands) Do you work out or something? (PETER rubs his shoulders) I mean, that's almost freakish. (offering a bottle) Strawberry mead?

LILA (She takes the bottle and swigs it.) You're an interesting guy. I appreciate that about you. Now, go take that weirdness and get Chloe on her feet. I'm relying on you, bud.

PETER Oh, I don't think you–

LILA (She claps PETER on the back) Go get em', tiger.

CHLOE Oh, I remember when we went to the beach. Matthew loved the beach.

PETER (He hesitantly crosses to the couch and sets the box on the coffee table.) Yeah... Break-ups, uh, suck?

CHLOE (Slurring, she shows PETER the phone screen.) Look at him. He has such a nice smile..

PETER (He sits beside her.) Yeah, he's, uh, not really my type.

CHLOE (sharply) Well, he's not your boyfriend. (pause) He's not my boyfriend. (She begins to sob.) (beat) What's in that box?

PETER Mead. Strawberry mead. It's Lila's favorite, I'm pretty sure.

CHLOE Oh. Oh. You like her, don't you? (PETER stays silent, avoiding CHLOE's gaze. CHLOE gasps.) Oh em gee! You like-like her.

PETER (Visibly flustered.) What? That's just– that... The mead. Yes, let's talk about the
mead. The mead is very good. I brewed it myself. In my basement.

CHLOE (She shoves him, attempting to be playful. PETER rubs his shoulder.) Shut up about the mead! This is adorable. You guys would be perfect for each other. You're so... Peter, and she's just so... Lila. You've come to the right gal, Pete-y-pie. I'll totally set you up.

PETER I wish you women would stop hitting me. Anyway, no matter how I
may feel for Lila, I really don't think she's interested in me.

CHLOE You don't know that.

PETER No, but...

CHLOE No buts! You can't give up before you try. You like the girl? Put on your big boy pants and get her. You're a smart, genuine guy. (pause) Just like I thought... (She winces.) Matthew was. (She sobs again.)

PETER Oh, jeez. (He offers her a bottle.) Mead? (CHLOE ignores him and continues to sob. PETER sighs.) Hypothetically, if I were to approach Lila, how would I... do that?

CHLOE (She brightens.) Well, first of all, you have to smell good. (She leans forward and sniffs him.) Not too bad, not too bad. You could do a little bit better than Axe Body Spray, but nobody's perfect. You seem well-groomed. Your hair's not too long, not too short, just how Lila likes it. (She leans forward until she is eye to eye with PETER, who is looking a little uncomfortable.) You've got dreamy eyes. Wow, really long eyelashes, too. Gosh, I wish I had them.

PETER Please don't take them from me. Anyways, how do I... talk to her?

CHLOE (squealing) Oh, she makes you nervous. How cute. (She pinches PETER's cheeks. He bats her hand away.)

PETER This conversation is futile. (He starts to stand up.)

CHLOE (She pulls him back down.) Wait, wait. I'm helpful, I promise. (She sighs and thinks for a moment) I guess... Well, I always talk about what I love. And that can mean anything. I usually talk about Lila, because she's my favorite person in the universe. She's just so Lila, you know? (she grins) I mean, she got us spots at Gigi's party tonight. Do you know how hard that is?

PETER I've heard.

CHLOE So what do you... (She leans forward and flicks his nose. PETER
winces and bats her hand away.)... Love most in the world?

PETER Mead. Brewing it, specifically.

CHLOE Mead? (she laughs) You know what? That'll get the job done. Talk about mead.

PETER Alright. Honey is an essential ingredient in brewing mead, as it acts as a natural antiseptic, which prevents bad things from growing and helps the yeast settle in more easily. Historically speaking, the first mead was allegedly the product of some farmer not fully emptying a barrel of honey. It rained—

CHLOE That's fantastic. Real good stuff. Save it for Lila, though. She'd love to hear all the mead lore.

PETER (smiling) You think so?

CHLOE Obviously. (She takes a bottle and sips from it.) Wow, that's really good.

PETER That's my special brew.

CHLOE I want to ask what that means, but at the same time, I'm good not knowing. So, when Lila walks into this room, you're gonna knock her socks off, right?

PETER I don't know about that. I was just gonna talk to her. I'm not interested in taking her socks off.

CHLOE What? No, it's just a– (LILA enters carrying a tray of charred cookies. CHLOE clumsily pushes PETER to his feet.) Go get 'em, tiger.

LILA (Placing the tray on the coffee table.) (disappointed) Welp, they definitely are burned.

CHLOE (gasping) Burned? Where? They look perfect. Right, Peter? (She looks at him expectantly.)

LILA (frowning) Really? (She also looks at PETER, who examines the
cookies)

PETER No, I'm pretty certain they're inedible. Baking isn't for everyone. (CHLOE face palms. After a moment, LILA laughs.)

LILA (shrugging) I guess not. Oh, well. (she sits on the couch)

PETER (Peter smiles, then glances at CHLOE, who gives him an encouraging nod. He sits next to LILA.) Did you know that honey can pick up the characteristics of the food bees eat? (rambling) And that color and taste can come through in the mead. For example, a hive feeding off of black berries will likely have a blue-ish color and berry taste. You see, mead is only as good as your ingredients. (CHLOE gives PETER a hesitant thumbs-up)

LILA (blinking) Wow, I did not know that. And you decided to enlighten me because...

PETER (blushing) Well, I... (he sighs) Chloe said I should talk about what I love. So I did.

CHLOE (abruptly rises, looking between LILA and PETER) I'm going to...powder my nose. (she exits, stumbling.)

LILA (suspiciously) What's up with you?

PETER Nothing. (pause, then blurting) I think you're really pretty. And funny. Strawberry mead is your favorite, right?

LILA Yeah, it is. (blushing) So, what, you have a crush on me or something?

PETER I suppose.

LILA (rolls her eyes, then sighs.) Fine, I'll go out with you.

PETER I didn't ask–

LILA I'm free tomorrow. (CHLOE enters, but stays out of sight.)

PETER Alright then. Tomorrow. (They smile at each other, sharing a tender moment. CHLOE squeals. PETER and LILA startle.)

CHLOE Oh, oops. Am I... interrupting something?

LILA Of course not.

CHLOE (hesitantly) If you two want to go to the party, feel free to leave. Honestly, I'm fine here. I'm really fine. I'll, like, watch a movie or something. Like the notebook. And I won't cry.

LILA It's okay, Chloe. I'm alright here.

CHLOE (She sits next to LILA.) Really? Are you sure?

LILA Yeah, I'm sure. I think I'll survive missing out on Gigi's attitude and dodging puddles of beer and vomit.

CHLOE (she sits next to LILA) Matthew posted with another girl. I guess he was really serious about the whole 'I never want to see you again.'

LILA What? That little piece of– (she begins to stand)

CHLOE (She pulls LILA back down) Lila, really. It is what it is. He just sucks. But I do feel... better. It's a weird kind of closure, you know? Knowing that there's no secret feelings. He's just done. So, I've decided to be done, too. (beat) I bet those cookies would be pretty edible if we dunked them in some milk. Let me grab some. (She exits.)

LILA (calling after her) Hey, would you grab that deck of uno on the kitchen table?

CHLOE (offstage) Yep!

PETER (pause) I could, uh, show you how to brew mead tomorrow. And we can go to Olive Garden or something of the sorts.

LILA I would love that, Peter (She takes PETER's hand and squeezes it.) (CHLOE enters with a deck of Uno and three cups.)

CHLOE Are you guys ready to get your butts kicked?

PETER Are you? (Lights go down as CHLOE sits and they begin their game, laughing)

END SCENE

THE LAUGHING BUDDHA
by Chloe Taylor, 12th Grade

The next time you find the glimpse of shiny smooth copper, face-up
Upon the chilled   rocky   concrete

You'll remember

My small   forgotten   statue   sitting
Upon your makeshift   cork   counter top.

But do you remember me?
Can you see me? Hidden away in the back?

With my silk   red   cloth   draping over my soft   gentle   folds
And my smiling cheeks
Pulling the edges of my face up into my contagious laugh
Awaiting the touch of your soft fingertips
Upon my hand painted   stained
Belly.

Just one touch. Come on, you know that I'll keep my promise.

To bring you the good fortune just in exchange to feel those pressed fingers
Upon my belly.

Just look at me, just once

But

As the time   passes
And the bits of dust pile up to fill the cracks and crevices of my satin wrinkles

The steady breeze will cloud my eyelids
And I'll see you walk by once more.

Maybe you have forgotten about me

You   don't remember
the last time you've picked up
Shiny   bronze.

And I don't remember the last time I've felt the touch
Of your soft fingertips

And with that
I think we both have forgotten about the promise.

SPOOKY SCARY PLASTIC SKELETON
by Nyah Parker, 10th Grade

"Hey, I'm going to sit John next to you," Mr. Connor said, placing the class life-sized plastic skeleton right next to where I was sitting in the back of the bus. I rolled my eyes because Mr. Connor was way too attached to that thing; it was like his only friend.

The bus rumbled to life, its engine groaning as we veered onto a winding, uneven road.

Rain drummed against the windows, a restless, rhythmic tapping. With every jolt, John's plastic bones clattered. I didn't see the point of spending an hour on the road just to visit some dusty fossil museum. All I wanted was to sleep, but between the rattling dummy beside me and the constant shake of the bus, that wasn't happening.

Half an hour in of staring out the window at the gray dead trees pass by, the bus lurched over a deep pothole. Before I could steady myself, an icy grip closed around my hand. I turned—John's eyeless gaze bore into me, his fingers clamped tight around mine.

"John!" I hissed, trying to shake his bony fingers off mine while looking around in case someone was looking. "What on earth are you doing? Let go! Someone could see!"

"I will not hide my love!" His voice came out flat. "I don't care what anyone else thinks! I love you!" The words sent a cold shiver down my spine. The rain hammered harder against the windows, as though it too was reacting to the bizarre, creepy confession. "I... LOVE... YOU!"

The nausea I felt came more from annoyance than fear. This had been going on the whole school year and I was done with John tormenting me. "No, John," I said firmly, placing my other hand on his cold shoulder bone. His bones rattled softly beneath my fingers. "We can't be together. You're an adult, male, plastic, skeleton, and I'm just a human girl. It just won't work." John went quiet. He didn't move for the rest of the ride, his bony hands folded in his lap, staring out the window as the rain blurred the world outside.

As we filed into the museum, Mr. Connor wheeled John along like an elder, his fingers tightly gripping the handles, guiding him with a care that felt way too personal for a plastic skeleton. I trailed behind, my arms crossed tight, trying to shake off the strange moment we'd shared on the bus.

I needed to shut this down, but then I saw her. In the center of the exhibit hall, bathed in soft, muted light, stood a real skeleton. Not plastic—this one was the real deal. The display read, "Lucy."

"Hey, Mr. Connor," I said, trying to sound enthusiastic. "I think it'd be pretty educational if John met an actual skeleton. What do you think?"

Mr. Connor gasped dramatically. "That's brilliant! John deserves to connect with his kind!"

Before I knew it, John was wheeled right up to Lucy. I crouched down beside him, my fingers brushing against the cool glass of the display case as I whispered, "John, meet Lucy.

Lucy, meet John. You guys are both made of bones. Kinda."

John didn't respond right away. His empty gaze shifted from Lucy to me, the air around us colder now, as if the rain had somehow seeped inside the museum. Then, in a flash of cold fingers, he grabbed my wrist and looked up at me.

"She will never be you," he whispered, his voice full of strange certainty. I frowned. Maybe this wasn't going to work. Maybe John would never let go, always holding onto the strange affection for me he had built in his hollow plastic heart. What was I supposed to do?

"John," I said softly, my voice quiet against the soft hum of the storm outside, "Maybe that's a good thing." He loosened his grip. I continued, my voice gentle, but firm, "Someone like me could never love someone like you. But if you try to get to know Lucy—maybe by reading her story?" I pointed to the small plaque under the skeleton's display name. But as I read, something caught my eye. "What's this?" I said, noticing a folded note tucked behind the plaque. John stiffened, his bony frame growing tense, but he said nothing. I unfolded the note and began reading aloud.

"Dear Lucy,

We can't be together. It's not just the rules—though trust me, the museum director would not approve—it's the reality of our situations. You belong in the exhibit, frozen in time, and I'm just a guy with a flashlight and a keyring, making sure no one taps on the glass too hard. But I have more than that too. I have life and a family. That doesn't mean we can't still be friends. I'll still check in on you during my rounds, still make sure no one disrespects your space. You'll always have a special place in this museum—and in my heart.

-Dirk, the security guard"

John stared up at Lucy, his expression unreadable. "You know," he said with an emotional rasp, "You know how it feels. You and I—we aren't so different, are we? Maybe... maybe this is meant to be."

I patted the top of John's skull and winked at him. "I'll leave you two alone for a bit."

And as I turned away, the soft patter of rain outside became a comforting rhythm, blending with the quiet hum of the museum. I knew then that John would be okay. Maybe even better than okay. He'd found someone who could truly understand him.

CREATIVE DIFFERENCES, A PLAY
by Aiden DuVall, 11th Grade

Edward Moreau: Younger painter, trying to become famous
Charles Dubois: Old art critic
Antoine: Often goes to art exhibition

1880's Paris, France. Towards the end of the Realism movement.

AT RISE: An art exhibition. EDWARD MOREAU Is showcasing his art, ANTOINE is
examining it.

ANTOINE Well, it is certainly unique; It is less detailed but seems more human in a way. It's certainly odd but it's great to see something new.

EDWARD MOREAU Thank you, monsieur! This piece is very important to me, and possibly the art world itself.

ANTOINE It (pause) looks (pause) What exactly is the meaning of this painting? It's certainly different from the other pieces here.

EDWARD MOREAU Yes, exactly the point! [CHARLES DUBOIS WALKS BY]
Oh! Monsieur Dubois! (EDWARD MOREAU waves to CHARLES DUBOIS) [CHARLES DUBOIS looks at EDWARD MOREAU and walks over]

CHARLES DUBOIS Moreau, it's good to see you made—(CHARLES DUBOIS stops and stares down the painting on the wall, and covers his mouth with his hand and gasps) (uncovers mouth and yells) What is that?

EDWARD MOREAU Pardon monsieur? Is there a problem?

CHARLES DUBOIS (Stutters) What is that? What happened Moreau? Please tell me this is a sick joke.

EDWARD MOREAU A joke monsieur? I knew you would be confused but not unreasonably harsh towards this piece. [Both characters are now angrily shouting]

CHARLES DUBOIS This 'piece' (pause) this is a piece of garbage. Are you trying to make me look like a fool, Moreau? I expected better from you than to pursue something so vulgar like (pause) this.

EDWARD MOREAU Vulgar? What is so vulgar about this? Is there a problem with impressionism?

CHARLES DUBOIS Monsieur Moreau, this is a professional art exhibit, there is no room for "impressionism" or whatever you call this vomit. There is no blending, and every single brush stroke is visible; it looks blurry, how could you ever call this art?

EDWARD MOREAU And you call everything else here art!? Every piece looks the exact same, it's all a copy of neoclassicism, the only difference is that they're painting poor people. I ask you how could you call any of the other pieces here art when you've all been copying the Greeks and Romans? There is no meaning to these paintings anymore, they're the exact same ideas with little deviation.

CHARLES DUBOIS They should have little deviation; these pieces are the closest
things to perfection! The academy has conditioned all these artists to perfect absolute beauty! Why would anyone change that to something so pedestrian as that!?

EDWARD MOREAU (starts gesticulating) To blazes with the Academy! The academy
is just a bunch of elite, royal children pandering to rich politicians in order to get a quick Franc or two! Personally, the thought of self-expression only being limited to the rich sickens me. [CHARLES DUBOIS grabs the painting off the wall and holds it in front of EDWARD MOREAU and ANTOINE]

EDWARD MOREAU What are you doing, you fool!?

CHARLES DUBOIS (Ignoring EDWARD MOREAU and looking at ANTOINE) Monsieur, what do you think about this piece? Surely you would understand my disdain.

ANTOINE Not entirely, I think it— [EDWARD MOREAU interrupts ANTOINE]

EDWARD MOREAU Put that down Dubois, your fat fingers are getting oil on the surface! [CHARLES DUBOIS turns to EDWARD MOREAU slowly]

CHARLES DUBOIS (very calmly) Oh, are my fat fingers messing up your
(sarcastically) masterpiece? [CHARLES DUBOIS breaks the painting over his knee, ANTOINE and EDWARD MOREAU are in a stunned silence]

EDWARD MOREAU (Stuttering) You. You buffoon! You lizard-skinned ape! [EDWARD MOREAU grabs his handkerchief out of his pocket, walks over to CHARLES DUBOIS and smacks him in the face]

ANTOINE (Shakes head from side to side, and puts his hands on his hips) (Annoyed) Oh dear lord. [EDWARD MOREAU's face gets really close to CHARLES DUBOIS]

EDWARD MOREAU That 'vomit' you said, Dubois? I will make you choke on it. [CHARLES DUBOIS put up his fists]

ANTOINE (Angry) Gentlemen! Be civil. This is an art exhibit. If you're going to brawl, at least head to the alley where the other barbarous rats are. [EDWARD MOREAU and CHARLES DUBOIS look at ANTOINE slowly and stare for a few seconds and then look back at each other]

EDWARD MOREAU (Bearing teeth, pretending to be polite) Monsieur Dubois, would you like to handle this with civility and duel me properly?

CHARLES DUBOIS Moreau, I would love to watch you bleed.
End Scene

Scene 2: Two weeks after scene two. It's midday.
AT RISE: In a field outside of Paris. Edward and Charles stand 5ft from each other, Antoine between them.

ANTOINE It's (pause) it's just (pause) a painting, though. [EDWARD MOREAU and CHARLES DUBOIS are staring each other down]

EDWARD MOREAU Monsieur, it's not just about art; it's about resisting the ivory tower of the rich that control what it 'should' or 'can' be.

ANTOINE (Puts his hands on his head) Oh dear.

EDWARD MOREAU Your argument is as well structured as that tangled eyesore that
looms over Paris.

CHARLES DUBOIS The Eiffel tower? You hate it like everyone else, and I'm
guessing you think it's ugly, too. How (pause) hypocritical.

ANTOINE Let's get on with this, please. Do you gentlemen remember the agreements and terms? [EDWARD MOREAU and CHARLES DUBOIS nod]

CHARLES DUBOIS Monsieur Moreau, will you be able to keep your composure?

EDWARD MOREAU I will be fine.

CHARLES DUBOIS Very well then. [ANTOINE steps backwards from between them]

ANTOINE Alright gentlemen, go ahead. [CHARLES DUBOIS and EDWARD MOREAU step toward each other and start dueling, very poorly] [CHARLES DUBOIS is struck on the forearm]

CHARLES DUBOIS Sacré bleu! My arm! [ANTOINE walks over to CHARLES DUBOIS and glances at the blood on his arm]

ANTOINE It seems that monsieur Moreau has won. [EDWARD MOREAU lowers his sword and steps back]

EDWARD MOREAU (low chuckle) I can already see my art splayed across your walls. [CHARLES DUBOIS wipes the blood off his wrist with his sleeve]

CHARLES DUBOIS Moreau, don't pretend that you want to inspire, I know that you do this for fame.

EDWARD MOREAU (Ignoring Charles Dubois) Thank you, monsieur. I think that you meant to apologize. So, I suppose my art is?

CHARLES DUBOIS I suppose it's unique in its own way.

EDWARD MOREAU Pardon, monsieur?

CHARLES DUBOIS Your art is unique. It's certainly not like anything I've seen. Moreau, why improve upon something that is already perfect? Moreau, changing the art world would be a step backward.

EDWARD MOREAU (Outraged) No, I won't take that, no monsieur! (pause) Dubois, is your pride so large that if you were to swallow it, you would choke to death?

CHARLES DUBOIS Monsieur, the only choking I would ever do is if I'd praise your paintings. We agreed that I would allow the exhibition of your "painting," not that I would absolutely bow and praise it. I believe that people are entitled to their opinion, mine being that your art isn't fit for the walls of Diogenes' barrel-house.

ANTOINE Gentlemen, please, calm down. [EDWARD MOREAU points at CHARLES DUBOIS]

EDWARD MOREAU (Yelling) Not until this wretched imbecile complies with what we
agreed upon! We had an agreement.

CHARLES DUBOIS Yes, we did. I'm just not sure you remember it correctly. Or I'm
sure that you just don't want to remember it correctly. If you don't want to follow it as it was agreed, I can do the same.

EDWARD MOREAU Pardon, monsieur?

CHARLES DUBOIS I don't have to display-—

EDWARD MOREAU (Interrupts CHARLES DUBOIS) (stuttering) You-you-you shut your mutt looking mouth you soggy, sloppy pile of useless lard! [EDWARD MOREAU starts walking towards CHARLES DUBOIS]

CHARLES DUBOIS (sighs) Alright monsieur Moreau, my apologies, I'm sure we can
work something ou—

EDWARD MOREAU (Interrupts CHARLES DUBOIS) (mocking him) "Work something out" Oh we can "work something out" alright.

CHARLES DUBOIS Excuse me? [EDWARD MOREAU tries to stab him in the stomach, CHARLES DUBOIS tries to parry, saving himself]

CHARLES DUBOIS AH, you egg! How could you? You fool. You would kill me over
some paintings!? [ANTOINE is watching in surprise]

ANTOINE I will not be a witness to a murder with the most foolish reason being over a painting.

CHARLES DUBOIS Are you really willing to die on this hill, Moreau?

EDWARD MOREAU If I can't live in a free world, death would be preferred.

CHARLES DUBOIS Very well, then. [They both thrust their swords at each other, but before any hits land, the curtain falls]

TAKING MY FAMILY FOR GRANTED
by Radley Hafner-Fournet, 11th Grade

2013: I remember holding my twin baby siblings when they were born. Their round fuzzy heads nuzzled into the crook of my elbow. All the aunts and midwives watched closely to make sure my clumsy five-year-old body could hold them. And in that moment I learned that babies smelled like warm cotton, that they breathe in whispers, that their bodies are like small sacks filled with bones and flesh, and that they unforgivingly stare right at you. The moment lasted only a second before my own childish curiosity drew me to the gifts that family had brought for me.

Spring was my favorite season: all the pastel colors eluding to summer, cherry blossoms would be in full bloom, their sweet scent covered by pesticides which made my eyes sting. Some petals would fall around me like ballerinas spinning and twirling to the songs of the Sandhill Cranes that fly in the sky above me. I lived by two cherry orchards during my life, and all before the 2021 chlorpyrifos ban. I think about this a lot. That 86% of farmers in the United States used chlorpyrifos as their preferred pesticide. What I think about more is the tested, proven brain damaging properties of chlorpyrifos and the effects its has on children...anyways the cherry blossoms. Now my favorite season is fall, its rusty dark colors signaling to the coming cold.

The year is unclear. I never paid attention to time when I was an only child. Why would I? When I had the world spinning to my rhythm. But if I were to guess I would say the year was anywhere between 2010 and 2012. Sitting on my small mound of sand that I called a hill. My hill was located in the middle of a private orchard, the privacy allowing me to imagine all my silly stories. From my sliding glass door, across my yard to the fence, using the critters dug-outs under the fence as my secret way in. But the secret is out of the bag...and soon there are two little beings chasing after me. And the world no longer dances to my drum but rather to these little demons. And now, I start keeping track of the years.

"I will never have children," I tell my mom on a regular basis. Her reply is always something along the lines of, "Wait till you're older. Then we'll see."

2016: Election year, Donald Trump vs Hillary Clinton; a year of nerves and hushed whispers. Unlike most of my past memories, the day Trump was elected was crystal clear. I was woken up to my mother who was in a hysterical state, and my father whose hatred of the world just doubled in feeling. Being only eight and my siblings just three, we were extremely confused at the heavy emotions at hand. In fact, we were probably hoping that these supposedly unfortunate events would lead to a movie day to keep us out of our parents' way in their moment of mourning and for us to be entertained.

I did not care much about my two siblings; they were too pudgy and small. They couldn't pronounce their R's so their speech was slurred and annoying. Because babies are stupid I would trick them. Make them run after me with their tiny little legs, making them hope for a sliver of their cool older sister's attention. They would run till they cried.

"Just play with them. They love you."

How I treated my siblings in the past is my biggest regret. Looking back from a parental perspective, I think my parents tried their best to keep our petty fights to minimum. Sibling rivalry is a big issue amongst families. Much so, that siblings will turn even the smallest thing into competition like who gets to sit in the right back seat of the car. It doesn't seem like something to argue about, but siblings can turn the smallest thing into the most important. Sibling rivalry simmers down in adolescence but is very prominent in early and middle childhood. Me and my siblings had intense rivalry for the longest time until we stopped caring. Caring in general, about what they were doing, eating, and going. We all stopped caring to the point of not asking, talking, and arguing. A new fear started to form for our parents.

2020: Covid-19 plus another election year. I am a big thinker, but during the years of Covid I took my thinking to a crazy place. I became fascinated by all these fast easy clips of information through social media. Questioning who I was and what I stood for. Everyday, something new to take from my screen to infuse into my beliefs. Putting my family on a backburner, especially my siblings. It was so easy, when you're held up in your home going through puberty, to just listen blindly to what's being fed to you on social media.

"Come eat dinner honey."

"No. I'm feeling depressed right now" Becoming detached from your family is a dangerous thing. I can look back now and confidently think *how stupid were you?* But I was what? Thirteen? I think that midlife crises are real but I also think preteen crises are very much real as well.

2022: I am now in school, after being homeschooled my whole life. Eighth grade. An extremely humbling experience. That's all I'll say.

Then...slowly....I started to look at myself outside of my body. And just float there. Observing. I started to lose my hotty confidence. It withered and died, shedding itself off me. Leaving me with new skin shining with regret, shame, embarrassment, and self awareness. During this time I developed a mindset of guilt, putting weights on my shoulders for reasons I honestly can't say. Not that I was guilty of something; more that I felt guilt over everything. It's know as maladaptive guilt; the guilt we feel when we haven't hurt or wronged another person, but we feel that we have. All my childhood lightness floated away leaving me heavier than ever, and this feeling of unexplainable guilt settled in. I felt extremely humbled by the world around me. I started to move slower and noticed things: How my siblings don't chase after me anymore. Now they are the ones who are annoyed.

How my mom brow furrows with concern when I am around, and how my easy going dad sighs a little deeper.

2024: a new election year and once again Trump is trying his luck. My sister and brother are both eleven, almost twelve. My parents have given up on elections altogether. And then there's me, sixteen going on seventeen, currently sitting on a couch reliving all the times I've taken my family for granted, which I will probably continue to do for all my living days, for I am just human.

IF I DIE IN THIS SHED...,
by Sydney Boettcher, 12th Grade

Content Warning: Suicide

Dear Friends and Family,

If you have found this note, it is because I am dead. When I said I was working on a project in the shed, that wasn't the whole truth. I was building a bomb. In our room, at the bottom of my sock drawer, you'll find maps of Canada and Michigan, as well as a map of the Midree-Norton Oil Pipeline. I was going to take my bomb, take my car, and know that I might never come back. Never in a million years did I think I'd become an eco-terrorist.

I'm sorry I wasn't more careful, but I'm not sorry for what I did. I fought for my future, for my son's future. I didn't want the people I love to watch the world end in front of them. I'd rather not have the pre-apocalypse become post, not when I could do something about it. So I did. I marched, I gave speeches, I was arrested, I was released on bail, I signed petitions, I wrote letters to my local representatives, and I marched again. But nothing changed. The gears kept on turning. There was no disruption, there was no discomfort. We were and are still peaceful. It's funny actually. I can remember the exact moment I became disillusioned with peaceful resistance: it was when I saw the Harvest Oil wedding on live television. The heiress to the fossil fuel throne, her holy matrimony officiated just a few hours north of the city I was protesting in. The reporters couldn't stop talking about how beautiful her dress was. They glossed over the fact that she was ending the world. This is what I've accomplished, I thought to myself. I'm out here getting pepper-sprayed so they can be happy.

I'll admit it, I almost surrendered right then and there. Maybe I could have lived out the rest of my days happily, welcomed the end with opened arms and closed eyes. But to me, to do nothing was a horrific act of apathy, and it played right into their hands. I found myself in the hotel room thinking, at what point do we escalate? At what point do we decide it's time to try something different?

When I told my colleagues how I felt, they all tried to talk me out of it. Most of it was a blur. zthey all told me things I had already said to myself, but one reaction stood out to me. It was after the protest had ended. I was sitting on a park bench smoking a cigarette, when my friend Nancy sat down next to me. She didn't say anything for a long time, but eventually she asked me, "What if you blow yourself up?"

Without thinking I responded, "I don't really care." I didn't correct myself, I guess that was how I felt at the time. She looked at me solemnly, like I was already dead. She nodded, wished me the best, and got up and left. That will probably be the last time I see any of them.

When news gets out about my death, this is my statement for the press: "They will defame me, and claim that I am sick. They'll call this violence, they'll call this unforgivable. But this was necessary. If I die in this shed, it was not politics that killed me, it was not an imagined radicalization. It was the robber barons and the politicians whose pockets they've lined. My blood is on their hands, another drop in the bucket. And if I am the last one to fight back, nothing will change because nothing has changed. If they had their way, we would stay on the path they've given us, decades of bad choices by a greedy few that very well could doom us all. If you don't already understand why I did this, then I don't know how else to explain it to you. For some of you people it is easier to learn to die then it is to learn to fight."

Actually, just publish the whole letter.

Here are my last words (my actual last words will most likely actually be "oops" or "wait, I missed a step" but, regardless): I don't believe in life after death. Part of me hopes I'm wrong. Maybe I'll be seeing all of you later. Maybe I'm burning in Hell. I took out life insurance, the total sum of which I leave to you, my wife. Put it in Jasper's college fund, or something. To Morgan, Kylie, and Jimmy: I'm sorry, you're going to have to find a new drummer. If it hasn't already happened, tell Eddie I said happy birthday. His present is under my bed. To Grandma and Grandpa: it's not too late for you to make things right. To everyone: do not make me into a reason not to fight back, I'd rather not become a martyr against my own cause. Break windows, burn down offices, blow up pipelines. Let those who profit from mass death know their capital is not safe. Although if you do end up going through with that last one, make sure you're a little more careful than I was when handling your lead picrate.

Sincerely, Bobby

IGNORANCE IS BLISS: THE INDUSTRIAL MISTREATMENT OF POULTRY
by Isabelle Plamondon, 12th Grade

Highly Pathogenic Avian Influenza (HPAI) within poultry has been widely covered by the press, but the causes for such a virus have conveniently not been covered nearly as much. They mainly talk about how it's affecting the price of eggs and meat as factory farms; solution when birds catch HPAI is to slaughter all of them. This is because of how contagious it is and the high mortality rate. So it's believed that this is the most obvious solution, when in reality it's nothing but a patch job because there has been hardly any effort put forth into making a preventative or a cure. It's just easier to slaughter them all instead of spending the time and money on a solution or something to better the situation, which in the end is costing us more money, time, and resources.

As for the causes of HPAI and other viruses and bacterial infections in poultry farming, they can be related to birds' immune systems shutting down from stress. This stress is caused by the inhumane conditions they are forced to live in. These inhumane conditions include overcrowding, selective breeding, and lack of sunlight or access to the outside world.

Overcrowding became a normal practice in factory farms in order to save money on space, production, and electricity: an example of this being the warehouses and battery cages poultry are kept in.

Battery cages, primarily used in laying hen facilities, are cramped wire cages with a slanted bottom so eggs fall into an easily collectable ledge outside the cage. Each cage, roughly housing four to nine hens, provides less space per bird than an A4 sheet of paper. The hens endure constant discomfort, leading to physical and mental suffering.

They will spend their entire lives, roughly two to three years, here before they are brought to slaughter and a new batch replaces them – it is notable to mention that a hen can live up to ten years and lay for around six. One scientist, Nobel Prize winner Dr. Konrad Lorenz, said: "The worst torture to which a battery hen is exposed is the inability to retire somewhere for the laying act. For the person who knows something about animals it is truly heart-rending to watch how a chicken tries again and again to crawl beneath her fellow cage mates to search there in vain for cover."

Despite minor modifications over the years, these cages remain virtually unchanged. But cages aren't the only thing used for overcrowding in the poultry industries. When Cage Free Acts are passed in states, like ours, factory farms switch to using warehouses.

As a result, there has started to be a shift in how factory farms are raising laying hens. When Cage Free Egg Acts are passed, they are put in "Cage Free Aviaries" which provide similar conditions to the meat production warehouses. The only difference is that there are some nesting boxes along the base of the walls, and there are roosting bars suspended from the ceiling. This is a little better on the hens, but it's still not much better than their previous conditions. Additionally, only fourteen states have made this change.

Warehouses have been used primarily for the meat production side of poultry. This is because birds used for meat, like the Cornish Rock Cross, broad-breasted varieties of turkeys, different varieties of geese, and Pekin and Muscovy ducks, are selectively bred to grow at a much quicker rate than normal. As a result, they could suffer breast blisters from the wire cages and their bones would become more brittle than they already are. Plus, birds used for meat production tend to be much more violent in stressful environments. So much so that stress- induced cannibalism isn't uncommon. So, warehouses are definitely the better option so that market value doesn't go down, but is this costing us our moral values and the possibility of better nutrition?

Warehouses might be marketed as the better option, but are they really the better option when the conditions the birds are living in aren't any better outside of a cage? The fact is, meat birds are often kept closer together in warehouses than hens in battery cages. They are kept like sardines in a tin can, so close together that they can't even lay down without being on top of each other. Every time the automatic feeder dumps their feed into the feeding bins, it's a trampling race to get to food. They are selectively bred to be constantly hungry and constantly growing. The pecking order becomes skewed as a race for food can turn into a bloodbath in seconds. These factory farms try to prevent this by putting red bulbs in the warehouses to mask any injuries from any of the birds because if they see a weak link, they cannibalize in the hope of having more room, sustenance, and less stress ("Factory Farming: The Industry Behind Meat and Dairy | PETA").

I've seen it first hand. The assembly line of chicks coming out of hatcheries and being handled by workers like a toddler with a toy, the cramped spaces and battery cages, the droopycombs and pale faces because artificial lighting does nothing for a Vitamin D deficiency, and the stench of hundreds, even thousands of birds toppled onto each other. It's a startling sight for anyone who isn't aware of their conditions. Even a simple google search will render you speechless; I know it has for me in the past.

But you know what they say: ignorance is bliss right? People tend to believe that if they don't know where something comes from, they'll be better off because what can they do in such situations? What kind of impact can one person make when the task at hand seems impossible?

Well, the truth is, it's not an impossible feat to change the regulations and laws associated with factory farming. In fact, Europe is well on its way to reform their animal welfare acts and provide more assessment programs where veterinarians are more involved in the evaluation of animal welfare on factory farms. This helps open up more veterinarian positions and helps keep animals healthy and public health concerns down. They have even started going cage free and requiring more space for all animals so they have more room to exhibit natural behaviors and they won't have to experience the stressful and overcrowded environment of "traditional" factory farms.

The United States, on the other hand, has had a very slow process of reform. They have started requesting that poultry research facilities go cage-free and instead use warehouses and aviaries. It is all optional though, which means it isn't really being enforced, just suggested. This is because of a lack of awareness of situations on our part. The only reason it's a slow track is because we don't have enough people advocating for livestocks rights and the ethics around factory farms.

What can be done to change these regulations? Well, some solutions include supporting local or small-scale farmers, advocating for legislative changes, and something as easy as reducing your food waste.

Local and small-scale farmers tend to have a lot more ethical and humane treatment of animals. They also need others' support to keep afloat, so you're helping your community while helping society as a whole.

People can advocate for stronger regulations and enforcement of animal welfare standards in factory farming through lobbying, supporting animal welfare organizations, and participating in legislative campaigns. This can include pushing for bans on inhumane practices like overcrowding and antibiotic use. Even reducing your food waste can help reduce the demand for factory farming by decreasing the overall demand for animal products. People can reduce food waste by meal prepping, proper storage of food items, and utilizing leftovers. This can also help those struggling financially.

Ultimately, consumers like you have the power to influence the food industry through their purchasing decisions. You have that power. So, will you ignore your moral compass, or will you be part of the change you wish to see?

OK BASS
by Jacob A. Trick, 12th Grade

Junior year was a year of growth. It was a year when I finally got the courage to fix= myself up. It was a year of self-discovery and hope, from simple things like dressing how I wanted to dress to more drastic changes like chopping off my greasy hair. Junior year was a time of me finally caring about my grades, caring about what my interests were, about my life in general.

Towards the end of the year, I had gotten more and more passion for writing and music. I listened to what I wanted to listen to, I enjoyed what I enjoyed: I wasn't just fitting in. Music= which before I would repress because nobody else around me liked it, I ended up listening to. Something so simple ended up being such a shifting moment in my life as an adult.

I wasn't really an adult yet. I was still seventeen; I would be an adult on September eighteenth. However, I felt as if I needed to make a shift due to the lack of effort before. I skipped class, I didn't care about grades, and I ended up ignoring certain friends; instead opting for a party with one friend and way more strangers who I did not care for. Junior year was good and allowed me to change, but I still had way more to go. Often I'd found myself doing whatever my friends were doing because, what else would I do? But who cared? The end of the year was here and I was finally going to make a change; this was going to be my summer!

Nothing changed. Not as in, I wasn't a junior, or it wasn't summer but more so, my plans for the summer didn't happen: at first. I spent a lot of my summer lying in my room. Why wouldn't I? I needed a break and it was about damn time. I had just worked my ass off for the past three years, and the next year is my last. That summer, my senior year summer, I won't be free. I'll be at a job saving for college, or I'll be getting ready for college, and I'll be morphing into a true adult.

Even with that restful sentiment, I felt hollow. Even when I would remind myself, "It's fine to sleep in. You'll wake up eventually," I still felt hollow. The two weeks I wanted off turned more so into a month. A month of either going into work or sleeping in. I wasn't writing, I wouldn't go on drives, I wasn't hanging out with friends. My last summer was being wasted because I didn't have the energy for anything.

I was still here, still alive, and still awake. So eventually it kind of kicked in that "Hey, why don't you just do something?" Sure, It was easy to tell myself that, but a lot harder to follow it. Not impossible, just hard. Nonetheless, I did exactly what I said. I bought a bass, a Schecter. It was a shiny glazed maroon color. The strings were bulkier than I had originally expected. The fret board had almost a diamond like design which paired nicely with the logo. After being stuck in awe I decided to get it set up with the amp.

I didn't know what I was doing, and I refused to get lessons because I thought that would ruin the "fun" and "creativity." Slowly, I began learning how to properly pick at the strings, how to properly lay my finger on the fret, learning some notes, and how they connect to the strings themselves. I was getting a routine slowly, making sure to get up and practice bass every day. I began cooking dinners more often, cleaning my room instead of rotting in clothes and Nature Valley wrappers.

I wish I could give an exact answer to what the shift was, but I can't. Of course, it wasn't solely the bass that fixed my problems, no, why would it? That shiny object that gave me routine was amazing, but overall I think I saved myself. A simple hobby, but a simple hobby of self- expression. A simple hobby that kept a routine going for me. A dream I had as a kid that I was finally chasing.

For quick reference, I can remember a specific event that happened around fourth grade. My friend decided he would get an electric guitar because our other friend had one. His was blue, white, and made vibrant sounds like we have never heard in person before. Then, my friend got a navy blue and sleek tan guitar which also made vibrant sounds, like I have never heard in person before. I was in awe, listening to them discuss the guitar itself. Every morning before school we sat in the same wooden booth with a cheap table that could hardly stand. Enough was enough. I would get a guitar myself!

I had always wanted an instrument anyways, and since my crush at the time liked electric guitars, I decided I wouldn't be late to the table this time. So, I talked to my dad about it; getting an AMP, an electric guitar, and that's it (I didn't do much research). While I was talking to him about it, he mentioned to me how we had had this same conversation before. The big difference was before I had mentioned a bass, not an electric guitar. Since I was a dumb kid who didn't care about anything, I just opted to not get a guitar.

So during the summer, more and more, I played the instrument; learning songs, notes, and how to tune it. It was a dream I had always wanted to follow, and I was finally following it. Keeping structure and routine, I had something to work on over the summer that really gave me joy. I enjoyed learning how to play songs, I enjoyed picking at a string just to make a random booming sound. More and more as time went on I found myself getting into a healthier head space; a more motivated head space.

I found myself hanging out with my friends more, keeping my steady routine going. I had passion, I had personality, I enjoyed where I was in life. Still, it wasn't a smooth road; I did end up breaking a string, getting mad at the bass because the plucking sounded bad, and just overall pissed when it wouldn't make the sound I was looking for. Who cares? That lasted for five seconds. So, eventually, I just got over it as that was a part of learning. Part of learning is feeling pain about doing something wrong, so later when you finally play the song you've spent hours practicing, you feel accomplished!

When it hit the end of July, I had a vacation planned; My friends and I were going to go upstate towards a little town called Baraga. It was a seven hour drive and we wouldn't arrive 'til midnight. TThe house had no AC, and we were all burning alive. Still, we made it work and while I will be honest some parts I hated (obviously), other parts I enjoyed. I wasn't so cynical about everything, I enjoyed the hiking and the trip. So what if my friends fought with each other or with me? We were on vacation, I was enjoying life.

My mindset had completely changed, finding more joy and passion in life than I did before. Listening to Rage Against the Machine or Jeff Buckely, I discovered more messaging in music. I discovered how you can be self expressive and get your message out into the world. Learning bass at the same time inspired me; I was able to do what these bands have done. Being able to learn songs, learn notes, play along to the songs themself. Something so little ended up waking me up in the middle of summer

Lollapalooza was then just around the corner: August first. Going to such a big festival targeted just around music, with some of my favorite bands was so freeing. Something I had been waiting for all summer finally came around. This festival I was able to go off on my own, meet new people, and enjoy new sounds. I was exploring my passion for music, and I had my best concert experience at said festival (even if it smelled like sweat, beer, and mulch).

Then the end of the summer came, and school was starting back up. I wasn't scared, or nervous: mainly just excited. Writers Studio was so interesting to me, and when I arrived I felt like I belonged there. Everyone was always there so early, so it encouraged me to get there earlier and actually wake up earlier. High school itself was nice. I have a friend in my class and have made friends in other classes.

To tie it all together, I think this is the best way to put it. I was trapped behind a stone wall, using my hands to try and escape. Obviously, that doesn't work; you're going to need something to break the stone. So instead of a bass, just imagine a hammer, chipping away at the stone, cracking into the bright unknown outside. Eventually I made it to that outside. I made it out of my stone trap. I wasn't going to pine away in fear of the unknown. I used my tools, my mind, and I brought myself up off the ground, and fixed myself. Playing the bass is pretty awesome.

TRAPPED
by Kaihe Brown, 12th Grade

The brick room was windowless. The only source of light came from the buggy fluorescent lights that buzzed continuously. Vivian had been sitting for eight hours at the table. The metal folding chair was uncomfortable. Her mind was racing. She wondered what was happening, where she was, and how long she had been there. She nervously scratched her neck implant as she waited.

Suddenly, the door opened with a loud squeak, and a woman in a lab coat walked into the room, her heels clicking against the ground. She sat down across from Vivian, typing on a tablet. She spoke in a monotone.

"Good evening, Miss Balaena, how are you feeling?" the woman asked.

Vivian took a moment to respond. "I-I'm fine," she managed to stutter. "W-who are you? . . . Where am I?!"

The woman moved slightly in her seat, not looking up from her tablet. "My name is Dr. Richter. I'm here to ask you a few questions about the incident. Is that ok?"

Vivian froze for a minute. Incident? What Incident? She thought to herself. Finally, she nodded her head.

"Excellent," Dr. Richter finally looked up at her, "Now, from what we understand, your AV was flying on a path from Liberty City to New Neo, is that correct?"

Vivian nodded, feeling herself begin to sweat. "T-that's right." She scratched her neck implant again.

"Right, but when we checked the AV serial number, it was registered under A man named Logan Sionas and not you." The doctor looked at her tablet to read the name before looking up again.

"Yes, Mr. Sionas is my boss."

"I see," the doctor began to type on her tablet again. Vivian began panicking again.

"Why am I here?"

"And where do you work?" the doctor asked, not looking up

Vivian froze for a second, her eyes wide as she began to tear up. She wiped her eyes. "Nerv Biometrics," she responded.

"And why were you flying in your boss's AV?"

"Mr. Sionas asked me to deliver a file to our Research and Development site in New Neo."

"Why didn't you deliver the file digitally?" The doctor asked, continuing to type on her tablet.

"We didn't want to risk any hackers stealing the files from the net," she answered. "So

Mr. Sionas lent me his AV to fly with a supply convoy to the site." Dr. Richter began typing on her tablet.

"I see." There was a short pause for a moment, Vivian felt the deafening silence between them before the doctor asked another question. "Would you mind telling me how the flight went?" Vivian felt her mouth fill with saliva. She quickly swallowed before she could respond.

"We were flying through a heavy storm, so I felt anxious about flying by myself. I guess the AV was hit by lightning because the AV started shaking a lot and everything suddenly went white with a loud bang. The next thing I know, I was suddenly out of the storm and started landing at a random airport in Nevada."

"What was the date of this?" the doctor asked, looking directly at Vivian.

"March 17." She answered, trying to back away from the doctor's intense stare as much as she could in her chair.

"What year?" The doctor asked, her voice taking a direct and slightly stern tone. Vivian shuddered at her voice.

"20- . . . 2046?" Vivian asked meekly and confused. What could she mean by 'what year'? She thought to herself.

The doctor furrowed her brows as she immediately started typing on her tablet again. Vivian began to panic.

"Ok, seriously," Vivian slammed her hands on the table, "WHAT IS GOING ON?!"

There was a long pause between the two before the doctor broke the silence. "Alright,"

She took off her glasses and set her tablet down on the table. "You see, Miss Balaena, you have been missing for three years," she spoke, finally looking over at Vivian.

Vivian's eyes widened. "What? What are you talking about? What do you mean I've been missing?!" she shouted.

The doctor continued, "That's the thing... we don't know." The doctor admitted. "When your convoy reached its destination, they realized that your AV was missing. They checked the convoy's flight log and found that during the flight your AV's signal miraculously disappeared."

This has to be a joke! Vivian thought to herself. *I'm not missing. I'm right here!*

"Naturally," the doctor continued, "An investigation went into your disappearance. They searched all over, trying to find out what happened to the AV." Vivian could feel her breaths shallow as she listened to the doctor. Her eyes began to tear up. "Eventually, when the investigation found nothing, officials gave up looking, and you were presumed dead." Vivian felt herself start to cry in shock as she continued. "So, when your AV eventually ended up in Harry Reid International Airport, the control towers were confused. Eventually we had gotten word of the incident, and we came in to investigate." She couldn't believe what she was hearing. It had to be a joke. It couldn't have been 3 years. "But that's all for now. Thank you for cooperating." Vivian watched as Dr. Richter started to leave, and began to panic.

"W-wait, don't go, you can't just leave me—" Before she could finish, Dr. Richter had left the room, leaving Vivian alone in the white room again. Finally, after everything Vivian had just heard, she began to break down crying. Vivian scratched her neck implant.

WHERE IT ALL BEGAN
by Ava Heiler, 12th Grade

A bright color catches my attention; the annoying chatter of a sister slowly gets tuned out. I don't know why it grabbed my attention. But I couldn't look away. The bright blue kept drawing me in. A book, an ordinary book is what called to me. I was fifteen, and never before had I held a book willingly, yet here I was. The soft, yet rough pages made me yearn to keep a hold on it. The smell I knew well. But the smell felt new at that moment. Then the annoying chatter came back. My sister was begging to leave without the book. But I refused, and that was where my addiction began.

My dream—to be a writer—began with that one book. For years I wanted to be a part of the police force, but just a few simple words in ink changed me. They changed my perspective. I want to know the feeling, the feeling of writing a book. I want to experience the struggle and the relief when you finally escape writer's block. I want to know the excitement when your book takes off and people love it. I want to go to writing conferences to sell my books and interact with other authors I admire. In the article "A Day in the Life of a Writer," Beth Revis writes about how early she would wake up and how she could barely have time to eat breakfast before she had to go to meet and greets. She loved being able to meet admirers but overall, she had a very stressful schedule.

The more I read, the more that passion for writing came to life. The more I went to libraries or bookstores I felt at home. The more I read the more inspired I felt to try writing for once, and when that pencil hit the paper for the first time... I was stuck. I thought writing would be easy, not hard, but instantly I was hit with writer's block. Coming up with characters was hard enough as it is but writing a whole book was going to be the end of me. So, I put the pencil down and I kept reading. In the article "Living a Writer's Life," Jackie Yeages writes how there are tons of struggles writers deal with. First, it's finding out what to write about, then finding someone to be your agent, finding a publisher, and if you happen to become a big-time author, the trips are even more hectic.

As years went on the more curious I became about being a writer. I was doing research about how to start out as a writer left and right, but I came up with nothing to satisfy my thirst. I would research about other authors and how they began their journey or simply how to start out as a writing and what to look forward to.

I don't know how to start this journey and I'm afraid I never will. I know I'm running out of time to choose my path. I feel like I'm having writer's block in general about life.

As I read, I connected with a book, "King of Pride" by Anna Huang. I hear about some people connecting with a book, but I never thought it would happen to me. This book sounded like my life. Not everything was the same, but it was about an inspiring writer who is struggling to even finish one book. Connecting to a character helped me realize that I'm not alone, even though that person wasn't even real.

I go back to that day when I was fifteen. At the time I didn't know it. But that's when my journey began, the dream of becoming a writer. Flashes of the color blue, the smell of fresh wood coming from new pages, and my sister's annoying chatter all come back to me. People say your life flashes before your eyes when you die, but I'm not dead nor am I dying. I see this as a reminder of what my purpose is.

The first step I took towards my dream was joining a writing class and bought my very own computer so I could practice my writing whenever I could. Going into the writing class I was surprised about how different it was compared to what I believed I would learn. I simply thought we would just learn how to write and how to use correct punctuation. But I ended up learning so much more. I learned how to write poetry, professional letters, plays and even journalism articles. I struggled at first but as time went on I finally started to get it and even improve on my writing skills.

I want to keep trying to reach my goal, that goal to release a book and have that thirst quenched. I know it's going to be hard but I will keep pushing till I make that dream come true. Until then, I will work my butt off till I get somewhere and can proudly call myself a writer. In the article "What You're Writing Life Looks Like as a Professional" Emily Cavanagh writes about how she soon found out that it was not going to be easy. She had to get a job and even though she continued to write it took her a long time to publish. Till this day Emily still thinks back to the day when her college teacher warned her in her class that being a writer is hard work. She writes, "Only now do I get it."

GLOOM- AN EXCERPT
by Landon Foster, 12th Grade

"Are you guys clear? We're facing large numbers of people." Gloom radioed to Leah and Iris.

"We are facing some difficulties, but yeah we are making our way smoothly," Leah radioed back.

"Good. Gloom out." Gloom shut off the radio. "Let's let them pass." Gloom nudged Chloe.

A large group of guards were huddled by a white pickup truck at a dead end of a road. These guards didn't look like Spanish civil workers, but more like a private militia. They all wore the same thing: camo coat, camo pants, and an AK-47 strapped around their backs.

Chloe backed up a little and huddled by the wall of the brick building they were hiding behind. Gloom did the same in front of her. Gloom knew she was probably very afraid of what was ahead. The guards were talking in a language neither could understand; however, it was not a language that would be normally spoken around here.

"Do you know what language they are talking in?" Gloom whispered to Chloe."It doesn't sound like Spanish."

"I think it's Russian. I've only heard a little bit of Russian, but it sounds a lot like it," Chloe whispered back.

"Maybe we should try to take another route around them," Gloom whispered. "Come on, we can go around them through the forest." Gloom pointed towards a forest to the left with his thumb.

"I'm following you."

Gloom slowly started making his way up the small hill behind the building they were using as cover. Once he reached the top, he laid down and helped Chloe up. Once they were up they both crept through the small group of trees. Once they were out of the trees, they both stopped to scout the surrounding area.

"It looks like we have a clear path to the target building." Gloom said, holding up a photograph of the building from the folder.

"Looks like this will be easier than we thought." Chloe smiled.

"Don't get cocky. We still need to get there." Gloom started to crouch his way down the hill and back into the narrow alleys between rock and buildings.

After some sneaking, they both stumbled upon the target building. "We are at the target. Where are you guys?" Gloom radioed.

"We ran into some trouble. We are nearly there," Leah radioed back.

"How many dead?" Gloom whispered into his earpiece.

"None. We just had a close call," Leah said back. "Leah out."

"They'll be here soon." Gloom layed down. "We have some time to waste."

"Time to relax I guess." Chloe laid down beside him. "Are we really going to not kill anyone? I mean you know how Iris is."

"Oh, trust me, I know. The plan is to not kill anyone but plans are subject to change. That's why I have a plan B." Gloom shut his eyes.

"Oh yeah? What's that?" Chloe asked.

"Kill every single person in this town." Gloom smirked. "But hopefully it doesn't turn into that."

WAR PLAN RED: CHRONICLES OF THE NORTH ATLANTIC
by Tristan Breeding, 11th Grade

The air hung heavy with the putrid scent of salt and diesel, a reminder of the unending struggle that had consumed the crew of the Fifth Fleet the past few weeks. The North Atlantic, once a serene expanse of endless blue, had transformed into a battlefield, its surface churned by the relentless clash of steel and fire. The fog, a new companion, shrouded the combatants in a veil of uncertainty, amplifying the already palpable tension.

Admiral Thomas "Tommy" O'Connell, a war hero from the Mexican invasion just 3 years prior, his face etched with fatigue and worry, gripped the railing of the bridge of the USS Essex, his flagship carrier. He surveyed the scene before him, one only of churning waves, smoke plumes, and the occasional flash of gunfire. He tasted the salt spray from the waves, pushing his tongue back and forth in disgust. He couldn't stand the taste of salt. His lone eye, however, was fixed on the horizon, where a dark smudge against the sky hinted at the presence of the British.

Tommy was a fierce, but ready admiral. He was raised in a military family that fought right alongside President Theodore Roosevelt, and thus quickly rose to an admiral. He fought in WW1 on a Heavy Cruiser as a captain, and engaged in several conflicts in Central America throughout the 20s and 30s. He foolishly said he enjoyed war, despite losing an eye and 3 fingers in a terrible accident. Now, in 1937, a new battle would be fought. One between two naval superpowers, fueled by the anti-American rage of Oswald Mosley.

Tommy knew what battle was approaching him. The British Navy and Air Force had been constantly harassing his naval force in the North Atlantic for the past few weeks, but today, things were different; a great fog had descended on the battlefield after the morning skirmish against a lone submarine. Tommy couldn't afford to lose anymore people, or ships, in this invasion force towards Newfoundland.

“Report from the scout plane, Sir,” a young ensign named Mark announced, his voice barely audible above the roar of the engines, his hands seemingly soft amongst the jagged water surfaces. Mark, a 25 year old college student, had signed up just months prior. Even though he'd always wanted to be a politician, he felt driven by a deep sense of patriotism after hearing of the horror enacted by the British in the news. Mark had always been obsessed with literature and reading, owning a small library in his house. Mark had been torn between signing for the Navy or the Army, he wanted a job close to home, and reluctantly sided with the Navy after his uncle, Admiral O'Connell, recommended him as an ensign for the USS Essex.

“Give it to me, Mark,” Tommy commanded, his voice but a mere growl.

Mark read the report, his voice trembling slightly. “Sir, the plane found a large force of enemy bombers approaching our position. They're heading straight for us, sir.” Tommy's heart pounded in his chest. The British had been relentless, probing at their defenses, testing their resolve while safe from their holdings in Newfoundland. He had been anticipating this moment, knowing that the enemy would eventually make a decisive move.

“All fighters, scramble! Heavy cruisers, prepare to engage! Damage control… standby!” he barked, his voice echoing across the bridge. His orders soon reverberated through the ship by fatigued crew members.

The Essex shuddered as the fighters roared into the sky, a flurry of silver against the blue backdrop of the sea. The cruisers, their guns trained on the horizon, waited for the order to open fire.

“Fire at will,” Tommy yelled to his crew. His order echoed through the ship, a deafening roar that vibrated through Tommy's bones as the guns roared to life. Tommy ducked into the carrier's superstructure, and observed the battle. Flames erupted from the sky, streaks of yellow and orange against the grim gray and blue canvas, followed by the black plumes of smoke. The British bombers, sleek and deadly, were relentless. They swooped low, their guns spitting fire, and Tommy could see the Essex shudder under the onslaught. The air was thick with the smell of burning oil and cordite. Tommy flinched, the sound of the guns a constant, jarring rhythm. He pressed himself against the cold steel of the window, hoping for a miracle, hoping the Essex would be spared. After a loud bang, Tommy's carrier rocked. Tommy's hand tightened. He didn't know what the future held, but he knew one thing for sure: he would face it, just like he had faced every other challenge in his life. Mark ran in, wiping off sweat from his dirty forehead stained in grime and oil.

After catching his breath, "Sir, the Yorktown," Mark reported. Tommy's monobrow furrowed. The Yorktown, his sister carrier commissioned just a few months ago, had been taking the brunt of the British attacks over the campaign. He hoped they were still holding their own.

Mark continued, "They've been hit, sir. A torpedo bomber got through and struck them amidships. They're reporting severe damage! I'm sure you felt it!" A wave of dread washed over Tommy. The Yorktown was a vital part of their fleet, a newfound symbol of American strength and resilience. Losing her would be a devastating blow.

"We need to get those bombers before they reach the Yorktown," Tommy said, his voice tight with urgency. Tommy ran out of the superstructure and with Mark, manned a 7.5 centimeter anti-air gun.

The battle raged on. The air throbbed with the deafening rhythm of explosions, each one a thunderclap that shook the very foundations of the ship. The screams of the wounded were like a chorus of agony. Fighters danced in a deadly game of chess, their guns, the pawns spitting fire against the British bombers, the wings, epic rooks clipped by the blasts of exploding bombs.

Each flash of light was followed by a deafening roar, and the air itself seemed to crackle with the energy of the battle. The cruisers, behemoths of steel, unleashed their fury. Their shells, each one a fiery meteor, tore through the air, shattering British formations. Planes exploded in a shower of sparks and debris, their pilots plummeting into the cold, unforgiving sea. The water itself churned and boiled, a unique maelstrom of destruction.

But the British were relentless, their bombers swarming the Yorktown, their torpedoes finding their mark. The Yorktown, once a majestic symbol of American strength, was now a pyre of burning steel. Flames licked at the sky, devouring her decks, turning her into a raging inferno.

Her once proud hull, now riddled with gaping wounds, groaned under the weight of her own destruction.

Tommy moved back to the superstructure and watched in numb horror as the Yorktown, a monument to American courage and sacrifice, vanished beneath the waves. The screams of the men trapped below, the cries of those who had jumped overboard, echoed in his ears long after the ship had disappeared. He felt a crushing weight of sorrow, a sense of profound loss, for the lives extinguished in this senseless battle. He knew, with a heart-wrenching certainty, that the world would never be the same again.

"Sir, the Brits are retreating," Mark announced after dismounting the anti-air gun, his voice, panting and barely above a whisper, almost buried in the ambience of war, "We seemed to have shot the lot of them down."

Tommy looked out at the churning sea, the fog still clinging to the horizon, obscuring the remaining British planes movements.

He returned to his crew, his eye meeting theirs, a shared understanding passing between them. They had fought bravely, but they had lost a sister, a friend. They had endured the fog of war, but the fog of grief would linger long after the guns had fallen silent. Tommy took off his cap in hard-felt pain.

He had seen such violence, such destruction, but this time was different. The air was thick with the smell of smoke and gunpowder, the sound of explosions deafening. He had witnessed the death of his shipmates, their faces frozen in expressions of terror and pain in his mind. What remained of his hands trembled, his heart a heavy weight in his chest. He couldn't fathom how he could possibly continue, how he could face another battle, another loss. He threw his hat across the flight deck.

He had watched in disbelief as the Yorktown was destroyed, a powerful symbol of American strength reduced to a smoldering wreck in a moment's notice. He had felt the fear, the despair, the helplessness that gripped him as the British pressed their attack. In his mind, he knew that this was not a war to enjoy. The thought of fighting, of facing the enemy again, filled him with a wave of nausea. He wanted to run, to disappear, to escape the horrors that had consumed him. But in his mind, he knew that he couldn't go home, not back to rural Louisiana where nobody cared about his admiralty; he had to stay, to fight, to win, and to prove himself. He wanted to run back to Wisconsin, to a wife that disliked him and an adopted kid that barely noticed him every time he returned from sea. His hat fell into the weary sea.

He saw the faces of his crew, their eyes hardened by the battle, their resolve unbroken. They had lost so much, but they stood defiant, their courage high. They had fought back with all their might, refusing to surrender to the British onslaught. He saw in their faces the reflection of his own struggle, the same fear, the same despair, but also the same unwavering determination to fight for their country, for their freedom. He would stand and fight alongside his men.

The fog of war had lifted, revealing the grim reality of the battle. The sea was littered with wreckage; the air was now thick with the smell of death—a mix of gunpowder and blood.

But the spirit of the American sailors remained unbroken, their determination to prevail unwavering. The war was far from over. He knew that. But as he looked at the faces of his crew, their eyes filled with a mixture of grief and defiance, he knew he couldn't abandon them. He wouldn't. He would stand with them, fight with them, until the last enemy had capitulated, until the flag of freedom flew over a world free from tyranny.

Contributors

2025 NWS Scholarship Winners in Partnership with GTRCF

Lola Russell is a senior at the Greenspire High School and Career Tech Writers Studio. She is passionate about storytelling, and plans to attend college next year to study film.

Tess Tarchak-Hiss is currently a junior at Traverse City West Senior High. She explores the world around her by watching a copious amount of *Great British Baking Show* and playing roller derby as her alter ego Gretchin' McFreakon.

Keira Wesley is a senior at Traverse City Central High School, and will be attending Michigan State University in the fall to major in Linguistics. Growing up, she fell in love with writing; it gave me her voice that she, as a very introverted person, didn't have before. Through writing, she became passionate about research, politics, and literary analysis. She can't wait to continue writing in college and beyond!

Katelyn Popp is a Junior at West Senior High and has lived in Traverse City for the majority of her life. School is her number one priority, but in her free time she enjoys writing, reading, playing tennis, and spending time with her friends and family. Although her plans for continuing education are in the mathematics field, she will continue to enjoy literature in her free time.

Solé Demeuse is a graduating senior at Traverse City West Senior High. Solé is the current editor-in-chief of West's Student Newspaper, *The Occidentalist*, but also enjoys playing tennis, reading, and spending time with family outside of writing. She will be attending the University of Wisconsin in the fall to major in communications and minor in journalism.

Jack Schripsema is a senior at Traverse City West Senior High School. He has a passion for the outdoors; whether it's surfing, fishing, or exploring, he's always out doing something. In the fall, he will be attending the Ross School of Business at the University of Michigan with the goal of utilizing business to give back to the communities around us.

Elyana Marschner is currently a senior at West Senior High School and plans to attend Ferris State University in the fall majoring in dental hygiene. This is her fourth year as part of the varsity track team.

Sam Milks is a 12th grade student attending Traverse City West Senior High School and NorthwestEd Career Tech Center in the Writer's Studio program. He is an artist with his hands in an array of hobbies ranging from graphic arts to crochet. He also plans to join the Cybersecurity field after graduation.

Ani Free, an Ohio transplant now attending Traverse City Central High School as a junior, is an avid reader passionate about writing. This love began in elementary when she first explored the world of Tolkien, inspiring her to write her own adventures.

Salome Flowers is a senior at West Senior High School. She loves being outdoors, art, and being with friends. She looks forward to pursuing a science based degree at Michigan State University to help her on her journey to becoming a large animal veterinarian.

Memoir Moments

Lincoln Montgomery is a 4th grader at Long Lake Elementary School. He enjoys writing, and video games. His number one favorite thing to do is play Roblox.

Wren Gotts is a homeschooled fifth grader and proud member of the Sokaogon Chippewa Community. She lives with her three brothers, and sister, all older, and her mom and dad, and dog named Dottie. They love living in Michigan and travel for acting and powwows. Wren loves Science, English and Minecraft and Interlochen Arts Camp. When she isn't writing she puts on her hot dog suit for auditions.

Wyatt Wagner lives in Custer, MI. He is homeschooled and enjoys learning about history. He loves learning about how things work and fixing things. He also loves to take care of his chickens. Wyatt enjoys playing outside, building forts, and camping with his family

Writers Create II

Reagan Bulloch is a middle schooler in the Great Lakes area. She loves skiing, drawing, sledding, and ice skating, she also loves to swim, boat, and tube. When she is not reading or doing homework she is writing, her favorite school subject is social studies. Reagan loves to write about real things. She is also excited to share her story with you.

Nora Bruinsma is a 3rd grader who is homeschooled. She is the oldest of four children. Her family has a pet dog named Sophie. She loves soccer, art, and piano. Nora also plays the mandolin. She started writing short stories for her siblings when she was seven years old. Nora continues to write more as she gets older.

Lily Wagner lives in Custer, MI and is homeschooled. She is in the sixth grade and LOVES books (especially the Warriors book series). She likes cats and many, many other animals. When Lily is not writing she can easily be found reading, snuggling with her two pet rabbits, playing outside, camping, horseback riding, and LOTS more! She has two younger siblings and a wonderful Mom and Dad.

Desmond Andrick is 12 years old and lives in Omena, Michigan. He is homeschooled and loves writing stories, reading, drawing, and playing video games with his younger brother.

Ziva Erlenbeck is a Traverse City 6th grader who spends her time reading, writing, studying, drawing, and spending time in nature. She has 13 chickens and is interested in zoology, herbalism, and science. When she becomes older she would like to be a zoologist, herbal practitioner, herpetologist, or biologist. Some of her favorite animals are snakes, horses, most birds, cats, and lizards.

Maggie Forsman is a fourth grader in Northern Michigan. She enjoys hiking, swimming, and walking around the neighborhood. She loves decaf coffee and getting up early, especially on snowy days and weekends.

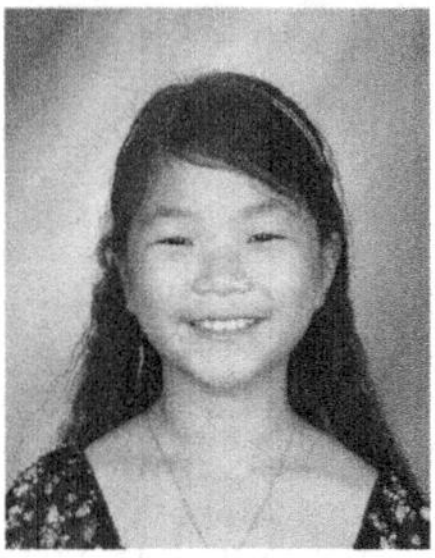

Irene Hong is a fourth grader in Michigan. She likes to ice skate, multiply numbers, and play with her friends. This is her first class with the National Writers Series.

Antrim Raising Writers: Language Lab

Nora Hornibrook is an 8th grade homeschooler and classical ballet student. She enjoys engineering, learning about astronomy and working with her hands. Nora lives in Petoskey.

Levi Hornibrook is a 5th grade student from Petoskey who is homeschooled. He is a member of the Petoskey District Library Chess Club who loves to play in tournaments. He enjoys poetry and playing piano and violin. Levi's favorite book is the *Redwall* series by Brian Jacques.

Jacob Stephens is an amateur writer who likes to play outside and spend time with his family. He attends Bellaire middle school and hopes to be a teacher someday.

Juju Pine Juju is an 8th grader at Suttons Bay Virtual School who loves to read and write. She enjoys spending time outside with her friends and family, playing softball, and camping.

Journalism

Gracie Gregory is a middle-schooler in TC. She loves to dance, listen to music and hang out with friends and family. Gracie also loves to play music and is taking piano and voice lessons. This is her second NWS class and also her second published writing piece.

Ronin Wells is a 5th grader who attends Central Grade School in Traverse City.

Adrian Reece is a 7th grader at West Middle school. She plays the bassoon in the school band and plays basketball. Her favorite subject is ELA and she enjoys writing, reading, and listening to music.

JJ (Josiah) Brudi is a 6th grade homeschooled student from Traverse City.

Peighton Kelderhouse is a 7th grade student at East Middle School in Traverse City.

Addison McGurn is an eighth grader at West Middle School. In her free time, she enjoys kayaking in the summer, playing the oboe and piano, and spending time with her pets and family. Addison can't wait to have her fourth piece of writing published, and to further involve herself with The National Writers Series.

Manistee County Poetry Club

Thomas Racine is an eighth grader at Manistee Middle High School, where he is a band member and an actor. In his free time, Thomas enjoys writing short stories, plays, and poems, playing games, and scootering around Manistee.

Goldilocks Framed Me! Fractured Fairy Tales

Kayla Cosens is a 7th grader who lives in Northern Michigan. She enjoys playing softball, basketball, and walking in the woods.

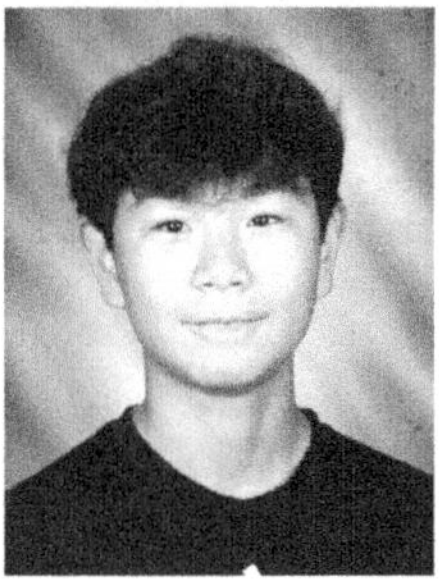

Albert Hong is 14 years old and is an MLS Next soccer player on Vardar. He loves to play sports and hang out with friends.

Marin Henry is 13 and lives in Traverse City, Michigan with her mom and dog. She enjoys running, swimming, being with her friends, and, of course, writing.

Color the World With Feelings: Sensory Poems

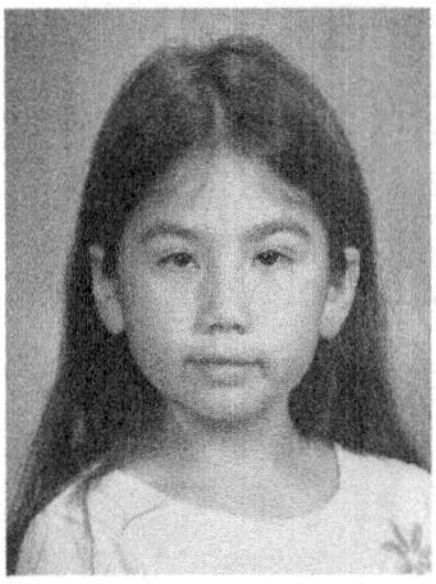

Hannah Erlenbeck is a third grader in Michigan and she loves to write, draw, ski, swim, and climb!

Joanna Bruinsma is in the second grade. She likes to dance and perform gymnastics. She likes to play basketball with my friends.

Back to the Beginning: Circle Stories

Autumn Heck, the writer of one of these stories, is a 5th grader who loves to write and draw. She moved a lot and found comfort in art and stories so she made this story for you!

Aubrey Babcock lives in Traverse City, Michigan. She attends Central Grade School and is in 5th grade. Her hobbies are writing, doodling, reading, piano, and swimming. Her inspiration for her circle story is that she loves making bracelets. She happily lives with her family, and her beloved kitten, Kiiko.

Chantry Halt is in 4th grade at Central Grade Elementary in Traverse City, Michigan. She lives with her mom and sister. She loves to read, write, draw, and sketch. She is ten years old and really likes to be outside. Her favorite book is not just one: she loves the *Keeper of the Lost Cities* series.

Anna Cosens is a 5th grader in Northern Michigan. She enjoys running, volleyball, and gymnastics, but her favorite activity is basketball. She loves spending time with family, friends, and her two yellow labs Lily and Honey.

Willa Selle is in 4th grade and loves to read and draw—that is why she wrote this story about a drawing contest. She has three siblings; Gwen, Cliff, and Vivian. She also loves skating! Her passion is playing piano, and she loves making food. Her family is very good at supporting her
with those things.

Kennedy Kraus is in 5th grade and is loving it. She enjoys track or any kind of running and is pretty darn good at it. She is Christian and the oldest of three children. Kennedy LOVES reading and writing. She loves anything that has to do with learning and is always excited to do more and do better.

Fiction Inspired by Myth, Legend and History

Ethan Konopacki is 18, in twelfth grade, and is a fantasy and history lover. He was born in Wisconsin and resides in Michigan. He also loves to read mystery books from authors such as Agatha Christie, C.J. Sansom, and Jeff Lindsay. Writing and publishing a book is his current goal.

Spring Break Staycation!
Write 50-Word Short Stories

Fionnagan VandenHeuvel is a seventh grade homeschooler who lives in Alden, Michigan with his parents and brother. He likes to telemark ski and alpine race, play Magic The Gathering with friends, and go on nature walks with his dogs, Winnie, Birdie and George. He loves stories, especially realistic fiction books and Garfield comics.

North Ed Writers Studio

Addison Seivertson is a Junior at Traverse City Central High School. She also attends the Writers Studio class at Career Tech. Addison enjoys writing and reading in her free time.

Sadie Hodges is an eleventh grader from Traverse City Central who attends Writers Studio at Career Tech. She loves writing, theater, and spending time with her dogs.

Alex Morgan is a 12th grade Homeschool Student in his last year of Northwest Education Career Tech. He enjoys writing fictitious stories and hopes to recreate the feeling of renewed hope he got from stories when he was younger. He's also a fan of Poptarts.

Kacie Blanchette is a 12th grade student at Kingsley Area High School and NorthwestEd Career Tech. She spends her free time writing, reading, and playing with cosmetics. Kacie does anything from dyeing hair to painting nails.

Hunter Arnold is in 12th grade. Hunter attends both Kingsley High School and Career Tech. She enjoys participating in the Northwest Michigan 4-H program.

Eileen Knight is a student at Traverse City West Senior High School and Career Tech Writers Studio. She's an active member of the theater community, as she's enrolled in Advanced Theater at her homeschool and has past experience as a volunteer actress in the Traverse City Young Playwrights Festival. Recently, she's established herself as a Young Playwright, with her play "BETWEEN LOVE AND MEAD" chosen to be produced in the annual festival.

Chloe Taylor is a senior at Mancelona High School and a member of Writers Studio. She enjoys painting, drawing, and listening to music. After graduating, she plans to attend Ferris State University for Television Production and Digital Media.

Nyah Parker is a homeschooled sophomore in the Kingsley, Michigan area who also attends NorthwestEd Career Tech. She enjoys listening to all kinds of music from pop to opera. Nyah often incorporates her love for drawing into her writing process, using sketches to inspire and develop her characters and stories.

Aiden DuVall is a junior from Buckley Community Schools and goes to the Writers Studio program at Career Tech. He is a 2025 winner of the Young Playwrights Festival and enjoys researching a multitude of random topics.

Radley Fournet is an adventurous seventeen-year-old, and a junior at Greenspire High School. She has spent the last couple years connecting with her writing and voice. Along with a passion for writing, she enjoys dancing, hiking, and swimming: anything to activate her mind and body.

Sydney Boettcher is a senior at Greenspire High School and a second-year student at Career Tech. After high school, he plans to pursue further education at Northern Michigan College. Assuming he ever finishes writing it, he hopes to one day publish a novel.

Isabelle Plamondon is a senior at Suttons Bay High School and a second-year student at Career Tech Writers Studio. She enjoys singing in choirs and musicals, writing, and raising animals. After high school, she hopes to study forensic behavioral sciences and make a difference in the world through her future career and her rhetoric and journalistic style writing.

Jacob Trick is currently a senior at Central High School who is currently pursuing writing in Career Tech's Writers Studio program. Aside from that, he enjoys listening to artists such as Hum, Thundercat, and Massive Attack. Additionally, he is currently learning bass in his spare time and works at a local Co-Op.

Kaihe Brown is a second-year student of the Writers Studio program at Northwest Education, and a Senior at Elk Rapids High School. Kaihe is a true artist at heart, always following whatever creative itch he has that week, always using himself as his target audience.

Ava Heiler is eighteen years old and a senior in high school whose dream is to become a writer. Heiler fell in love with reading at the very beginning of high school as a freshman. As years go on, and her mind continues to play tug of war with her future, writing unexpectedly wins.

Landon Foster is a 12th grader at West Senior High and Career Tech Center. He enjoys watching sports and playing video games. He has 4 siblings and 1 cat.

Tristan Breeding is an 11th grader who attends Writer's Studio at Career Tech. Tristan Breeding resides outside of Mancelona and would like to be a lawyer.